crude

D0031839

THE STORY OF OIL

Sonia Shah

SEVEN STORIES PRESS

New York • London • Toronto • Melbourne

First trade paperback edition, May 2006

Seven Stories Press
140 Watts Street
New York, NY 10013
www.sevenstories.com

IN CANADA
Publishers Group Canada, 250A Carlton Street, Toronto, ON M5A 2L1

IN THE UK
Turnaround Publisher Services Ltd., Unit 3, Olympia Trading Estate,
Coburg Road, Wood Green, London N22 6TZ

LIBRARY OF CONGRESS CATALOGING-IN-PUBLICATION DATA
Shah, Sonia.
  Crude : the story of oil / Sonia Shah.— A Seven Stories Press 1st ed.
    p. cm.
  Includes index.
  ISBN-13: 978-1-58322-625-4 / ISBN-10: 1-58322-625-7 (hardcover : alk. paper)
  ISBN-13: 978-1-58322-723-7 / ISBN-10: 1-58322-723-7 (paperback : alk. paper)
  1. Petroleum. I. Title.
TN870.S495 2004
665.5—dc22
                      2004012307

College professors may order examination copies of Seven Stories Press titles
for a free six-month trial period. To order, visit www.sevenstories.com/textbook/
or fax on school letterhead to 212.226.1411.

Book design by India Amos

Printed in Canada
9 8 7 6 5 4 3 2 1

Contents

List of Tables

For the Love of Oil

Oil creates the illusion of a completely
changed life, life without work, life for free.
. . . The concept of oil expresses perfectly
the eternal human dream of wealth achieved
through lucky accident. . . . In this sense, oil is
a fairy tale and like every fairy tale a bit of a lie.

—Ryszard Kapuscinski[1]

OUR SPECIES HAS basked in the strange and
wonderful properties of crude oil for millennia. But it was only over
the last century that we built whole ways of living upon its power,
harnessing crude to make cars run, planes fly, houses warm and lit,
hospitals sterile, and supermarkets stocked with fresh fruits and
vegetables.

Today, one-sixth of the entire global economy is dedicated to the
staggering effort of harvesting oil from its uneven accumulations
within the earth's crust. From birth to death our mobility, health,
and sustenance all depend, in various ways, upon crude oil and
its progeny. Newborn babies slide from their mothers into gloved
hands, are swaddled in petro-polyester blankets, and hurried off
to be warmed by oil-burning heaters. Later, strapped into steely,
oil-fed motors, their soft breakable bodies gloriously extend their
reach and power.

So long as the pipelines course with crude, our reliance on oil
isn't a fact we think about very often. But every so often, we are
struck with a paralyzing anxiety. How much is there? How long will
it last? What will come next?

There are many reasons why we might worry about our reliance on crude. After all, we use the stuff 100,000 times faster than it can accumulate underground. And we've already depleted the easiest and safest sources of oil.

But our apprehensions are generally sparked by a more mundane trigger: rising oil prices. In the wake of the oil embargo and Iranian revolution in the 1970s, the price of oil more than tripled, forcing Americans to take their first baby-steps toward moderating oil consumption. But then, in the 1980s, despite the ongoing depletion of oil, the price of a barrel of oil plummeted, and the zest for conservation faded.

And so it hit even harder when, in the middle of the first decade of the new millennium, the price of oil shocked us once again. This time, a confluence of factors threw the delicate balance between supply and demand into pandemonium. China consumed more oil than expected, while a series of hurricanes crippled oil facilities in the Gulf of Mexico. As the price of oil rose, so did the anxiety. Hollywood movies spun elaborate conspiracy theories about the oil supply. Editorialists speculated darkly on the end of oil, and webmasters warned of "Petrocalypse Now!" Talk shows discussed the possibility of an ever-growing China depriving Americans of their oily birthrights. The term "peak oil" entered the public lexicon.

The fundamental facts are not hard to understand. Every year, the world demands about 2 percent more oil than it did the year before, while the flow of oil from known oilfields declines by 3-5 percent. Since the 1960s, oil explorers' finds of new oil have been ever smaller, and since the 1980s, they've been finding those smaller accumulations less frequently. And so the oil industry slakes growing desires for crude by slurping faster on the reserves of oil discovered decades earlier. At some point, that endowment of oil will be spent, and the flow of crude will start to inexorably decline.

Some analysts say if we invest sufficient effort and money we can stave off the peak by a few decades. Others, more pessimistic, say the beginning of the end is a matter of years, or even months.

The oil industry has, indeed, been pronounced dead before. In 1909, Standard Oil was beheaded, and the oil industry was predicted to fade into oblivion. In 1960 the Organization of Petroleum Exporting Countries (OPEC) was formed, depriving Western oil companies of access to the most plentiful oilfields in the world. In the 1980s the rate of discovery of new oil started to decline. In 1997 the Kyoto Protocol was forged. And yet, the industry has survived, and thrived.

That's not to say there's been no fallout from these near-death experiences. In the beginning, oil drillers did little more than dig holes in their own backyards to produce oil. Today, oil companies must enlist the best minds of scholars and the blood of soldiers to fortify their sprawling tangle of arteries pumping oil to the world's machines. But the accumulated scar tissue would hardly be revealed through the simple pulse-read that is the price of oil. Despite the increasing difficulty of keeping the pipelines full, oil has not always become more expensive. In part, that's because it isn't consumers but distant ecosystems and future generations that suffer the lengthier pipelines, longer drills, stepped-up security, and environmental disruption that costlier oil requires.

In the coming years, the oil industry may be able to continue to keep the pipelines full with heavier oils, distant oils, and oil-like substitutes. But if the higher costs are pushed onto people and places separated from consumers by time and space, judging by the price of oil we may never know it.

If so, we may not experience oil's death throes as a prolonged period of painfully high prices for ever-scarcer oil, but rather as other kinds of seemingly disconnected disruptions. Up in the air, the century's explosion of carbon from the planet's crust hangs over us, ominously. The malignant spawn of petro-states send us cryptic messages of Armageddon. The most powerful nations on earth vie for the last forests, fresh waters, and farmlands to feed their oil-hungry economies. These—not the price of oil—may be our canaries in the coal mine.

If that is so, one could reasonably take a look around and surmise that the question isn't when the end of oil will come. We're in it already.

What next after crude? Again, there are roughly two camps. According to conventional wisdom, the West's high-tech, hydrocarbon-based society lies at the pinnacle of a natural, inevitable development path. There is no need even in the face of oil's decline, according to this view, to veer off in a new direction. We can continue using as much energy as we have over the last century of oil. We'll just get the stuff from other sources, whether coal, natural gas, nuclear power, or biomass.

An alternate view holds just the opposite: that the petro-life is an anomaly, based on the improbable discovery of relatively rare, finite accumulations of energy lurking under the ground during an era of unusually stable climatic conditions, a development as unlikely as winning the lottery. According to this view, the discovery of oil, the harnessing of its power, the rapid development of a society nourished and sustained by its short-term riches, despite its long-term and far-away costs—none of this was preordained or inevitable. If the very basis for this aberrant way of life is receding, there is no reason left to cling to its pathways. It is time, then, to adjust to radically new ones.

Whether we decide to maintain our oil-drenched society or chart a new energy future at least partly depends on how we understand the circuitous path behind us. It depends upon our story of oil, from its birth hundreds of millions of years ago to its abrupt exhumation over the last century and a half, a story told, in part, in the pages that follow.

INTRODUCTION

Oil Is Born

THE STORY OF oil is written on a time scale that humans can scarcely grasp, but it starts with something innocuous and seemingly peripheral: the slimy dregs at the bottom of the sea.

The outer crust encasing the earth is just 100 to 200 kilometers thick, a mere fraction of the way to the center. It is like a cracked eggshell, fragmented into about eight large plates and many smaller ones. Along with the burning star that is our sun, the Earth is primarily energized by its own interior, a hot core left over from the planet's creation more than 4 billion years ago. The fury of that heat becomes apparent when volcanoes erupt, vomiting up the innards of the planet. That heat drives the plates into constant slow motion—as much as ten centimeters a year.[1]

Throughout Earth's 4.5-billion-year history, these moving plates press against each other, forming mountains; tear apart, leaving huge depressions; slip under and slide past each other. Their rocky surfaces bear the scars of their journeys. Ice scrapes on rocks in the middle of the burning Sahara Desert and tropical rainforest plants buried in the middle of North America allow geological detectives to unravel the mobile plates' ancient pathways.[2]

A watery shroud swathes the cracked crust of our gigantic ball of heat, sloughing off the outer layers and sending them into motion. The water enveloping the planet in clouds, oceans, lakes, rivers, groundwater, and glaciers constantly circulates, melts, rains, freezes, and evaporates. The frenzy of water's activity along the surface of the earth shapes its face, eroding mountains, cutting grand canyons, slowly slipping ever downward through the tiny spaces between the crumbs of soil into the rocks below.[3] When the weather turns cold, the water inside the rock freezes, expanding and shattering the rock. All of these processes slowly but surely break the mountains down.[4]

The products of that weathering and erosion, sediments, slip down the land, settling in puddles, washing into streams, and finally slipping into the sea. Rivers swirling with sands and sediments rush toward the ocean. As they approach the sea, the rivers' flow slows, and the suspended sediments start to sink. On the floor of the sea, the layers of sediment slowly build up. The bottom ones get buried under progressively more and more weight and eventually turn hard and compressed. They become rock.

The ocean teems with tiny crustaceans, worms, and algae, microscopic life on which the entire food chain hangs. The seas are cloudy with them. But among the three kinds of sea creatures—the ones fixed on the bottom, like corals; the ones swimming around, like fish; and the tiny creatures that simply float with the currents and tides; the tiniest are by far the most prolific, producing up to 80 percent of the total organic matter in the ocean.[5]

Those hordes of miniscule marine creatures are called plankton. The term "plankton" refers less to a specific kind of organism than just a strategy: those creatures that are too small or weak to swim well and who thus choose to float along the currents and tides, hoping for the best. Phytoplankton, microscopic one-celled photosynthesizing organisms, are the engines of the sea. They form the basis of the food chain under the water by feeding on sun and carbon dioxide, and then raining down to sustain the creatures below, swallowed in bits by other plankton or in great mouthfuls by those that swim.

The goal in life for plankton is not to sink. They must stay within the layer of the water that gives them enough light and warmth, and this struggle tends to keep them quite minute. In order to avoid predators, they hide by making themselves transparent or schooling together in great clouds or by simply becoming smaller and smaller. Particles of food suspended in the surrounding water nourish them.[6]

Especially prolific are the diatoms, half-plant half-animal creatures that reproduce by division, and which can lurk for years, undead, waiting for the right opportunity to come alive again. The longest ones measure eighty micrometers. After they die, their glasslike shells sink to the bottom, joining the discarded fish bones and teeth littering the seabed, infused along the coasts with incoming sediments from rivers.[7] The tiny shells of these and other single-celled creatures fall to the bottom and mix with the mud to turn into what geologists call carbonate "ooze."[8]

Plankton remains and other sediments can blanket the sea floor with about .1 millimeter of organic rubble a year. Over 10 million years, that adds up to an entire kilometer. Indeed, the accumulated remains of coccoliths, tiny shelly spheres about ten micrometers in diameter,[9] formed most of the towering white cliffs that loom over both sides of the English Channel.[10]

Most of the organic material that starts sinking to the bottom never reaches the seafloor. It gets eaten by fish or demolished by burrowing bacteria. But in fits and bursts at specific times and locations, organic sediments are preserved unrecycled and are buried untouched. If conditions are precisely right for those silty layers to accumulate, they may, in time, turn into oil.

The slime in question, this preancestor to oil, is packed with carbon.

Carbon is the building block of life, the stuff plants turn into food and that we breathe out as carbon dioxide. It is the black sooty stuff that makes up coal and graphite along with the hardest material on earth, glittering diamonds, as well as countless other substances when partnered with other elements. An entire branch of scientific inquiry, organic chemistry, is devoted to studying carbon.

Billions of years ago, carbon-containing meteorites and other small, solid celestial bodies bombarded the earth, steadily increasing the amount of carbon on the newborn planet.[11] There are about 49,000 metric gigatons[12] of carbon on Earth today,[13] making it the fourth most plentiful element in the universe after hydrogen, helium, and oxygen.[14]

Carbon circulates around our planet, sinking into the earth, spewing out in volcanoes and wafting up into the atmosphere. Seven hundred and fifty gigatons of carbon hang in the atmosphere, accounting for less than 1 percent of the world's carbon. At those lofty heights, carbon envelops the planet in a warming shell, letting heat in but not out.[15]

The vast majority of the world's carbon—more than 30,000 gigatons—resides in the world's oceans. (About 10,000 gigatons are locked in methane hydrates, a crystallized form of methane that forms under cold deep seas.)[16] The ocean and the airs above it conduct a gentle, give-and-take conversation with carbon, whispering the element back and forth depending on which side's concentration is greater.[17] Carbon dioxide dissolves in seas and ocean currents carry the carbon-laden waters down into the dark depths. Phytoplankton also turn the carbon from the air into food, storing it in their watery tissues. Other hungry creatures take with their bite of phytoplankton all of its stores of carbon, passing the carbon along the food chain.[18]

A similar process occurs on land as plants transform carbon into food and living tissue by photosynthesis. Animals eat the carbon-rich plants, growing their bodies and exhaling the byproducts, carbon dioxide, into the air—where plants can once again breathe it in. In total, forests and the rest of terrestrial life hungrily eat, breathe, and exhale another 3 percent of the world's carbon.

When fused with hydrogen, carbon repels water, which is why oil won't mix with water. Oil, along with natural gas and coal, is a hydrocarbon, so named because it consists of hydrogen and carbon. The simplest oil molecules are long chains of carbon atoms with hydrogen atoms hitched along the sides and ends of the molecules. A single carbon atom with a few hydrogens attached to it is methane, a light gas. A chain of three carbons is propane; four carbons is butane. A chain of eight carbons is octane. As the chains and rings of carbon get longer and longer, they stick to each other better. The hydrocarbon gets thicker. Thirty-carbon chains are waxy; refiners string even longer chains together to make plastics.[19]

For creatures like plankton that are composed mostly of water and live in water, a barrier of water-repelling material is crucial. It is what separates them from the sea that surrounds them, the thin barrier between the animate water inside and the inanimate water outside. Not surprisingly, a key component of planktonic cell membranes is made of chains of hydrocarbon molecules. If you zoomed in on the cell membranes of marine algae you'd see it: a chain of fifteen or seventeen carbon atoms strung together, holding the incoming waters at bay.[20]

Hydrocarbon-rich plankton corpses pile up in the sediments at the bottom of the sea. As more and more rich organic sediments collect on top, each layer is buried deeper under the subsiding seabed. When the sediments have sunk several kilometers underground, their compaction expels much of the water. Because much of the organic material comes from plankton, and minus water, plankton contains water-repelling hydrocarbons, the layers become rich in hydrocarbon. Over millions of years, the sunken, hydrocarbon-enriched layers harden, turning into thin sheets of dark chocolate brown or black rock.[21] If you took a chunk of it and put it under a microscope, you might see bits of shell, pollen, and even whole microorganisms fossilized there in the hardened rock.[22]

Once buried deeply, at least seventy-five hundred feet down, these sedimentary layers will turn into a hydrocarbon-impregnated shale or mudstone. Under increasing pressures as they get closer to the center of the earth, the organic-rich layers are gently heated at temperatures of around 180 degrees Fahrenheit, as warm as a hot cup of tea. Cooked over millions of years, the hydrocarbons in the rock mature. The heat splits the large molecules into progressively smaller ones and the hydrocarbons in the rock become lighter, less viscous, and much more volatile. The water-repelling cell membranes of single-celled marine creatures get squished and simmered into oil, which now infuses the shale, or "source rock" as petroleum geologists call it, in drops and blobs.[23]

If the rocky layer continues to descend into the earth's crust, going deeper than eighteen thousand feet, the pressure becomes too great, the layers too sunken, and the heat too intense. The oil "cracks" into the smallest and lightest molecules of all—methane, or natural gas.[24]

Just over a fifth of the world's carbon has been entombed this way, resting in the earth's crust.[25] Before people started to unearth oil, geologists from the U.S. Geological Survey figured around 2 trillion barrels[26] of carbon-rich oil were secreted underground. By unleashing oil from its silent tomb and burning it, we send the carbon locked in oil's hydrocarbons back into the atmosphere. During the last ice age, the carbon blanket in the atmosphere was only half as thick as it is today. Now, as more carbon wafts up to weave itself into that blanket, it thickens, keeping the planet warmer and warmer.[27]

If the world's oil all resided underground in deeply buried layers of shale, that carbon-rich, plankton-blessed rock, people would have never known about it. Part of the story of oil is how it moves and gets trapped in places where humans can get at it.

Oily shale and mudstone source rocks are full of oil, it is true, but it is practically impossible to get the oil out of that sludgy rock, as it is too dense. Of course, people have tried. There's a massive amount of oily shale in Colorado, deposited by a gigantic lake that covered parts of Utah, Colorado, and Wyoming more than 60 million years ago. Today, the lively lake is gone, but its oily sediments remain unburied, what one petroleum geologist dubbed an "unborn oilfield."

Chunks of Colorado's rich shale burn almost like coal, as railroad workers discovered when they used the rocks to encircle their campfire. There are tons of oil in that shale; if people could get it out, the amount would be roughly equal to all the world's conventional oil.[28]

In the 1980s, Exxon, desperate for a new source of oil, spent over $1 billion trying to get oil out of Colorado shale, ultimately abandoning the project when the price tag zoomed to $8 billion for a measly fifty thousand barrels of oil a day.[29] To deliver the unborn oil, the company would have to mine the rock, crush it, and then heat it, producing more waste than would fit into the hole they dug to mine the rock to begin with.[30] The procedure is also highly polluting, releasing three to six times more greenhouse gases into the atmosphere than conventional oil production, according to Greenpeace, which has campaigned against shale oil development.[31]

Instead, people look for the places where geological forces have moved the oil out of the shale into a rock more suitable for drilling. That happens when the shale layers get squeezed, as the constantly moving plates start pushing and pulling on the rock. Millions of years of such pressure on the rocks squeezes the oil out, buoyed by its own relative lightness. A migrating stream of oil can travel long distances, sometimes more than a hundred miles.[32] Where does it go? Crushed under tremendous pressure, under thousands of feet of shifting layers of rock, the oil searches for the easiest route out, through the tiny fractures and pore spaces in the rocks that suffocate it. It is a tortuous path, twisting and turning amid the miniscule gaps, aiming for the sun.[33]

The rock layers are heavy, but not all of them are very dense. Say the migrating oil encountered a rock made from a buried beach of white fine sand that had fused together into a porous sandstone. Even under great pressure, up to a quarter of the volume of that fine-sand-beach-turned-rock will be empty space. The even-sized sand grains stack upon each other like a pile of ping-pong balls, leaving plenty of room between them. Or say the traveling oil met up with limestone that had been lifted back up to the sea and exposed to fresh water again. The acidic water would have dissolved passageways for itself as it trickled through the rock, leaving behind a network of tiny connected veins. Or it could run into a buried reef, with its countless tubes and passageways created by living creatures, likewise riddled with connecting holes.[34] Such a porous rock will start to soak up the oil like a sponge. The oil-saturated sandstone or limestone becomes what is known as a "reservoir rock."[35]

The oil-soaked sandstone, this oily sponge, must also have a lid on it. Otherwise, the oil will keep on trickling out, dispersing itself over vast areas and becoming so spread out it will be impossible to collect. Something impermeable must sit on top of the sandstone, forming a kind of seal for the migrating oil. The very structure of the rocks may change in a way that could trap the seeping oils. An impermeable rock layer, perhaps more shale through which water and oil won't flow, might be shifted into place above a stream of migrating oil, curling over it like an overturned soup bowl. Over millions of years, those curved layers (called "anticlines" by geologists) can capture the oil in the porous rock layer below. Natural gas from deeper layers may drift upwards and also become trapped above the oil, along with water migrating amidst the rock.[36]

Sometimes, if there are multiple layers of shale, sandstone, and salt, over and over again, the salt will tend to float upwards, because it is lighter than the other layers above it. The bulging salt layers will push up the sedimentary layers above them, forming a kind of dome. When the shale's oil is squeezed into the sandstone, the dome will bar its further movement. Anticlines formed by salt domes are excellent traps for oil.[37]

However, years of erosion can occasionally wear down the rocks that entomb such oil-filled traps, bringing an entire oilfield to the surface. It happened in Alberta, Canada. All of the light oil and gas quickly dispersed into the air, leaving behind only a tarry, oily sludge—the infamous Alberta tar sands, a dead oilfield to shale's unborn one.[38]

A worthwhile oil reserve, then, must have thick layers of oil-rich source rock, porous reservoir rock, and an impermeable "cap" rock, all in the right position to form a trap, and pressurized and heated to just the right conditions. It is an elaborate sequence of events that takes place over millions of years, enlisting the carcasses of billions of creatures, the rising and falling of seas, and the shifting of tons of rock. All told, earth has given birth to 2 trillion barrels of oil, a labor that appears as improbable as it is quite awesome in scale.

Kenneth Deffeyes is a retired professor of geology from Princeton University, a cheery rotund man who grew up in the oil patch. His fondness for the oil he's spent his life scrutinizing, for Shell, Princeton, and the various oil companies for whom he's consulted, compels him to roll down his car window when he drives by a refinery, in order to take a deep breath. The story of oil's unlikely ancestry appears to fill him with glee. "If any one of these conditions is missing, tough luck. If one of them is only partially developed, you get a small oilfield," he says. "The chances of rolling a seven with the dice six times in a row is rather small!"

"So it does look like accidents on the highway, where you get a lot of little fender benders and a few of these giant pileups with forty cars in it," he goes on. "Well, the Middle East is a giant freeway with a forty-car pileup. It is a place where everything was just right."[39]

Around 180 million years ago, a warm shallow sea washed just above the equator, splitting the single continent that had previously covered the earth into two major subcontinents, Laurasia and Gondwanaland. Ancient reef-building organisms slowly built their wondrous reefs in this sea. It's been named the Tethys, as in the mythical daughter of the Greek god of heaven and the goddess of earth who bore three thousand ocean nymphs and all the river gods.[40] The Tethys sent its warm, equatorial ocean currents and its diversity of shelly and fishy Jurassic and Cretaceous life flowing all the way around the globe.[41] Dolphin-like reptiles and sea-going crocodiles cruised its waters, with forty-foot plesiosaurs as kings of its underworld.

Up on the land, dinosaurs stomped amidst the spiky, pineapple-like cycads. Our ancestors among them, the early mammals, were just tiny vermin, "the cockroaches of their day," as paleontologist Michael Benton put it, although we would claim the Tethys' products of that time as our own, much later.[42]

For more than 100 million years, the Tethys sea floor collected rich layers of sediments, as abandoned shells, plankton, and other organic sediments descended gently on the seabed. Then the seas lapping up on the shore receded, leaving behind a salty crust on top of the organic layers. Sands rushed in and buried the salts. This happened over and over again, leaving thick sequences of source rocks, reservoir rocks, and evaporites. Slowly, the layers began to sink, which compressed them into that essence of ancient life, oil.[43] Those sunken sea-bottoms of the Tethys now contain about two-thirds of the world's oil.[44]

Much of it got trapped in the Middle East. Around 15 million years ago, the sea-floor under the Tethys was consumed into the earth, its sediments scraping up onto the surface. The continents of Arabia and Asia that once lined its shores collided. The impact smashed the land, throwing up the soaring, snow-capped Zagros mountains, which lie in today's southwestern Iran. The southwest side of the mountains was left with a huge depression, the Mesopotamian basin, one of the largest sedimentary basins in the world, where the organic-rich sediments of the now-vanished Tethys came to rest. Meanwhile, the stress of the massive continental smash rippled, folded, and faulted the rock, squeezing the oil out of its deeply buried layers. The oil started to migrate. The long-gone beaches and reefs of the Tethys, buried and turned to sandstone and limestone, sucked up the migrating oils. In some places the salty layers sealed them in salt domes; in others, the stresses folded the sediments, forming huge anticlines that trapped the oil.[45]

With trillions of barrels of crude oil migrating through the twisted crevices in the rocks underfoot, it isn't surprising that some of it managed to find its way to the surface. Some of it would simply vanish, evaporated into thin air. Some would linger, collecting in muddy pools, trickling down cliff faces, or burbling up under rivers, creeks, and seas.[46] Bacteria would feed on the rich hydrocarbons, swirling in black puddles. In tropical seas, bacteria would crowd hungrily around the warm seeps of oil clouding the water, forming mounds later colonized by reef-building creatures.[47]

Newly evolved humans walked out of their ancestral Africa, using the land bridge formed by the crash between Africa and Asia that had swallowed the Tethys, and settled in the fertile valley between the Tigris and Euphrates Rivers. It wasn't long before they found the remains of that ancient rich sea. Its oils were slowly oozing out onto the fertile soils basking in the sun.[48]

The first thing they noticed was the otherworldly sound. Natural gas percolated through the fissures under the ground, sending up a ghostly echo. It sounded to the people above, craning their ears to the earth, like the voices of the gods of the underworld. They found oily pools and gathered some of the strange liquid, divining the future from the shapes that the liquid would make when thrown into water. Soon the stuff was put to more practical use, gummed onto boats and houses to create watertight seals. The seeps were so plentiful that the Mesopotamians were able to dig up over fifty thousand kilograms of solid petroleum sludge. They found some light liquid oil as well, but deemed it useless. Pliny declared it too combustible and therefore "quite unfit for use."[49]

The Persians filled pots and other vessels with a stinky volatile mix of sulfur and crude oil, which they'd set afire and then hurl at their enemies. The ancient Greeks greased their arrows and lances with petroleum to make flaming torches. By the seventh century A D, the Byzantine Empire had perfected a liquid combustible made primarily of boiled petroleum called "Greek Fire," which set hearts trembling throughout the region for centuries.[50] They used the combustible mixture to fend off waves of attacks from Muslims, Western Europeans, and Russians. Soldiers cavorted with long tubes full of crude, which they would light and throw into their enemies' faces. Muslim states used incendiary warfare—weapons made fiery with oil—to fend off Christian invaders.[51]

Tethys' hydrocarbons inspired godliness as well as aggression. In Baku, the ancient Persian city that is now the capital of Azerbaijan, some of the oil escaped with gusts of natural gas and burned continuously. The Persians worshipped those miraculous everlasting fires. The prophet Zoroaster, born in Azerbaijan or Iran more than two thousand years ago, created a new religion based on fire worship, which flourished as the official religion of Persia for over four hundred years. His followers, the Zoroastrians, tended perpetual fires in their temples. When Muslim Arabs conquered Persia in the seventh century, extinguishing the eternal flames, the Zoroastrians fled to India. Today, 270,000 Zoroastrians in India and Iran pray to the sacred fire five times a day, a modern testament to an ancient wonder, pure combustion spurting out of the belly of the earth.[52]

Oil has become so enmeshed in our lives that, like the air we breathe and the ground underfoot, many of us barely notice much about it, aside from a slightly pungent odor at the pump during the weekly five-minute ritual of refueling the car. But oil, as part of our planet, its legacy of life, and its capacity for change, is not something we can so easily separate from our own organic earthbound selves, pouring it into our machines at arm's length, noses held.

The way oil is created, its ancient pedigree, its tortuous journey to the places in the earth where we can find it, its elaborate chemistry—all of this makes it precious. Yet, it has rarely been treated as such. Once we encountered oil, we wallowed in it, consuming crude about one hundred thousand times faster than it could possibly accumulate again. [53]

CHAPTER ONE

The Eclipse of Coal

By THE MID-1500s, England's forests were dwindling. People needed to feed their fires and they turned to a strange, fiery black rock that they clawed out of the ground. They didn't know it at the time, but the rich rocks they found were the ancient condensed remains of ferns and other plants that had rotted in swamps eons before: coal. Burning it wasn't a great option. The black coals reminded them of the black swellings of bubonic plague. The smoke made them sick. Extracting coal was time-consuming, dangerous, and inconvenient. The mines held poisonous and explosive gases, and were apt to unexpectedly fill with water. But it was better than the alternative: freezing to death among the denuded hills of England.

And so, coal was dug out of the ground to feed Britain's fires, coating the cities with a thick layer of grime and filling the skies with low-hanging dark clouds. By the 1700s, the coal that ran in shallow veins close to the earth's surface was gone. They'd have to dig deeper to get more, risking even worse flooding and explosions.[1]

Continuing to rely on such a difficult, costly fuel source would be risky, possibly even foolhardy. The amount of energy needed to pump the water out of those deep holes that burrowed beneath the water table might be equal to, or even greater than, the amount of energy that the lumps of coal that came out of the ground could pay back.[2] Yet coal was already a business worth fighting for. Mine-owners calculated that they could still profit from bigger and deeper mines, even if they had to foot the bill for more workers and more machines, as long as they could recoup their investments by selling even more coal.

In other words, the more depleted the coal became, the more trouble it would be to get more out and, at the same time, the more coal they'd have to sell to make it all worthwhile. Yet the topsy-turvy formula worked. By consolidating, hiring more workers, and attracting greater investment, coal mining soon became one of the biggest, most capital-intensive industries in Britain.

In 1712 the steam engine was invented and quickly employed to drain the water out of ever-deeper coal mines. The steam engine, "the most wonderful invention which human ingenuity had yet produced," wrote historians, bestowed "the art of converting fuel into useful power for the benefit and convenience of humanity."[3] The additional coal made accessible by the steam engine was used, in part, to fuel the steam engines and the fires that smelted the iron to make the engines. It was a self-sustaining cycle that allowed both coal production and iron production to intensify, driving the price of both down. Soon, the industrial revolution—that frenzied partnership among iron, steel, and coal—was banging along. Britain, with its huge coal reserves, and its formidable Navy kept honed by accompanying the coal convoys down the English coast, sat at the very top of it.

Coal bestowed power in the eighteenth and nineteenth centuries, but it came at a price. Coal's black smoke was so thick that it could be seen hovering over English cities from miles away, in some cases blocking the sun's rays entirely. Londoners, squinting by their sooty windows, switched on their lamps to read the morning papers. Children toiled in the coal-fired factories, and even worse, in the dank, toxic coal mines themselves. "For watching the doors the smallest children are usually employed," noted economist Friedrich Engels, "who thus pass twelve hours daily, in the dark, alone, sitting usually in damp passages without even having work enough to save them from the stupefying, brutalizing tedium of doing nothing." Children dragged themselves homewards after their long shifts in the mines so tired that many were found, hours later, asleep on the road.[4] Deprived of sunlight, subject to poisoned air and explosions, they died in droves. Most of the poor in mid-nineteenth-century Manchester didn't survive to see their eighteenth birthdays. Those who did aged prematurely. Some of the tragedies that befell coal workers were hidden, for a time, by coal-mine owners who conspired with local newspapers to censor coverage of mine explosions.

Nevertheless, London was affectionately dubbed "The Big Smoke," a smog-shrouded city that Lord Byron romantically described as "a wilderness of steeples peeping on tiptoe through their sea-coal canopy."[5] Painters such as James Abbott McNeill Whistler, Joseph Mallord William Turner, and Claude Monet captured the city's foggy phantasmagoria, and Charles Dickens wrote of coal's "soft, black drizzle." Jack the Ripper stalked his prey under cover of coal's thick brown haze.[6]

Across the Atlantic, a different story was unfolding. People found tons of black coal, but they also found something else, a liquid fuel that would slowly gain in popularity until it overtook coal altogether.

By the 1850s, people in northwestern Pennsylvania had noticed the black grease floating on top of their creeks and springs. Skimming it off the top, or soaking their rags in the oily waters, they used the liquid for the first thing that would come to mind in those rough days: to try to ward off the bewildering array of illnesses that plagued them. At the time, cholera, yellow fever, influenza, and smallpox epidemics ravaged the North American populace. Some entrepreneurial types started selling the oil under the name "Seneca Oil," as a cure for worms, deafness, toothaches, and dropsy.

When set alight, oil's long chains of carbon split apart, releasing the energy stored in their powerful bonds. Afterwards, oil's hydrogens and carbons pair off with the oxygen in the air, forming carbon dioxide and water.[7] The amount of energy stored in a gallon of oil is equal to the amount in almost five kilograms of the best coal, or more than ten kilograms of wood or more than fifty well-fed human slaves toiling the day away.[8] Oil contained so much energy that it could be used with abandon and still release much more energy than was required to get it out of the ground.

The men in Pennsylvania had a better idea than time-consuming hand-digging for this miraculous new liquid. They would drill an oil well, just as they had drilled wells for water and salt. First they'd find the oil seeps in creeks and hills and then they'd stab the earth nearby to get more out. In the famous story, in 1859 Edwin L. Drake, a former railroad conductor, drilled a hole on a farm where seeping oil was collected; at sixty-nine feet, the hole started, incredibly, to fill with dark fluid.

Explorers of all ilks criss-crossed the globe, hunting for the tell-tale leaks that might produce riches when tapped. On the other side of the ocean, Russians drilled the seeps whose eternal fires had so entranced the Persians. They shipped the oil from Baku in tankers—the first was called the *Zoroaster*—across the Caspian Sea. Around Baku, the smoke from the two hundred refineries that distilled the oil was so dense that the area was known as "Black Town." Russia's dirty oil started filling lamps across Asia, along with oil extracted from dripping rocks in Indonesia by Royal Dutch Shell. Entrepreneurs with dollar signs dancing in their eyes braved the hostile lands and people of Persia to drill along oil seeps there.[9]

By 1862, drilling near known oil seeps in Pennsylvania was bringing up 3 million barrels annually. They called it oil "production," a funny term given that they weren't "producing" anything, but taking something the earth had made countless years before humans had evolved. It took just thirty years for sixteen thousand farmers, entrepreneurs, and speculators to drain Pennsylvania's oil, by piercing the earth in as many places as they could and siphoning the oil out as fast as was then technically possible. When the oil wells abruptly ran dry, it was like a plague had fallen upon the nearby towns that had mushroomed around the wells. Having no idea how much oil there was underground or where it came from, they hadn't seen the end coming.

Unlike coal, which could essentially be thrown into a fire pit as soon as it came out of the ground, crude oil required energy-intensive processing in order to be truly useful. The oil that bubbled out of the ground was a messy mix of thousands of different kinds of hydrocarbons, the mushed remains of the cell walls of ancient algae, in various states of pressurized decay. There'd be some long chains of carbon, with seventy or more carbons linked together, as well as light gas, tiny little hydrocarbons with just four carbons linked together, and everything in between besides. The mix would vary from crude to crude, depending, in part, on how deeply buried the oil had been.

The different hydrocarbons in crude oil all burned at different temperatures, which was a problem when trying to harness the energy of their explosive combustion. The various fractions would have to be distilled into their various pure components, so that machines could be tailormade to specific types of hydrocarbons. To do it, refiners would essentially boil the crude.

As the crude gets hotter, different fractions reach their varying boiling points and turn into gas. At room temperature, the methane immediately evaporates. At more than 100 degrees Fahrenheit, the 8-carbon-chains—octane or gasoline—turn to gas and drift off. At around 500 degrees, the 16-carbon-chains, the diesel, evaporate. At over 1,000 degrees, even the tarry 80-carbon-chains, the coke, start to stew. In modern refineries, each constituent is lovingly captured, as its vapors rise in giant steel towers, cooling as they float higher and higher.[10]

But in the nineteenth century, there was only one fraction that was deemed useful. That fraction was kerosene, which was used to illuminate the nineteenth-century night, marking a considerable improvement over scarce sperm whale oil and the flammable turpentine people poured into their smoky lamps.[11] American refiners distilled as much kerosene as they could; like Pliny, they considered gasoline worse than useless because it was so volatile.[12]

John D. Rockefeller, a stern, pious entrepreneur from New York, built his fortune on the market for kerosene. Rockefeller considered his task in almost spiritual terms, delivering light to a world of darkness. "Give the poor man his cheap light, gentlemen," he told his colleagues.[13] But in reality it was big business, and hugely lucrative. Rockefeller made it so with his merciless quest to expand his oil empire and dominate markets. He deployed secret front companies to underprice competitors, forcing them out of business. He controlled the means of transporting the precious fluid, extracting deep discounts from the railroads for train transport of his oil. The company countered the inevitable public outcry with clever deceits. "We should . . . parry every question with answers which while perfectly truthful are evasive of bottom facts," proclaimed one executive.[14]

Then, in the early hours of October 21, 1879, a sleepless Thomas Edison watched blearily as an electric current zapped through a glass globe in his New Jersey laboratory. Emitting a dim reddish glow, the world's first incandescent light bulb had been invented, and the electric power industry crackled to life.[15]

Society's desire for kerosene rapidly dissipated in the face of the new light. Yet Rockefeller and the other oil barons were swimming in oil. With the Pennsylvania fields wasted, the nascent American oil industry had moved on to Ohio and Indiana in the mid-1880s, where oil had also been dribbling out of the ground. A new market had to be found, and fast.[16]

The railroads forged in the heat of the Industrial Revolution, ferrying coal, steel, and people, coupled with horse-drawn carriages, defined transportation in the nineteenth century. Both required sizable inputs of energy to power their motion. Rail transport required tons of steel and sweat to build the trains and the rails, and then coal and humans to power and maneuver them along the tracks. Animal-powered carriages required less energy input, just room and board for the creatures and materials to build the carriages, but were likewise less powerful and more limited in terms of range and utility. The ratio of the amount of energy put into the system versus the amount of energy released was, in other words, stubbornly constant.

In 1860, a small contraption that could radically increase the ratio of energy input to output had been invented: the bicycle. This compact simple machine could make human motion almost four times more powerful, catapulting an hour's exertion from a three-mile slog into a twelve-mile sojourn. It required little maintenance and its humble materials could repay their energy investment handily. Unlike the train, which relied on mountains of coal, and the carriages, exploiting animal metabolism, the bicycle was small-scale, human-powered, and efficient. (This is true even by today's standards. Modern trains require 210 kilocalories of energy to move a single person a mile forward. A bicycle can do it with just 20 kilocalories, the amount of fuel in a bite of banana.)[17]

The bicycle had quickly taken the world by storm. "Thousands of riders acquired a taste for speedy mechanical road transport," wrote car historians Jean-Pierre Bardou and Jean-Jacques Chanaron. It was a completely new way to move, because unlike the trains, which only traveled at certain times, and to and from certain places, bicycles could take their riders virtually anywhere and were "entirely under their own control."[18]

Perhaps it was inevitable, with trains steaming about and bicyclists sweating over their handlebars, that the two forms of transport would eventually merge. In 1886, four years after the invention of the light bulb had pulled the kerosene market out from under the wobbling oil barons, German engineer Karl Benz attached a motor to a tricycle. Inspired, two American bicycle mechanics designed their own motorized vehicle in 1893, a gasoline-burning automobile.

The new inventions didn't exactly overwhelm train-horse-and-bike society. Three years later, the bike mechanics hadn't sold even a dozen of the autos.[19] The *New York Times* was not impressed. In the January 3, 1899, edition, they wrote:

> There is something uncanny about these newfangled vehicles. They are unutterably ugly and never a one of them has been provided with a good or even an endurable name. The French, who are usually orthodox in their etymology, if in nothing else, have evolved "automobile," which being half Greek and half Latin is so near indecent that we print it with hesitation.[20]

Besides being ugly and indecent, cars weren't very efficient at transporting people. Even today's cars require three times more energy than trains and thirty times more energy than bicycles to transport people a given distance.

But cars could be fast, and what's more, unlike the coal-powered trains, cars needed oil to speed along. Coal might compete with oil on some applications (after all, coal was much more abundant) but for this one, oil definitively trumped coal.[21] Coal was bulky and its energy was given off too slowly for machines that would need to be turned on and off quickly.

By 1900, Americans had built four thousand of the new gasoline vehicles, holding automobile races and other events to entice the public.[22] The fluid needed to propel the new machines continued to turn up in new and unsuspected regions. In 1901, an amazed public learned that essentially by chance, the premonition of a one-armed mechanic, oil had been struck under a salt dome in Texas, gushing out of the ground under its own pressure in a column twice as high as the derrick. Geologists and explorers renewed their hunt, this time looking for salt domes over which to position their drill-bits.[23]

With oil flowing so profusely, it wasn't long before American car production surpassed Europe's—the birthplace of the bicycle and the motorized trike—churning out forty-four thousand cars in 1907.[24] In 1909, automaker Henry Ford announced he would "build a motor car for the great multitude,"[25] and it was only a year later, with Ford's affordable Model T's zipping off the assembly lines, that gasoline sales surpassed those of kerosene.

These new vehicles would go on to conquer the pedestrian, the bicyclist, and the railways themselves, paving over their rights-of-way with smooth asphalt for their immense engines, creating a thirsty new market for the oil industry in the process. Bicycle paths, like those linking Pasadena to Los Angeles, were abandoned half-built, as investors fled from the two-wheeled future they had earlier envisioned.[26]

The oil empire that Rockefeller founded, based on secrecy, consolidation, and market dominance, had found its *raison d'etre*. Although Rockefeller's Standard Oil monopoly was beheaded in 1909, fed on a fatty diet of gasoline sales, Standard's subsidiaries would slowly regenerate into the gigantic uber-companies from which they sprang.[27]

Britain had taken the plunge and converted its warships from coal to oil in 1912, even though the country itself had coal reserves but no known sources for oil.[28] It was like switching to an all-fruit diet while sailing the Arctic seas; they knew they'd have to take the stuff from someone else's country, and they already knew where: Iran. The British government had bought into a new British company, Anglo-Persian Oil, today known as the more familiar BP. The company had struck oil in Iran and the crown took it upon itself to protect BP's access to Persia's abundant hydrocarbons.[29]

Across the Atlantic, motorized warfare was off to an inauspicious start. In 1916, General John Pershing enlisted two thousand of the newfangled vehicles to travel two hundred miles into Mexico to hunt down revolutionary leader Pancho Villa. But so undeveloped were the roads and untested were the new machines that "at the end of the campaign," writes highway historian Lee Mertz, "all two thousand vehicles lay strewn along the line of march in various states of breakdown."[30]

The following year's military exploits proved no better for the reputation of the automobile. The Americans were preparing to send 2 million soldiers, with their horses and fodder, across the ocean to join in the First World War. But how to get them there? All of those men and animals, spread out over the continent, would have to be amassed on the U.S. east coast in order to board ships across the Atlantic to Europe. That appeared impossible. Desperate, the military decided to try trucks again, despite the troubles during the campaign against Pancho Villa.

The nascent auto industry produced thousands of trucks to carry the soldiers and their equipment to ports on the east coast. Once again, the decrepit roads stymied the effort. Where they existed, the roads were impassable. The dirt paths were swamped in mud and obscured by piles of snow. The new trucks, those pinnacles of oil-industry and car-making technology, couldn't get through. The trucks ended up being loaded onto trains, which carried them to the next section of passable road, while crews worked around the clock to clear snowdrifts.[31]

Still, the Allied forces didn't lose faith in the internal combustion engine and its magic fuel, a faith that turned out to be worth the trouble. Britain and the United States unleashed the fury of their agile, petroleum-burning machines—about 163,000 oil-burning vehicles and 70,000 airplanes—vanquishing Germany's bulky coal-fired ones. Black gold was crowned king. Ten days after Germany surrendered, in November 1918, British statesman Lord George Nathaniel Curzon declared the Allied forces' triumph as petroleum's. "The Allied cause had floated to victory upon a wave of oil," he said.[32]

Back at home, demand for light clear gasoline continued to grow. In 1930, essentially by luck, oil explorers discovered the bountiful oilfields of East Texas. Texan oil flowed from a geological formation, at the time unexpected to hold crude: an "angular unconformity." As jubilant oil hunters fanned out searching for more, General Motors, Standard Oil and Firestone banded together to take over the nation's streetcar companies. Between the world wars, only about one in ten Americans owned a car, as most urban residents traveled by electric streetcar, which whisked commuters along their steel tracks leaving just the bumpy margins of the roads for automobiles.[33] As Texas's oil spilled forth, the companies boldly attempted to force consumers to opt for gasoline-burning cars instead, curtailing electric trolley services and replacing them with unpopular diesel-burning buses.[34]

Meanwhile, chemists were beginning to unlock the mysteries of a small but popular set of natural and semisynthetic materials called "plastics," from the Greek word "plastikos," meaning "able to be molded."[35] These elastic substances derived from all kinds of unlikely sources—amber, horn, wax, bitumen, shellac (from the secretion of the lac beetle), and gutta percha—and their unusual properties made them uniquely useful. Gutta percha, a dark-brown material from the Malaysian palaquium tree, was used for sheathing the first submarine telegraph cable. Shiny hard buttons could be made from casein, a paste of milk curds mixed with formaldehyde. Flexible but firm tires could be made from rubber trees, grown in plantations in Southeast Asia, and mixed with sulfur to form "vulcanized rubber." Celluloid, cellulose from cotton mixed with vegetable oil into a dough that could be molded into shapes or pressed into thin sheets, was used to capture early photographs and to form into billiard balls, replacing earlier ones made of elephant tusk ivory.[36]

At first, chemists thought these jelly-like compounds were actually a multitude of small molecules somehow held together. But then the truth came out: these elastic materials consisted of single molecules of unheard-of lengths. Some could have hundreds of thousands of atoms strung together in long flexible chains.[37]

With this insight, chemists set about building similar molecules, cracking, reforming, linking, and de-linking carbon chains, much as refiners did. The best compounds they came up with indeed were extremely malleable. Some could even be melted, molded, hardened into shape, and then melted and molded again. They could be stretched out in thin sheer sheets, cut into slivery threads and woven into fabrics, or shaped into poles and platforms to build furniture. The new synthetic plastics didn't *have* to be made out of oil—coal, alcohol, or natural gas could all be changed into the necessary building blocks—but with the gush of byproducts from refineries, oil was the cheapest and easiest option.[38]

In 1940, *Popular Mechanics* magazine predicted that "the American of tomorrow" would be "clothed in plastics from head to foot . . . will live in a plastics house, drive a plastics auto and fly in a plastics airplane."[39] The Second World War would help make it so.

By 1941, Japan had taken control of the rubber plantations of Southeast Asia, cutting off the supply of natural rubber to the United States. For American soldiers and pilots fighting in Europe, this meant that a flat tire had become a death sentence. The U.S. government pumped over $3 billion into the fledgling petrochemicals industry, demanding a ramped-up supply of synthetic rubber, along with whatever other goodies the industry could devise. With a river of byproducts streaming out of the oil refineries—themselves working in overdrive to provide fuels for the war effort—the petrochemists outfitted soldiers not just with synthetic rubber tires, but with nylon parachutes, synthetic rubber life rafts, plexiglas airplane windows, and plastic raincoats. Other crude byproducts, such as naphtha and methane, were blasted into nitrogen ammonia for explosives.[40]

Out on the battlefield, oil's essential role in powering the machines of war was undisputed. Military leaders took aim at the veins and capillaries of the enemy's oil supply. Allied submarines targeted Japanese oil tankers, crippling the oil lifeline to that oil-poor country. Allied torpedoes sent over 2 million tons worth of Japanese warships and oil tankers to the bottom of the South Pacific. The sunken oil might threaten delicate coral reefs and fishing grounds many decades later, but it wouldn't power the Japanese war machine.[41] "Toward the end," commented one Japanese captain, "we were fairly certain a tanker would be sunk shortly after departing from port." By the first quarter of 1945, not a single drop of imported oil reached Japanese shores, and the Japanese started building their naval ships to burn labor-intensive coal instead.[42]

When the war was over, the U.S. government sold its chemicals plants back to the oil and petrochemicals industry for a fraction of their cost. Exxon nabbed a $2 million petrochemicals plant for a mere $325,000. Monsanto acquired one that cost over $19 million for $10 million. DuPont got a $38 million facility for $13 million. Off to a running start, refineries and petrochemicals companies "were now ready to supply copious amounts of petrochemicals," writes historian Peter H. Spitz, serving "pent-up consumer demand for products that could be made from these materials."[43]

The United States, with seemingly plentiful oil in Texas, Oklahoma, California, and elsewhere, had little need, at first, to plunder foreign lands for its black gold. But many fields were rapidly exhausted as the Second World War exerted its heavy demands on the industry. The technology that would allow the industry to sniff out deeper, more hidden oil reservoirs had yet to be developed. By the end of 1943, Secretary of the Interior Harold Ickes was sure the United States stood on the brink of an oil famine. "If there should be a World War III it would have to be fought with someone else's petroleum, because the United States wouldn't have it," he wrote, warning that "America's crown, symbolizing supremacy as the oil empire of the world, is sliding down over one eye."

Ickes insisted that "we should have available oil in different parts of the world," and "the time to get going is now." No matter how generous domestic oil reserves may have been, controlling the giant foreign oilfields that other countries would have to rely on could only elevate the United States' strategic power. After all, with more and more sectors of the economy reliant on oil, military prowess dependent on its riches, and popular support contingent upon a growing economy, securing access to oil was crucial to maintaining power. In 1944, then-President Roosevelt staked America's claim to the Middle East's oil. Arrangements were duly made with the British. "Roosevelt showed the [British] ambassador a rough sketch he had made of the Middle East. Persian oil, he told the ambassador, is yours. We share the oil of Iraq and Kuwait. As for Saudi Arabian oil, it's ours," as historian Daniel Yergin described the exchange.[44]

Elites in Western countries had been helping themselves to slaves, silk, spices, and other goods from less powerful regions of the world for centuries, from the Niger Delta to the Indian subcontinent. Oil would be no different.

In 1946, a Justice Department investigation found General Motors, Standard, Firestone and other oil, auto, and rubber companies guilty of attempting to control public transportation. But the miniscule fines levied against the auto and oil industries were nothing compared to the grand upheaval they had effected. By the 1950s, the electric trolley system of public transportation had been effectively dismantled. The abandoned trolleys rusted in Los Angeles' vacant lots, where homeless scavengers turned them into impromptu shelters. Commuters would have to either take the bus or buy a car.[45]

While the oil industry was swept up with increased demand, basking in its ability to create ever more products and dominate a wide variety of markets, the coal industry was mired in conflict. Exploited coal miners had been rising up in anguish. Between 1929 and 1954, the U.S. coal mining industry lost 5 million worker-days to strikes every single year. And for every interruption in the coal supply, fed-up factory managers would invest in the switch to reliable oil.[46]

The black environs of London, the coal capital of the world, had become murderous. Although the moths could perhaps adapt—the peppered moth famously turned black so it could blend in with London's dark, lichen-stripped trees[47]—the people, increasingly, could not. On December 4, 1952, the wind sweeping through London died down and a warm humid layer of air descended on the city. The 1,000 tons of smoke particles, 2,000 tons of carbon dioxide, 140 tons of hydrochloric acid, and 370 tons of sulfur dioxide that Londoners' coal fires had pumped into the air that day were trapped over the city. Five still, windless days followed, and the stagnant 30-kilometer cloud of smog smothering the city turned amber, then green, then brown, and finally black. The sulfur dioxide reacted with sooty water droplets in the air to form a soup as acidic as battery acid, which scraped Londoners' throats, unleashing a torrent of mucous and inflammation. Many didn't make it to the overflowing hospitals, but collapsed in the street, blinded by the black fog. Fifty corpses littered a single city park, and the undertakers started to run out of caskets. When the smog finally lifted a week later, over 4,000 had perished.[48]

Before the war, coal accounted for about half of U.S. energy use; by 1955, it was responsible for less than a third. By 1956, even the city of London banned coal fires.[49]

It took less than a century for oil to eclipse coal, following the arc of oil-rich America's eclipse of coal-rich Britain. It wasn't just that oil was so powerful and versatile it could be used for everything from lighting lamps and powering vehicles to making clothes. It was also that the riches that could be earned by its extraction triggered intense competition between profit-seeking companies. The more precious oil became, because of geological depletion or because access to its reserves was cut off, the farther the industry's operations would reach, and the hungrier these big companies would be for sales to sustain themselves. And so, oil companies penetrated one market after another, in some cases endeavoring to manufacture new markets, helped all along by the nations whom their black gold showered with war-making prowess.

Coal continued to be burned, of course: over a billion tons of it in 2001 America alone, mostly for electricity. But it would no longer be smoking away in front of people's faces. Instead of hundreds of thousands of little fires, the industry would burn a handful of gigantic bonfires, transforming coal's dirty energy into likable electrons before piping it into people's homes. During the coal era, the typical American family would shovel about three hundred pounds of coal into their stoves every week. Now the stuff they would pump into their machines would be fluid.[50]

CHAPTER TWO

Exile from Tethys

AFTER THE SECOND World War, with the spoils of war divvied up among the victors, the countries of the West started a happy expansion. Oil-engorged and stable, the economies of Europe and the United States boomed during the 1950s and 1960s, and fed on the petrofuels, technologies, and products forged during the war.

Since the embarrassment of the First World War, when America's trucks had to be ferried by trains because of the nation's pathetically rutted roads, the oil industry had partnered with automakers to lobby for a network of smooth black asphalt criss-crossing the country on which their war-winning cars could ramble. In 1956, while the last coal fire was stubbed out in London, their lobbying finally paid off. The U.S. Congress earmarked over $26 billion for the National Interstate and Defense Highway System Act, setting off a fit of road-building that would profoundly alter the country.

American families and industries used the smooth roads and their new automobiles to drive themselves away from the congested cities. Between 1950 and 1990, suburban sprawl had become so intense that some areas were gobbling up land four times faster than their populations grew.[1] The new suburban nation survived by virtue of a web of asphalt and a river of oil, allowing them to access food, fuel, and labor from the distant homes in which they had cocooned themselves.

Like the horse before it, the car became a kind of much-needed, beloved pet. Gallons of ink were spilled describing the love affair between Americans and their cars, a romance the auto industry spent billions advertising. From 1957's publication of Jack Kerouac's classic novel about hitchhiking, *On the Road,* to drive-in movies and hot-rodding, Americans of all stripes embraced car culture. In 1955, more than 50 million cars were registered in the United States; twenty years later, over 100 million were on the books.[2]

By the 1950s, the synthesis of ammonia used for nitrogen fertilizers by Standard Oil and Shell, among others, was growing exponentially. German chemist Fritz Haber had discovered how to use petroleum's power to make ammonia back in 1909, effectively unlocking nature's restraint on plant growth. Before Haber, plants relied on about one hundred genera of bacteria to capture the nitrogen essential for their development. Employing methane to create extreme heat (up to 600 degrees Celsius) and intense pressure (equivalent to being submerged under about six thousand feet of water), Haber transformed nitrogen from the air into NH_3, ammonia, which could be used to make nitrogen fertilizers. Petroleum had allowed Haber to capture the Holy Grail of inorganic chemistry, something that had eluded chemists for more than a hundred years.[3]

The result out in the fields was remarkable. Agricultural yields doubled between 1947 and 1979, and the global population of humans skyrocketed. Before nitrogen fertilizers, there were fewer than 2 billion humans on the planet. By 1979, there were well over 4 billion. Without nitrogen fertilizer, geographer Vaclav Smil calculates, about two-fifths of today's 6 billion souls would not be alive. "Never before have so many people—be it in absolute or in relative terms—enjoyed such an abundant supply of food," Smil writes.[4]

As the fertilized crops grew copiously, so did the farm operations that harvested them. Big mechanized farms were hooked on oil not only for the fertilizers and pesticides that produced their super-sized crops but also for the machines that would harvest them and the oil-fired transport that would speed the crops to distant markets.

Meanwhile, plastic was becoming the most used material in the world, found in everything from space ships, garbage bags, children's toys, prosthetic limbs, and X-ray equipment to nylon stockings, acrylic sweaters, Teflon pots and pans, vinyl floors, Velcro closures, life jackets, glossy paper, and printing ink.[5] The natural plastics, those quaint wooden, shell, and cotton objects, were demoted to mere artifacts, the last vestige of celluloid's heyday hanging on in the lowly Ping-Pong ball, quite possibly the only object whose market the synthetic plastics industry still hasn't been able to overwhelm.[6]

Plastic penetrated every sector of the economy, touting itself as the very stuff of life; the word itself summoned up the future, as Dustin Hoffman's character in the 1967 film *The Graduate* was famously told. It was true, to an extent. What else could possibly be used for airplane windows or football helmets or surgical gloves?

In the heart of the oil business, tucked away in Shell's petroleum research lab in Houston, a crotchety geologist, calculator in hand, dropped a bomb on the party. In 1956, geophysicist M. King Hubbert announced that, according to his calculations, the seemingly bountiful flow of oil from Texas and Oklahoma, along with the rest of the country's oil territories, would reach its zenith by the early 1970s, after which it would start to decline. No matter where they looked for more oil, no matter how heroically they pumped it out, whatever oil was under U.S. soil had already been found and half or so would be gone within fifteen years, Hubbert proclaimed. The bosses were not happy, recalls Kenneth Deffeyes, who shared a lab with the "curmudgeonly" Hubbert. "Shell hated it!" said Deffeyes. "Right down to fifteen minutes before he gave his talk, the head office of Shell was on the phone saying, 'Don't do it, don't do it!'" It didn't matter at the time, anyway. With the oil party in full swing, nobody believed Hubbert's gloomy prognostications.[7]

While increasingly comfortable middle classes enjoyed oil's bounty in the West, the people at the other end of the bulging pipelines and well-trammeled tanker lanes remained mired in dispossession and conflict. When Britain pulled out of colonial Palestine in 1948, it had handed power over much of the country to the minority Jewish population, increasing their share of the country's territory from 6 percent to 56 percent. The neighboring Arab states never agreed to the u n -sanctioned deal, and fighting commenced almost immediately.[8]

The Western oil companies continued to exploit Middle Eastern oil assets the way any private, for-profit company would: to maximize profit. The situation in Iran typified the situation. b p and the British government both raked in more money from the extraction of Iran's oil than the Iranian government. b p 's margin on Iranian oil was so good it was able to earn 250 million pounds in profit between 1945 and 1950. The Iranian government earned just a fraction of that, 90 million pounds, from royalties.[9]

Amidst heightened conflict at home and seemingly insatiable Western thirst for crude, it started to dawn on many in the oil-producing countries that the oil that coursed under their feet might properly be considered their national heritage, which could be developed for the good of society and its future generations instead of a foreign company's bottom line. In 1956, Egyptian president Gamal Abdel Nasser, fed up with "the great capitalist monopolies in the advanced developed countries" that "rel[ied] on the exploitation of the sources of wealth in the colonies,"[10] took over the hundred-mile-long Suez canal that coursed through the Egyptian desert, through which two-thirds of Europe's oil was ferried on tankers.[11] Nasser promised more to come. "I see the Iraqi people in shackles, facing fire and steel," he thundered. "We shall all defend our freedom and Arabism . . . and work until the Arab nation extends from the Atlantic Ocean to the Arab Gulf."[12]

Barred from the narrow Suez, which slashed the journey from the Persian Gulf to Europe almost by half, wary oil companies turned instead to the longer journey that avoided the canal. They wouldn't be able to afford as many trips. The tankers carrying the oil would have to be huge.[13] (In time, the tankers would grow so large that many wouldn't be able to pass through the Suez's constricted passages at all, even if they had wanted to.)

From there, things went from bad to worse. In 1960, the death knell for the early oil industry tolled. The Organization of Petroleum Exporting Countries (OPEC) was formed, a cartel that today includes Algeria, Indonesia, Iran, Iraq, Kuwait, Libya, Nigeria, Qatar, Saudi Arabia, the United Arab Emirates, and Venezuela.[14] One by one, OPEC countries kicked Western companies out, taking over their assets and declaring their country's oil the sole province of state-run companies, to be developed at a rate dictated by the logic of governance—or at least the self-interest of ruling elites—not Western profit-making.

The Western oilmen abandoned their suburbs in the Arabian sands and went home, angrily. The abundant oilfields holding up to two-thirds of the world's oil percolated underneath these countries.[15] Oil historian Daniel Yergin gives eloquent voice to their rage:

> They had created value where there was none. They needed to be compensated for the risks they had taken—and the dry holes they had drilled. They believed that they were being put upon by greedy, rapacious, and unreliable local powers-that-be. They did not think that they were 'exploiting'; their plaintive cry was, "We wuz robbed."[16]

Thus shorn of easy access to more than half of the world's oil and the great majority of it that lies in easy-to-find and cheap-to-produce areas (Western companies had already been barred from touching Baku's 300 billion barrels and the rest of the oil in the Soviet Union in 1917, along with the 13 billion barrels in Mexico in 1938), the industry turned to politically safer regions, with progressively smaller reserves and increasingly formidable environments, relying on technology to get them there. Meanwhile, the hungry engines of the global industrial machine were, by 1960, slurping up over 21 million barrels every day.[17]

The quest to find oil outside the oil-rich countries, where the stuff was literally leaking out all over the place, was Herculean. Crude methods, born of both greed and luck, had already exposed the majority of the world's oil. By 1950, all of the structural traps in the United States that were visible from the surface had been drilled.[18] By the mid-1960s, the majority of the world's giant oilfields had already been discovered, mostly on the lands that the Tethys had washed over, in Iran, Iraq, Kuwait, and Saudi Arabia, along with Venezuela.[19]

Oil explorers would have to pinpoint layers of source rocks that could be as thin as thirty feet thick, buried under tens of thousands of feet of rock.[20] If the migrating oil hadn't found its way to the top where someone could see it, or if the geological formation that had trapped the oil wasn't visible at or near the surface, how would the companies even start to look?

A lot has to happen before a company can position its drill to actually figure out what is under the ground. Geologists theorize on whether the geology looks "prospective." If it does, then access has to be secured. Finally the rigs move in, and the companies lay out anywhere between $5 and $30 million to drill exploratory wells, looking for oil, gas, or any tell-tale clues in the rocks that something oily might be there. A lot of times they are wrong.

Once oil companies knew they were in "oil country"—places where they had determined that oil burbled somewhere underfoot— they only had to sniff out the places where the stuff was trapped. Still, the success of exploration wells was bad even then.

Exploration geologists marked a tiny "X" on maps covering huge chunks of the earth's surface. The holes they'd drill would be just eight inches in diameter. "It's easy to miss the target, and a single unsuccessful wildcat (dry hole) often condemns the entire prospect," said one petroleum engineer. With millions of dollars at stake, "Precision is essential," he went on, admitting that "it isn't really possible because exploration geology operates with a minimum of information."[21] The key to success, exploration geologists said, was to use all the information you could get together and then proceed "in the presence of uncertainties."[22]

As much as geologists knew about oil and its movements, and the huge amounts of money involved when they were wrong about their guesses, nine out of ten exploration wells drilled in the United States were dry holes. Just one in a hundred exploration wells discovered a usable oilfield.[23] When, in 1975, two University of California geologists analyzed the three hundred thousand exploratory holes that had been bored in the continental United States, they concluded that more oil would have been found faster had the holes been drilled completely at random.[24]

Military technology, harnessed to hunt the enemy and under-written by the public, was transferred to the private hunt for oil, which many described in openly warriorlike terms. The mapping of the ocean floor for submarines, aerial surveys for picking out bomb targets, and seismographs used to pinpoint enemy artillery: all of these military technologies developed to wage war were put to service in the hunt for oil.

The seismograph proved to be the "most powerful new weapon of all," as one historian put it.[25] Translating the echoes of seismic waves pumped into the ground could reveal the deformations where they lay below unseen, just as a bat's clicking could find its mosquito. The reverberations from explosions of dynamite, a vibrating steel plate under a truck, or underwater bursts of air would be recorded by tiny microphones stuck into the ground or dragged behind boats.[26] Seismic information was recorded from top to bottom and side to side, yielding a two-dimensional slice of data about the rock.

By the 1950s, seismologists had started to record their echoes on digital magnetic tape, allowing computers to analyze the mountains of data.[27] As computers improved, so did the speed and sophistication of the data analysis.

From each oil strike, explorers would fan out incrementally, slowly leading them to slip off the side of dry land and wade into the shallow water. By around 1950, companies had drifted off the spent oilfields of Texas and California into the shallow waters off the coasts. As seismic surveys improved, they found that some oil was trapped under the water, untapped. The lure of a big find pulled them in deeper as effectively as an undertow.[28]

Geologists had suspected there might be oil bubbling from the thick marine sediments under the North Slope of Alaska since the 1920s, but the harsh Alaskan environment had kept them away. At the North Slope, an area larger than the whole of Minnesota, winter temperatures could plummet to 40 below. Add to that two months of continuous darkness and ground permanently frozen down to two thousand feet.[29]

By 1967, oil companies had just about given up on finding any oil in Alaska. There was one last exploratory well scheduled to be drilled, at Prudhoe Bay on the northern coast, where the Sagavanirktok River splashed into the Arctic Ocean. They almost didn't bother, but the rig was already there and only had to be moved sixty miles. "It was more a decision not to cancel a well already scheduled than to go ahead," explained the oil exec who ordered the well. The conflict in the Middle East had intensified, as Israel attacked and conquered the Arab-populated lands of the Sinai Peninsula, Gaza Strip, West Bank, and Golan Heights in June 1967. Any dribble of domestic oil, no matter how chilly, would surely be greeted with approval from American officials.

The day after Christmas that year, the drillers at Prudhoe Bay made an incredible discovery: over 10 billion barrels of recoverable oil situated thousands of miles away from the bloody conflict in the Middle East. It may have been just a fraction of the amount of oil sitting under Saudi Arabia, but Prudhoe Bay was the largest oilfield ever found in North America.

While oil companies set to work developing the harsh new oilfields, analysts debated over how to supply the oil to thirsty American engines in the lower forty-eight. Nuclear physicists suggested that nuclear-powered submarines might carry Prudhoe's crude. Others advised a fleet of jumbo jet oil tankers. A pipeline, in the end, seemed the most sensible idea. But heartbroken locals and environmentalists, worried about the fate of their beloved Alaskan wilderness, fought the proposal bitterly, winning a court injunction against its construction in 1970.[30]

Oil explorers' determination against the elements paid off across the pond in Britain as well. In the days when Middle Eastern oil was available for the taking, nobody in the oil industry was interested in the North Sea, bound by the east coast of Great Britain, Norway, and the Netherlands. That shallow sea was so turbulent that one of its storms had vanquished an entire invading armada back in 1588.[31] The equipment needed to even think about exploring or drilling in such a forbidding place was hardly available at the time; a few feet of calm shallow waters might be all right but somewhere like the North Sea was inconceivably difficult. Plus, it wasn't clear who owned the rights to explore or drill in it.

Still, geological clues as to the Sea's crude potential tantalized. In the early 1960s, a huge gas field had been unearthed in the northern Netherlands, and geologists found that the same rocks that spurted that gas lay on the other side of the North Sea in eastern England.

Those same hydrocarbon-rich rocks might extend underneath the North Sea as well.[32]

If so, it would be a tremendous boon to Britain, by then a fallen colonial power. Hopeful government officials resolved the ownership issues. Seismic surveys followed, showing plenty of "bright spots" where the pore spaces in the rock had trapped gas. The race was on.[33] In the early 1970s, BP and Shell pinpointed two of the North Sea's biggest oilfields, the Forties and the Brent fields. Eventually, oil companies would find over 16 billion barrels of oil under the North Sea.[34]

As in Alaska, draining the North Sea oilfields would be expensive and physically challenging, but oil companies could rest assured that their costly investments would be safe. Unlike in Mexico, Iran, or Saudi Arabia, the British and U.S. governments could be relied upon to drape a protective wing over their activities.

In 1971, while the industry readied their conquest of Alaska and the North Sea, Hubbert's unheeded prediction quietly came true. The government agency that regulated the amount of oil pumped out of U.S. wells announced that the oilmen could pump out as much as they liked. "The Texas Railroad Commission announced a 100 percent allowable for next month," read the obscure announcement in the *San Francisco Chronicle*, Hubbert's colleague Kenneth Deffeyes recalls. "I went home and said, 'Old Hubbert was right.'"[35] From then on, the taps in the lower forty-eight states would be fully on; if the flow of oil they provided was insufficient, Americans would have to look elsewhere for more. Oil production from the United States, save for Alaska, would steadily decline ever after.

The news may not have been heard very loudly outside the industry, but within it, "The world split," says Deffeyes.[36] "There were Hubbertians and non-Hubbertians. The non-Hubbertians were larger in number and tended to be economists, managers, and a lot of geologists," who insisted that the boys were crying wolf. They argued, variously, that higher prices would provoke more drilling and thus render more oil; technology would improve so that more oil could be pumped out of already spent oilfields; that previously inaccessible hunting grounds like Alaska and the North Sea would pour forth riches; that Saudi Arabia still sat on a goldmine and could easily make up any shortfall. But many insiders took Hubbert's predictions to heart, and "literally shaped their careers around it," Deffeyes says.[37] They didn't trumpet the news to the masses, but anyone watching might have noticed their minor exodus from the U.S. oil business, as shaken engineers, geologists, and others fled for more secure industries, some migrating into nukes, others, like Deffeyes, into the ivory tower.

CHAPTER THREE

Into the Cold

By 1973, the earth's crust was bleeding more than 55 million barrels of oil every day, over half of it from the Middle East.[1] With each barrel swallowed by the industrial world's roaring machines, there wasn't a drop to spare.

Then, in October of that year, Egypt and Syria attacked Israel, attempting to recapture territories lost in 1967.[2] The United States promptly arranged for aid to be sent to Israel.

For the ministers in a then-obscure cartel called OPEC, this was just too much. They decided to take a stand. What they did would make OPEC "a household word, not just an obscure acronym," noted the *National Petroleum News,* turning Western attention to the distant lands they unknowingly relied on "for the first time."[3] Several OPEC ministers voted to cauterize the arteries pumping life-blood to Israel's allies, embargoing shipments of oil to the United States and the Netherlands.

Over the next six months, the price of the now much scarcer oil skyrocketed from $3 to almost $12 a barrel. The effect on industrial oil-gorging economies was tremendous and long-lasting. Almost every product by then came with an embedded oil cost.[4] Between 1970 and 1980, consumer prices doubled. Unemployment rose. Inflation set in.[5]

Then-President Nixon considered forcibly seizing Middle Eastern oilfields, but American soldiers were already stuck in a costly unpopular war in Southeast Asia.[6] What else could the United States do? Its own once-prodigious oilfields were in decline, North Sea and Alaskan oil had yet to come into full production, and the country relied on imported oil for almost a third of its oil.[7] They'd have to settle for a slow buildup of forces in the region: maybe they'd be better prepared next time.[8]

In the meantime, as prices kept rising, the government reluctantly did the obvious: institute measures to curb energy consumption. Nixon instructed homeowners to turn their thermostats down and companies to shorten working hours. Gas stations were to ration each driver to just ten gallons each. No gasoline would be sold on Sundays. For the first time, vehicles would have to meet some minimum efficiency requirements. Later, President Carter would urge energy conservation, appearing on national television wearing woolly sweaters in the chilly White House. He pressured companies to reverse their historic switch from coal to oil and gas—and to go back to coal. In 1978, he instituted the "gas guzzler" tax, a penalty leveled at those who bought inefficient cars.[9]

"Governments, corporations, and individuals were entirely unprepared for this turn of events," writes historian David Hackett Fischer. "Many American families found their budgets strained beyond the breaking point."[10] A new government agency was formed to study how energy was used in the economy—it would come to be called the Department of Energy.[11] A new way of thinking about energy, power, and society sprang up in the book-lined thinktanks and universities, with groundbreaking works from political philosopher Ivan Illich, biophysicist Donella Meadows, economist Herman Daly, and others. But none of it made much sense to insular, oil-coddled Americans. Commented one finance writer, "To many Americans it was impossible to understand how their standard of living was now being held hostage to obscure border clashes in strange parts of the world."[12] Broke and uncomprehending, they waited impatiently in the endless lines at the gas stations. Disappointment turned to pessimism, and a widespread cynicism set in.[13]

President Gerald Ford instituted a stockpile of oil, to be used in a future emergency: the Strategic Petroleum Reserve. Ultimately, several billion barrels of oil would be squirreled away in Louisiana's salt domes for safekeeping should capricious oil suppliers play dirty again. The industrialized countries that depended on OPEC oil formed their own alliance to counter the cartel, the International Energy Agency.

The second "oil shock" arrived in 1979 when Islamic fundamentalists overthrew the Shah of Iran. America's shaking hand curled into a fist. Carter announced what came to be known as the "Carter Doctrine." From then on, the policy of the United States would be to smother any hostile act that might curb the flow of the Gulf's oil using "any means necessary."[14]

However dispiriting and difficult the 1970s oil shocks were to Americans, they were much worse on the countries of the developing world. Poorer countries couldn't simply cut back on Sunday driving in order to weather a quadrupling of oil prices. Their newly industrializing factories needed the oil to function. The oil-intensive mode of growing food prevalent in the West had taken hold, and those who eked out a life growing their own food on small plots had seen their lands bulldozed by the oil-fired machines, sprayed with oil-derived fertilizers and pesticides, and their monoculture crops carted off on oil-burning trucks and planes. Amidst the plenty that petroagriculture made possible, one out of every seven human beings still went hungry, yet at least in the short term, industrial farms would demand their crude to avert potentially even greater catastrophe.[15] Many Third World governments borrowed billions of dollars from commercial banks and institutions to pay for the expensive oil imports.[16]

A crushing debt grew. In 1970, the developing economies of the Third World had a manageable external debt, approximately $100 million. By 1988, the Third World's external debt had grown to a staggering $1.3 trillion. Just paying the interest on these loans constituted a massive transfer of wealth from the countries of the South to the bankers of the North.[17]

Meanwhile, the oil industry was enjoying golden years. Flush with cash from the pricey oil that was dragging so many economies down, oil companies invested in developing their perilous but politically safe treasure chests in Alaska and the North Sea.

In hot pursuit of "energy independence," the nation's new battle cry, Congress had decreed that the trans-Alaskan pipeline be given the go-ahead.[18] The old gangs from Saudi Arabia were resurrected. A $50 billion matrix of roads, rigs, and machines rapidly colonized the windswept, icy, coastal plains, ferrying in drawling cowboy-booted oilmen from the south. "The whiteout blend[ed] sky and earth in a deafening whiteness," remembers one oil consultant, fondly. "And here, where the opposite extremes of earth are found, here you find the commonality of the drilling rig and its crew, the buddies of those in Arabia. Some have been there themselves. I hear[d] the drawl, and I [saw] the cowboy boots and the tobacco spit again."[19]

The clouds of dust following the zooming trucks and tankers sent the wildlife running, hunters finally penetrating the tundra on the new roads made for oil. The oil empire exhaled almost a hundred thousand tons of pollutants into the cold air every year and leaked over a million barrels of contaminated wastes every day. The native Alaskans watched as strange new sores and lesions befell their moose and caribou, their children started coughing more, and their seals' skins thinned.[20] Yet the industry and the governments that supported it were determined to continue plumbing the most forbidding seas and braving the most extreme climates in pursuit of crude anywhere in the world—except for in OPEC countries.

The triangular island of Newfoundland lies off the eastern edge of Canada in the frigid North Atlantic. It is a snow-covered jag of rock, its poor soils supporting stark pine forests and reindeer-moss covered plateaus. The people who live there, "Newfies," are the poorest and least-employed people in Canada.

One hundred and eighty miles off Newfoundland's southeastern coast, a series of banks rise off the continental shelf. Cold currents from the Labrador Sea wash over the banks, carrying stately icebergs, broken off the Greenland ice sheet. Meanwhile warm waters pushed by the Gulf Stream rush in from the south. As the frigid waters meet the warm over the shallow banks, clouds of fog are belched into the air, and the waters below start to churn.

This patch of ocean has long been known as "iceberg alley" to the Coast Guard. The lethal combination of shallow water, fog, and icebergs over the banks menaced the busy shipping lanes linking North America to Europe. Some of these ice pillars could be as heavy as 5 million tons, soaring to three hundred feet above the water.[21]

The waters are rich in oxygen and nutrients, providing a perfect medium for plankton, the precursor to a lush food chain. For more than four hundred years, fishermen and women from all over the world braved the seventy-mile-per-hour winds and hundred-foot swells of the largest of the banks, the 350-mile-long Grand Banks, for what was once one of the richest fisheries in the world.[22]

In 1979, Mobil, after drilling and abandoning fifty dry holes, struck oil off the Grand Banks in a field dubbed "Hibernia." The news met with great excitement among political elites, oil execs, and the long-suffering Newfies. Hibernia became the "indisputable darling of Wall Street investors," with commentators guessing the Grand Banks could hold up to 10 billion barrels of oil. This was "big-league stuff," as one analyst gushed.[23]

But how to get it out? In order to drill exploratory wells off the forbidding Grand Banks, oil companies would need a new and improved kind of vessel, one able to withstand the blow of gigantic icebergs. They'd need something much better than the Titanic, which an iceberg had punctured near the banks in 1912, and it wouldn't come cheap. Drilling a single well under the ocean could cost four times more than even the most expensive wells drilled on land.[24]

The truth was that oil companies were extremely cautious about new methods. Mistakes were costly and nobody wanted to ruin a perfectly decent well with some untested gadget, no matter how efficient or groundbreaking it might be. "Making a huge up-front investment in a technology that might not be commercial for ten years may be a necessity, but it's not a pretty addition to the balance sheet," commented one analyst.[25] By the turn of the millennium, many were still lionizing the breakthroughs that made Halliburton and Schlumberger legendary names in the business, innovations pioneered in the 1920s.[26] As a petroleum engineer put it, the industry was "totally oblivious to other technologies that were not stamped with a big H or a big S."[27]

Oil companies approached the problem of taming the banks' icy tempest the same way they approached others: enlarge. In 1981, Mobil spent almost half a million dollars a day to send a towering rig to drill exploratory wells on the stormy banks. At fifteen thousand tons, the rig, called the Ocean Ranger, was the world's biggest. "The massiveness kind of terrifies you at first," the Ranger's captain admitted.[28] The platform was twice the size of a football field. As one reporter who ventured onboard put it:

> [The Ocean Ranger was] as square and solid as the Parthenon, which, with her eight massive supporting columns, she somewhat resembled. Towering thirty-seven stories from keel to derrick top, moored by twelve anchors with cables each a mile long, the Ranger seemed a temple of stability. Veteran ship captains were amazed to find that she hardly rocked at all, often less than half a degree. But the oil men who ran the Ocean Ranger just propped up their cowboy boots and smiled. Well, Oklahoma didn't move around under your feet, either.[29]

The rig was considered unsinkable.

The ship's able captain boasted forty years of nautical experience, but unlike most other vessels afloat in the sea, the captain didn't have ultimate authority over the Ocean Ranger. The person in charge of the ship wasn't a mariner, but an oilman. Even while drilling miles away from solid ground, "land-bound, oil-field tradition prevailed," as the *Washington Post* described. Once anchored for drilling, the captain wasn't even required to be on board the Ranger.

The captain watched, dismayed, as routine seagoing protocols fell by the wayside. Reports that the Ranger had discharged a hundred gallons of diesel fuel went unreported to the Coast Guard. The drilling workers wouldn't show up for their lifeboat-skills training. No pumps or alarms stood at the ready should the ship take on water. The captain, Karl Nehring, sometimes complained to the chief oilman about the various safety breaches. "Who's in charge, Karl?" he'd point out belligerently.

Fed up, Nehring resigned in January 1982.[30] Six weeks later, in a howling blizzard kicking up fifty-foot waves, the Ocean Ranger capsized and sank, killing everyone on board. A wave laden with chunks of ice smashed a porthole, splashing water on electrical panels and short-circuiting them. The valves that controlled the level attitude of the rig started to go haywire and the vessel tilted forward into the waves, taking on more water. Lacking survival suits or Coast Guard-approved lifeboats, eighty-four workers plunged into the waters, where the frigid temperatures struck them unconscious then killed them fifteen minutes later.[31]

Back on land, newly made widows took in the news. "I felt like my insides were made of paper, very white paper. I would even walk carefully in case something might rip inside," recalls one.[32]

A year and a half later, the vessel bubbled up to the surface once more. Obscenely it emerged from the depths, upside down, pontoons jutting into the air. Tug boats attempted to tow the monolith farther out to sea. But the Ranger couldn't be pried from the Grand Banks. It broke free over the banks' southern tip, and sank once again.[33]

Such tragic mishaps were compounded by expensive errors. In the early 1980s, oil companies spent over $2 billion building a gravel island fourteen miles off the north coast of Alaska and drilling into the freezing waters, looking for what they hoped would be an oilfield as big as the ones in Saudi Arabia. But the moving rock layers had tilted, and the migrating oils had spilled out, either being entrapped somewhere else or simply leaking and dispersing at the surface. The oil had been there, but the trap had failed. "We drilled in the right place," said one oil company executive. "We were simply 30 million years too late."[34]

All told, the stream of oil from the industry's discoveries after 1970 comprise less than a third of the oil powering humans and their machines, most of it from small fields that would peak and deplete rapidly.[35] In some instances, oil companies would end up burning more fuel digging and pumping oil from deeply buried fields than the sought-after wells themselves would provide.[36]

Yet it would make huge amounts of money for the companies. After all, the industry could wow its investors with finds of 500 million barrels or even less. At twenty bucks a barrel, such a find was a $10 billion asset. In terms of potential profit for the companies, these finds surely deserved the superlatives heaped upon them by companies and the news media. But in terms of global oil supply, world oil consumption, or the global distribution of oil resources—500 million barrels could slake today's global thirst for oil for about a week and was less than 0.1 percent of the amount of oil collected under the Middle East—the finds were miniscule.[37]

The Arab oil embargo, for all the panic and mayhem it triggered, had cut the flow of oil to the world market by a measly 7 percent, as non-OPEC suppliers upped their oil production to counteract the OPEC cuts. Had Western oil consumption been anything near temperate, this temporary constriction in the flow of oil may have been vaguely tolerable.[38] Instead, successive Western administrations lived in fear of a repeat of the 1970s oil shocks, shaping their military budgets, foreign policies, and economic packages in order to counter the perceived threat of its return.

CHAPTER FOUR

Rockefeller's Ghost

As the 1980s rolled around, inflation started to let up. New oil from Alaska, the North Sea, and elsewhere started to tip the scales away from OPEC oil, which by the early 1980s accounted for roughly one-fifth of the daily American oil diet.[1] By the time Ronald Reagan took the White House, the country was instructed to go back to doing what it did best: driving cars around and shopping. Reagan brushed off the cautious energy conservatism of the 1970s like unsightly dandruff. He ostentatiously removed the solar panels on the White House roof,[2] and let the energy efficiency requirements pioneered in the 1970s expire. The country didn't need an energy policy, Reagan thought, just "strategic reserves and strategic forces," as his budget director put it.[3]

By the end of the 1980s, the price of oil had fallen below the price of bottled water, and a network of American military bases, aircraft carriers, and warships ringed the Middle East's oilfields, guns at the ready should any trouble arise.[4]

In August 1990, the wrath of the Carter Doctrine fell upon Iraq when it attempted to annex neighboring oil-rich Kuwait. The United States responded with deadly force, followed by a regime of sanctions and years of aerial bombing.

Amenable Gulf countries such as Bahrain, Kuwait, Oman, Qatar, Saudi Arabia, and the United Arab Emirates were armed to the teeth so they could help the United States take on any trouble from Iraq, Iran, or other potential troublemakers in the Gulf. Between 1990 and 1997, the United States handed over more than $42 billion worth of weapons and ammunitions to these countries, in the largest arms transfer from any single supplier to any one region of the world ever, according to international security expert Michael T. Klare.[5]

After the dismemberment of Standard Oil, the world's first Big Oil company, the company's constituent parts survived separately as Exxon, Mobil, Chevron, Amoco, Sunoco, and Conoco. In 1999, amidst increasing demand for oil, Exxon and Mobil merged. Two years later, Chevron merged with Texaco. Rockefeller's ghost was rising; Big Oil was back.[6]

By 2001, oil companies penetrated slicks of oily rock in more than eighty countries from four thousand oilfields.[7] The lucrative hunt put the oil industry, valued at between $2 and $5 trillion, in control of almost a sixth of the global economy.[8] ExxonMobil's returns on investments made over the past three decades were nearly *triple* that of other top companies.[9] In 2004, after a spike in the price of oil, ExxonMobil posted the highest one-year operating profit of any company in U.S. history.

That year, humans burned over 29 billion barrels of oil. North Americans were by far the most prolific. On average, each American man, woman, and child accounted for nearly 3 gallons of oil consumption every day of the year, compared to the average Italian, who burned less than 1.5 gallons a day, the average South African and Brazilian less than 0.5 gallons a day, and the average Chinese just 0.21 gallons a day.[10]

The business of domestic trade in the United States relies almost completely on diesel-burning trucks, which convey 70 percent of the nation's goods from remote factories and farms. In 2003, trucks traveled five times as far as the average car with about one-quarter of the fuel efficiency—just over 5 miles to the gallon. But their numbers paled in comparison to the armadas of cars.[11]

The American automobile market had been technically saturated by 1990, when the average American household owned one car for each of its licensed drivers. And yet, Americans kept buying more cars.

The population growth of cars shot ahead of the population growth of the humans, with a new car rolling into driveways every three seconds whereas new babies appear only every eight seconds.[12]

Gone are the "family pleasure drives" of the 1950s. In 2004, American adults spent more time in their cars—over two hours a day—than with their own children.[13] Yet all the extra driving isn't transporting Americans any farther. Between 1995 and 2001, Americans spent 10 percent more time in their cars but traveled the same number of miles. Americans' beloved cars were meant to herald liberation, yet the faster this freedom spread, the more often drivers found themselves trapped in congestion. Americans burn over half a billion barrels of oil a year just getting to work; they burn another 12 million barrels idling in traffic.[14]

The way Americans live chains them to their cars, whether beloved or not. "I have to have my car," complained one driver. "I need it to get to the hospital, or see my family, or take my wife to a nice dinner," the eighty-year-old man said. "It's not a luxury. It's a big part of my life."[15]

Belching fumes into the air, crashing into each other, cars and trucks kill more than seventy thousand Americans every year.[16] And the cars are growing. Rather than continue their losing competition with more efficient Japanese cars, U.S. automakers tweaked the towering vehicles originally designed for the military into luxury four-wheel-drive cars dubbed "sports utility vehicles" and marketed them to sporty urbanites and safety-conscious families.

Between 1980 and 2000, automakers spent $80 billion advertising large cars and trucks, and between 1995 and 2001, the number of suvs on American roads doubled while vans and pickups increased by more than 20 percent. "You put a few more bucks into a car, enlarge it, and sell it for a lot more money," explained a marketing director from Chrysler. "There was no actual customer need for four-wheel drive," added a Jeep executive. "All of the suv market was psychological." The gas-guzzling suvs had been classified by Congress as "light trucks," and thus were exempt from the more stringent fuel economy standards required for passenger cars, regulators perhaps reasoning that suvs would never appeal to anyone outside of farmers and horse-owners. But by the time sales had started to skyrocket among urbanites, the Environmental Protection Agency (EPA) found it difficult to crack down. As an unnamed EPA official admitted to *New York Times* auto reporter Keith Bradsher: "We don't want to kill the goose that lays the golden eggs for the domestic [auto] industry."[17] With an average fuel efficiency 20 percent less than the average passenger car, suv sales pulled down the average fuel efficiency of the nation's light vehicles, which declined steadily from 1988 onwards.[18] Even when sales of suvs stumbled in 2005 in the wake of high fuel prices, automakers remained steadfast in their commitment to the oversized vehicles, with Chrysler planning to launch no fewer than 4 new Jeep models in 2006.[19]

More stringent fuel efficiency standards alone would probably not stem the oil bonanza in any case. Many technologies that let energy be used more efficiently had had the vaguely counterintuitive effect of actually increasing energy consumption, a turnaround noticed by scholars over a century ago. In 1865, many believed that technological progress in making engines more efficient and the like would reduce future coal consumption. But in fact just the opposite occurred. The more efficiently energy could be harnessed, the more savvy marketers would encourage people to consume. Energy analysts called it "Jevons' paradox." More efficient refrigeration technology led manufacturers to market bigger refrigerators, and more fuel-efficient cars led Americans to step up their leisure driving, they found. As long as more efficient technology drove prices down, the technology stimulated more energy consumption, not less.[20]

Today, crude has become so indispensable to American society that even temporary interruptions in the flow of oil can seem dire.

On July 30, 2003, for instance, a pipeline carrying gasoline from Tucson to Phoenix ruptured and had to be shut down, depriving Phoenix of one-third of its gasoline supply. Panicked drivers waited in lines at gasoline stations for hours, only to find the pumps had run dry. "I never knew that gas was going to seem like gold," said one alarmed suv driver.[21]

Bereft of cheap plentiful gasoline for their commutes to work, many Phoenix residents were forced to improvise. Within the living memory of some Phoenix residents, automakers and oil companies had felt they had to trick commuters into driving cars rather than taking public transit, but now, stumbling onto exotic-seeming public buses, Phoenix residents had little notion about how to behave, prompting local newspaper reporters to offer helpful tips. "As the bus approaches, signal the operator to stop," read one bit of news media advice, "by waving."[22]

The state's worried governor looked at the lengthening gas lines and cancelled her own travel plans, assuring Phoenix drivers that the gasoline supply would be quickly restored and that rationing "is nowhere near the top of the list" of solutions to the problem.

Although it isn't easy to opt out of Western car culture, neither is it impossible. Frank Hewetson, father of two, built extra seats into the back seat of his car. "The school run, if you are doing it just you and one kid," he proclaimed, "is fairly outrageous." And so, every day, he'd round up five more kids to pile into his car and drive to school, figuring he was at least helping remove a few cars from the congested roads. But then he'd be forced to drive on to work, "sitting there alone in the car, feeling really guilty." And once at work, he'd sometimes have to drive more.

Luckily, his employers had an old black tank in the corner of the yard. Every so often an outfit that collected the leftover cooking oil from fish-and-chip shops and converted it into biodiesel would come and pour the fuel into the tank. Hewetson didn't feel so guilty driving the company car around, burning old recycled fish-and-chip-shop oil rather than gasoline. Plus, he added, the exhaust smelled like french fries.

Along with domestic trade and the daily grind, the daily bread has become a daily toll for the oil industry. In 2003, industrial farmers around the world spread over 85 million tons of nitrogen fertilizer on their lands, requiring over half a billion barrels of petroleum.[23] In the end, the petrofoods they produced provided just one kilocalorie for every ten kilocalories put in to grow them, a complete reversal from the times when humans stalked their prey and tilled their small plots, expending one-tenth the energy they'd reap in food.

Nitrogen fertilizers increase yields at first, but over time, farmers have had to apply more and more in order to sustain the incredible bounty of the first harvests. The potent runoff of this excess of nitrogen poisons both land and water.[24]

Today, Americans eat food that has typically traveled between 1,500 and 2,500 miles to get from the farm to their plates. With abundant plastics for packaging and plenty of cheap oil and trucks, the network of factories, farms, and supermarkets that keeps Americans fed has had no reason not to spread out lazily. Centralized supermarkets ensure that even organic and locally grown foods incur a petroleum cost. If nearby farmers want to sell food to their neighbors through the local store, they must ship their produce hundreds of miles to and from centralized inspection centers first.[25]

Plastic packaging makes it possible for these foods to remain somewhat edible, but long-distance petrofoods are by necessity more processed and homogeneous than seasonally available local foods. American hybrid corn is a good example. Almost a fifth of the country's arable land is planted with corn, a crop that requires more petrofertilizers and pesticides than any other, packing more than a half-gallon into every bushel.[26] It isn't that Americans eat so much corn, as corn. American fossil-fuel-grown corn is an abundant feedstock to process and transform into myriad processed foods. Most animals raised for meat are fed corn, even if they then require antibiotics to tolerate the illnesses to which the corn diet makes them vulnerable. Even farmed fish are fed corn. Syrup made from corn saturates sodas, sweets, and snacks.[27]

The predominant activity of the modern industrial economy has become combustion. No less than 40 percent of the matter pumping through American society's veins is oil; 80 percent of its wastes are the smoky end-products of combustion. "Modern industrial economies, no matter how high-tech, are carbon-based economies," the World Resources Institute reported, "and their predominant activity is burning material."[28] The amount of energy in the crude oil that goes into U.S. refineries and chemicals factories is matched, one to one, with the amount of energy they need to consume to keep functioning.[29]

On the smoky margins of this global bonfire, Frank Hewetson, a tall, balding, fit man in his thirties, dons a dry suit and life jacket, and throws himself into the freezing North Atlantic, directly into the path of a giant tugboat pulling a towering oil rig into place. He floats in the water for hours, leaning his head back and staring at the stars. In the pit of his belly, he can feel the shock waves of seismic surveyors' blasting airguns, an experience he describes as surreal.

He delays the ships, for a time, but eventually Hewetson gets carted off.

As an activist with Greenpeace UK, Hewetson and his colleagues resist Western carbon-burning culture in a most visceral way. Their plans include campaigns much more ambitious than simply freezing in the dark North Atlantic sea; Hewetson and his colleagues board and occupy oil rigs themselves, using the most high-tech materials and machines produced by the hydrocarbon economy to do it.

"If the rig was working, we would be fairly worried about going anywhere near it with our petrol boats," he says.[30] So, slowly, they move in with their diesel boats, with their sparkless ignition systems.

If the weather is good, they maneuver the small boats near the gigantic steel legs of the rig. Beams, giant chains, and pipes dangle from all directions in the shady waters under the rig. The waves pound the little boat. The currents under the rig threaten to capsize the boat, sucking it under the rig's metal maze.

Hewetson jumps to the rig followed by two others. On his back he carries climbing equipment, drysuits, and food:

> We actually climbed up the anchor chain itself, which was quite scary because it was moving around. Each link is about two to three feet big, and we just free climbed it, basically. We tried to make our way up to the working platform, but the workers were stopping us, physically getting in the way, so we came back down.

On the way down, Hewetson spies a small metal balcony, "tucked up right inside where the chains were." He squeezes his sleeping bag out of his pack and "made myself a home." He stays there for a few days, one worker even surreptitiously handing him a hot cup of coffee. His presence stops the rig from working for a few days, bleeding precious summer working hours in the process.

Later, Hewetson's group hatched a plan even more audacious. They would hoist a self-contained pod, a rigid, well-equipped, airtight camping tent, onto one of the rigs. This would provide for a much sturdier, more permanent occupation than an impromptu sleeping bag. If they could somehow attach the pod to an oil rig, they might be able to stymie oil production for days or even weeks.

An aeronautics engineer designed and built the pod from bright yellow Kevlar, a bullet-proof fabric made possible by oil's bounty. One morning, Hewetson and the others set off to affix the yellow blister to the side of an unsuspecting rig. "We climbed up the oil rig and put a big pulley there. Then we took a rope from the boat through the pulley and down onto the pod, so when the boat went off, the pod went up and we roped it in."

Hewetson and the others maneuvered themselves onto the tiny yellow pod, clinging to the side of the rig high above the seas. They shut the hatch and sat tight. If they hung on long enough, the calls for radio interviews would start streaming in on the satellite phone they had set up in the pod.

Suddenly, a powerful spray of water rained down on them. The workers were hosing the pod, like old cobwebs under the porch. They'd positioned a crane nearby, set to pull the pod off the rig, with a net underneath to catch the activists should they fall out.

Hewetson, realizing their plan, strapped on a rope and jumped out of the pod. "I tied the whole net in a big knot. It was just a useless bunch of rope then." Later, the oil company took more aggressive action. They sent some people down on ropes to stand on the pod's hatch, trapping Hewetson and the others inside. Then, with the activists trapped inside the pod, they craned the whole thing up onto the platform. They smashed open the hatch and grabbed the activists out. The police took over.

That was the last Hewetson saw of the Kevlar pod. Exhausted, out of fuel and batteries, the MV *Greenpeace* steamed home.

The oil industry said that the West's giant, self-reinforcing edifice built of black grease brought prosperity, pointing to the strong link between GNP growth and oil consumption. The more oil countries consumed, the more their GNP would shoot up. The more fuel workers consumed, with bigger and more fuel-intensive machines, the more productive they were. The correlation had been well-documented for decades.[31]

Critics wondered whether a rising GNP indicated genuine growth or a mere "swelling." Running up an $11 billion medical bill treating the childhood asthma epidemic triggered in part by trucks' diesel fumes added to the growth of the GNP, after all.[32] Such dilemmas were mostly brushed aside, most aggressively by those in the oil industry. According to Rex Tillerson, the swaggering Texan vice president of ExxonMobil, the world would descend into poverty and insecurity if the oil industry were not allowed to hunt, track, and plunge their drills into every last corner of the earth. "It is clear that the discovery and growing use of hydrocarbons over the last century has contributed greatly to people's wellbeing," Tillerson said in February 2003. "Access to affordable and reliable energy supply remains essential to the continued progress, prosperity, and well being of the world's citizens." Regulations based on "misplaced" environmental concerns would waste the "limited resources" of private oil companies, restricting their ability to "provide the greatest good to society."[33]

Promoting variations on this argument, the U.S. government and the international lending institutions it dominates have ensured that the fossil-fuel economy doesn't end at Western borders, by affixing thick, oil-soaked strings to its loans to indebted developing countries. Between 1992 and 2002, American export credit agencies handed out over $30 billion for fossil-fuel projects to developing countries; the World Bank almost $25 billion.[34] By 2003, World Bank was spending fifteen times more on fossil fuel projects than on renewable energy projects, a ratio the Bank vowed to improve by 2009—to around five to one in favor of petro-projects.[35]

Ensuring that developing countries consume increasing quantities of oil is "crucial to the long-term growth of oil markets," the U.S. Department of Energy opined.[36] Carmakers and oil companies know that the next hot market for them is unlikely to be in the West, given that each licensed driver in the United States already owns a car. In 2000, automakers spent almost $10 billion advertising their cars outside the United States.[37] China, in particular, "offers huge potential for future growth" BP's annual report avowed.[38]

Today, congested, slum-ridden megacities such as Calcutta and Jakarta are rapidly vanquishing their well-trod footpaths and bike alleys for asphalt-paved roads for cars driven by the elite.[39] The effects can be seen from miles above the planet.

Ram Ramanathan, an atmospheric scientist, gazed out his airplane window, heading south from Mumbai, India. The thick brown city haze, from hundreds of millions of wood fires and flaming cow-dung patties, sped past the plane's oval windows as it climbed over the Indian Ocean. But almost a thousand miles later, as the plane glided over the open sea, the brown pall still hadn't lifted. "This is something big," he thought to himself.

Dust, ash, and smoke from Asia's poorly regulated industries have congealed into a giant dark cloud of smog, blocking out as much as 10 percent of India's sunlight. Ramanathan had flown through the two-mile-thick "Asian brown cloud," a permanent fixture now stretching thousands of miles over the skies of Asia.[40]

By 2020, the developing countries, led by China and India, are expected to consume almost 90 percent as much oil as the industrial-ized countries.[41] The growth in their demand for oil could outstrip oil demand growth in the West by almost two to one. It is only natural, according to the U.S. Department of Energy. Growing populations and burgeoning industrial economies in China, India, and the rest led to "rapidly rising consumer demand for transportation via cars and trucks powered with internal combustion engines."[42]

CHAPTER FIVE

Refining the Hunt

By THE MID-1980S, reports that oil output in Britain's North Sea had peaked started to appear in the newspapers. Like all oilfields, they had spurted their oil out into strategically drilled wells for a while, under their own pressure, but then started to lazily dribble; eventually, the trickle would come to a stop altogether. When a porous, oil-filled rock is first pierced, releasing the tons of pressure on the buried layers, the oil inside will rush from pore to pore towards the well. But once this initial natural pressure spends itself out, in order to keep the oil flowing, drillers must start what is known as "secondary recovery." Their methods, using pumps and shooting chemicals, gas, or soda water down the hole to keep the pressure going, can stave off the inevitable decline in output, but eventually it arrives, generally when about half of the oil in the reservoir has come out of the ground. After that acme or peak of oil production, the daily volume of oil flowing of the well starts to fall, never to climb back up again.

The UK government, desperate to keep the industry afloat, incrementally reduced their tax on oil developments, sending their tax revenues from their stormy oilfields falling by 87 percent between 1984 and 1994, according to researchers at the University of Sheffield.[1]

In late 2002, plans were afoot to abolish all royalty taxes on North Sea oilfields approved before 1982.[2] Thus liberated from fiscal responsibilities to the people on whose waters they drilled, companies could scrape the seabed for ever-smaller fields and still turn a profit. But it is extremely unlikely they'd find anything big there now. "It would be a very big surprise to discover another Brent or Forties field now," said a Shell explorer. "It's like breaking a pane of glass:

you pick up the big pieces first and then you get out the dustpan and brush and sweep up the shards."[3]

Big oil companies such as B P aren't interested in minimum-wage cleanup jobs. Their Forties field had peaked in 1979. They pumped whatever they could and then sold it in January 2003.[4]

By the late 1980s, the better part of Prudhoe Bay's oil had been drained as well. From a production peak in 1988, each well's output declined by 20 percent every year, despite a spate of drilling and the injection of gas and other chemicals to encourage more oil to ooze out.[5]

Meanwhile the beating heart of the world's oil endowment lay in the Middle East, much of it barely touched. By 1996, for instance, only about one-fifth of the most promising structures that geologists had pinpointed in Iraq—let alone any potential stratigraphic traps— had ever been drilled *at all*.[6] But Western oil companies remained anathema to many O P E C countries; the public resisted them and some countries' constitutions outlawed their involvement.[7] Under increasing pressure to privatize, national oil companies had started, by 2002, to "act in a more aggressive, commercial manner," as *Petroleum Intelligence Weekly* noted, but it didn't help the biggest Western oil companies much.[8] Still, only the tiniest trickle of Middle Eastern oil leaks into ExxonMobil and ChevronTexaco's coffers, making up less than 6 percent of those companies' total output in 2003.[9]

"Having so much oil already there" in the Middle East, admitted one petroleum geologist, "it does seem somewhat wasteful to have to go and immediately look for more." Yet that is exactly what industry geologists would have to do.[10]

The oil industry forks out hundreds of billions of dollars every year searching for new streams of oil to fill its emptying pipelines and rickety tankers. In 2003, the industry spent $136 billion looking for

new oil, approximately the gross national income of Saudi Arabia
that year. In 2006, the industry would spend $238 billion.[11]

Oil companies exploit the most high-tech tools money can buy
and ever-more-sophisticated geological insights to conduct their
search for crude. Their latest weapon, one that has improved the
industry's rate of successful discovery by an order of magnitude
according to some enthusiasts, is the three-dimensional seismic
survey. Whereas before the industry made do with muffled echoes
to determine what lay underfoot, with three-dimensional seismic
technology they could carve a clear glass window into the crust of
the earth and take a look.[12]

Throughout the 1990s, giant ships prowled the world's oceans,
towing behind them up to a dozen six-kilometer-long kerosene-filled
cables studded with tens of thousands of microphones collecting
seismic data. On land, surveyors cut a maze of seismic tracks through
oil-prospective regions, in a few months collecting enough information to fill twenty-five thousand CDs. Sending the data by satellite
to supercomputers onshore, or by fitting their ships with massive
computers, the data can, in a few months, be processed into a shim-
mering, three-dimensional image of the underworld.

Different colors indicate different kinds of echoes, and the whole
image can be projected onto large-scale 180-degree interactive
screens for oil execs and geologists to wander about in. The three-
dimensional movie domes have kitschy names like "VisionDome,"
"Reality Centre," and "Decisionarium."[13]

Ian Vann is a true believer in three-dimensional seismic technology.
The vice president and technical director at BP, Vann is a forceful,
white-bearded geologist with a thick Scottish brogue. He proudly
broadcasts his movie of seismic images to his colleagues. Wavy col-
ored lines on a flat dark screen slowly descend to reveal something
entirely unexpected: a tall, wildly jagged, three-dimensional structure. It's the oil- and gas-rich rock, hiding virtually invisible under
the flat strata atop it. The effect is eerie. Vann booms to the crowd,

in case anyone is not suitably impressed, that his movie requires "the largest parallel processing power available industrially!"

In fact, three-dimensional seismic is even better than that, he bellows. It "represents the evolution of technology within the last two years equivalent to the changes brought about by the launch of the Hubble space telescope!" It certainly makes Vann's passion for unmasking the geological secrets of the earth much more interesting. Members of the hushed audience nod their heads.[14]

Between 1994 and 2004, oil explorers found 426 oil and gas fields of over 100 million barrels of oil equivalent each. Since 1998, over 40 percent lay not under the familiar arid plains or even arctic tundra but deep under the ocean's restless currents and the sea floor's shifting sediments.[15] A software package eagerly touted by one of the world's biggest energy consulting firms summed it up in its title: it was called "DEEPE$T."[16]

The deeper waters off the Gulf of Mexico's continental shelf, for example, had been virtually ignored by oil explorers for years, even as they exploited the oil reserves in the shallow waters nearby. "The first and real killer was the stratigraphy," explains Chevron's former chief geophysicist, Lee C. Lawyer.[17] Conventional wisdom dictated that there couldn't be any oil in deep water. Only shallow seas, washing over the shelves of the continental plates that slipped under water, could have deposited the oil-rich shales and reservoir sands that turn into oilfields. How could any of that stuff wash all the way into the depths of the ocean? And even if some source rocks had formed in the deeps, the idea went, there wouldn't be any reservoir rocks down there to soak it up.

Checking into the veracity of this notion was virtually impossible, in any case. Anything that deeply submerged under water became invisible to traditional seismic methods. A highly mobile layer of salt hid all of the underlying geology.

Then, confounding conventional wisdom, Brazil's state-owned oil company discovered an oilfield under the ocean's depths in the mid-1980s. An entire realm of the planet, the deep oceans, hitherto written off as oil-barren wastelands, might be loaded with crude. Eyes opened, the industry whisked around to take another look in their own backyards. Armed with three-dimensional seismic technology, explorers set off into the deep water of the Gulf of Mexico to find their missing gold.[18]

In 1999, they found it. BP uncovered a billion-barrel oilfield under no less than six thousand feet of water, reverentially dubbing the field "Crazy Horse." This nominal homage was stymied when the Lakota raised an outcry over the despoiling of their ancestral warrior's name,[19] but an awestruck BP still aimed to spend $15 billion to develop oil under the Gulf's depths.[20] The now-renamed Thunder Horse would be tamed with what BP claimed would be the largest floating oil and gas structure in the world.

None of it would have been found without three-dimensional seismic, Vann declared. The seismic technology is twenty times better in 2003 than it was just three years before, allowing petroleum geologists to "see" the Gulf's deep water oil when before they were blind to it, he said. It still isn't easy. "Without 3D we wouldn't have a chance," agreed Lawyer. "With 3D, it is still a difficult problem. . . . Trying to sort out data that has been recorded after passing through a salt body is very difficult and often very misleading. . . . Mistakes are very costly," he pointed out. "Who could make money when the exploratory well cost more than $20 million?"[21]

With TotalFinaElf's 1996 discovery of a multi-billion-barrel oilfield off the coast of Angola, the hunt for oil in the deep water off the west coast of Africa had commenced along the coasts of Angola, Congo, Equatorial Guinea, Gabon, Ivory Coast, and Namibia. As the Society of Exploration Geophysicists put it, "West Africa—where oil-filled, undrilled, amplitude delineated, treasures await. Let's go!"[22]

In late 2001, a three-dimensional seismic survey company, Petroleum Geo-Service, had released seismic data indicating potential oil off the coast of tiny São Tomé, setting off a storm of deals in that 150,000-strong 1000 square-kilometer island nation, with PGS, ExxonMobil and others.[23] Advisors pushed the White House to set up a military installation on the tiny impoverished island, as a home port for oil tankers and the warships that would protect their precious cargo.

According to a State Department official:

> African oil is less sticky than the stuff you get in the Middle East, and much of it is in deep water far offshore, so the natives don't notice it being taken, whereas in the Middle East it's pumped out of the ground under the noses of Wahhabi fundamentalists. Then you have São Tomé, which is basically the only stable democracy in West Africa. It's perfect.[24]

The West African governments aren't driving a particularly hard bargain: "Fiscal terms for deep-water licenses are usually negotiable, work obligations are not excessive, license periods are long, and block sizes are generally large," enthused *Petroleum Economist*. The waters are relatively calm and warm, the waves rarely topping five meters. The only problem is, well, these countries are dirt poor. "The infrastructure for oil operations is generally poor, and facilities for constructing and maintaining high-tech structures and equipment are either not available or, at best, unreliable," *Petroleum Economist* moaned. Everything would have to be shipped in.[25]

The industry invested precious little of its own enormous income on the risky, long-term research needed to make technological break-throughs, proportionally speaking. The computer and pharmaceutical industries, for instance, spend between 13 and 20 percent of their sales income on research and development, the oil and gas industry devotes a mere 3 percent. According to a 2002 study, big oil and gas companies reduced their investments in R&D by over 40 percent over the 1990s, spending between $2 and $3 billion a year on "near-term proprietary needs" rather than the risky, collaborative, long-term research that they'd need to continue exploiting diminishing resources in the future.[26]

This was where university scientists came in handy. The highly trained academics toiling away in the ivory tower, the nation's brain trust, its repository of intellectual capital for helping solve society's challenges, could easily be shifted toward pursuing basic research that might lead to the next big thing in the oil industry. Most worked on miniscule budgets perpetually slashed by the federal government. A few choice grants could easily generate the kind of buzz in the academic world that would lead to university researchers subtly and overtly channeling their own and their students' research toward where the money was.

For financial giants like ExxonMobil and BP, scattering a few million dollars amidst the starving academic masses would hardly slow their stride. But the influx of corporate dollars could remake academic disciplines. Petroleum geology, for instance, the science of finding and measuring oil, shot at least twenty or thirty years ahead of the rest of geology. "We understand a lot more about where oil comes from, how it is formed, how to find it, simply because there was so much money to be made by corporations and individuals," says one petroleum geologist. "The investment and effort was way way way bigger than any other branch of geology."[27]

But it was more than just petroleum geology that could profit from the industry's new deep-water hunt. "There are many . . . disciplines central to the development of deepwater and ultra-deepwater," *Offshore* magazine enthused. "The list can go on almost indefinitely."[28]

A range of public universities openly transformed themselves into corporate R&D centers for the petroleum industry. According to *US News and World Report,* the University of Texas at Austin, Texas A&M University, and Stanford were the very best graduate schools in the country for petroleum engineering.[29] The University of Texas at Austin awarded more PhDs in petroleum engineering than any university in the world. Oil money funded Texas A&M University and the University of Texas at Austin directly; the universities shared in the oil income from 2 million oily acres in west Texas.[30] The oil industry and the National Science Foundation showered them with funds to create a joint research center on offshore technology, where academics and students studied how to make oil exploitation of the Gulf of Mexico more lucrative. They honed their oil platform and subsea well models in a giant, fifty-five-foot-deep tank of water fitted with paddles and fans to simulate the gusty, wavy ocean.[31]

Oil companies were graced with full access to shape and direct such university research. The University of Tulsa, for instance, took a $500,000 grant from ChevronTexaco. In return, the school would allow the company to be "intimately involved in every phase" of university research, "developing a powerful new collaborative model to help solve some of the industry's toughest challenges."[32]

BP, by underwriting some research at the University of London's Imperial College, gained access to "everything from the writing of briefing papers to major programmmes of fundamental research," BP's inhouse magazine boasted. Indeed, "BP effectively has access to the whole intellectual think-tank that is Imperial College," admitted one of the college's research directors.[33] According to Aberdeen University's public relations office, its Oil and Gas Centre was "genuinely committed to trying to do all we can to help [the oil and gas industry] through contract work and through consultancy and, where possible, training programmes," with funded positions such as the Shell Chair of Production Geoscience, the BP Arco lecturer in Petrophysics and the ExxonMobil lecturer in Structural Geology. According to an independent study, British taxpayers spend 40 million pounds a year subsidizing such research on fossil fuels.[34]

The aftershocks of oil industry largesse encounter a few breaks as they ripple through academia. Mount Holyoke geology professor Michelle Markley, for instance, didn't relish the idea of her beautiful rocks being punctured by oil drillers, but she, like most academic geologists, couldn't do the work she loved without relying in some way on oil industry funding. Markley, like many scholars of rock, lived for stone. Small rocks adorned the shelves and alcoves of her airy Northampton, Massachusetts apartment; whole slabs littered her office at Mount Holyoke's geology department. She chose her life's work after an incident with a bit of boulder. As a young student, a teacher explained that the pockmarks on the rock were imprints from raindrops that fell 2 billion years ago. It moved Markley to tears.

"Oil exploration and research geology have been evolving together for about a hundred years, so lots of the ties seem so natural that no one thinks twice about it within the field," she says. The oil companies collected the best earth-science data in the world, using the fastest machines and the most advanced technology. Three-dimensional seismic imaging was just one example. It is "truly innovative," Markley says. With improved imaging, structural geologists like Markley were able to pioneer a more sophisticated understanding of the faults, folds, and sedimentary basins they poked around in, so much so that three-dimensional seismic had even changed their guiding theories about how the earth's features moved and collided.

It is a two-way street. "The relationship between oil exploration and basic research is intimate," she says. "Much of what we all do is useful to the oil industry. Lots of geologists who are well respected for their basic research either work directly in the oil industry or are partially funded by the oil industry."[35]

And yet, unlike most academic research conducted under the grace of public subsidy for the advancement of human understanding, industry-related research culminated in a product, a lucrative intellectual property to be bought and sold to the highest bidder. And so, the results of oil-industry-friendly academic research were often not available to the public, as is standard in most other fields.

Albert Bally, a widely respected geologist who joined the faculty at Rice University after a three-decade career with Shell, openly admitted that his concept for a new textbook using three-dimensional oil-industry data would "revolutionize traditional structural geology," yet insisted that he'd leave out crucial information "to insure that the commercial value of the data would not be diminished." Students wanting to know where the beautiful three-dimensional images were shot from would be out of luck.[36]

Oil companies and the academics who work for them "are sitting on a shocking amount of great seismic data that the majority of academic geologists have never seen and never will see," Markley remarks. How all of that information, were it digested in the broader public and scientific community through publication, debate, critique, and reanalysis, would lead to new understandings is unknown. The few chunks of information that do occasionally filter out of industry's secret cache—like some of their three-dimensional data—indeed do make "a big difference," she says.

With support from academic engineers, geologists, and other experts, the industry has developed the tools they need to find and extract oil from its hidden nooks and corners.

A new technology called "directional drilling," for instance, allowed a single platform to claw into the ground from all directions. Now those deposits of oil, which would have been too small to be worth the expense of an entire rig, could be profitably developed, sending oil entrepreneurs to sniff out and encircle every last little bit. Directional drilling was "dramatic" and "so accurate," the American Petroleum Institute bragged, that companies could "target an area the size of a walk-in closet located more than five miles from the well and a mile or more below the surface." With this technology they could sap the oil coursing under delicate wetlands or fragile coral reefs, over which it would be impossible to directly position a rig. Directional drilling allowed them to increase the amount of oil siphoned out of reservoirs twenty times over.[37]

"Oil and gas at depths recently considered unreachable can now be tapped. Smaller accumulations once thought to be uneconomic can now be produced profitably. Fields under wetlands or cities can be accessed without disruption of the surface," crowed the Department of Energy's fossil energy office.[38]

With new methods of "enhanced recovery"—getting the second half of the oil out of the rock—every last bit of oil could be gained, as detergents, fire, water, bacteria, and soda water were all shot down into the well. Scientists were dreaming up new products to try every day. Geophysicists shot three-dimensional seismic images before and after the first gush of oil was taken out, tracking how the oil and gas moved in the rock. The technique was called four-dimensional seismic: three-dimensional seismic plus the fourth dimension of time.[39] Four-dimensional seismic imaging could target several millions more barrels of oil or its equivalent for a company's cache.

In other words, the industry could perform both as a lumbering giant and a nimble parasite. No ecological niche, no matter how tiny, fragile, or beloved, could consider itself safe from the drills.[40]

While seismic explorers pored over the Gulf of Mexico and the waters off West Africa, oil companies were struggling to tame some of the planet's most awesome forces in ice, water, wind, and wave in order to unearth Hibernia's riches. More than two thousand icebergs drifted around Hibernia's oilfields every year. Underwater currents could slam those icebergs into a rig even if the wind were blowing in the opposite direction.[41]

The scale of the development had started to smell bad during the early 1990s, as the federal and provincial governments put up ever-greater sums to lure investors into developing the oilfield. The locals were increasingly doubtful. "It's not a viable project in the strict sense of economically viable. If it was, why are we putting these massive amounts of subsidization into it?" a Newfoundland economist said. "Even with that, you're having difficulty to get people to say 'Yes we want to do it'."[42]

Then a cash-heady Mobil struck a deal with the Canadian government to attempt to exhume Hibernia's oil, icebergs or not. Their strategy: build the biggest, strongest rig ever. With a price tag of no less than $7 billion, Hibernia would be the most expensive oil development ever.[43]

First, the sleepy foggy town of Bull Arm was bulldozed for a new construction facility to build the concrete base of the rig, a behemoth of more than 400,000 tons of concrete and 69,000 tons of steel. By 1992, thousands of workers descended upon the newly built construction camps. They built a dock for the coming concrete base, in the process pumping out 38 million gallons of water. They built a pier, draining a small lake for a fabrication yard.

Two years later, the structure was floated out to sea where it was anchored. Workers by the thousands rode helicopters and barges out to the site to pour more concrete and steel into it. Forty barges circled the ever-growing giant, including one where concrete was mixed, another supplying power, and yet another holding more than eighty offices. It was an industrial city afloat in the ice and fog.

In Korea, Italy, and Canada, workers built the drilling derricks, the flare boom that would burn the natural gas that inevitably accompanied the oil, the lifeboat stations, helideck, and living quarters that would sit atop the concrete base. When these "top modules" arrived in the desolate province, they struck a reporter as "a many-tentacled space station inexplicably plunked down in the stark landscape of coastal Newfoundland." Over five days, the concrete base was gradually partially submerged into the icy waters while the top modules were lined up on top. (When Norwegian oilmen had attempted the same maneuver in the North Sea, their concrete base shattered and sank to the bottom of the sea.)[44]

Once combined, the resulting mammoth weighed 587,000 tons, heavier than five aircraft carriers.[45] Nine tugboats towed it to the stormy site, where 400,000 tons of iron ore were pumped onto it until the whole thing slowly sank to the bottom of the sea floor, more than two hundred feet down.

It had taken six years and over five thousand people toiling on three different continents to build. "I don't think that a more complicated civil construction project will ever be built," bragged Hibernia's construction manager in 1997.[46]

Unlike the rigs of the North Sea and elsewhere, swaddled in pipes, boats, machinery, and steel, the concrete fortress at Hibernia was fully enclosed upon itself; nothing except lifeboats hung over its sides.[47] More than forty wells spat oil into underwater pipelines leading into the rig, and then off to floating loading stations to be delivered to tankers.[48] By the late 1990s, the rig's two drills and several hundred workers were fighting off icebergs and storing over a million barrels of oil onboard.

The looming icebergs were shot off course by water cannons from the supply ships ringing the rig. Others were lassoed and dragged away. The rig itself was armed with a 1.4-meter-thick ice wall, spiked with sixteen serrated teeth.

Was it worth it? By the turn of the century, the consortium of oil companies that owned Hibernia, including ExxonMobil and ChevronTexaco, estimated they'd get just over 500 million barrels of oil out of the ice-ridden field.[49]

In the sapphire seas off West Africa, where oil companies were poising their drills over some of the deepest, most remote patches of ocean in the world, trials of a different nature presented themselves.

As in the new deepwater finds off the Gulf of Mexico, the oil finds offshore West Africa were not only generally smaller, they were out in the middle of nowhere, miles away from the complex of underwater pipelines, refineries, and oil terminals that ringed the oilfields of the North Sea and Alaska. If companies had to build entire infrastructures just to drain these small pools, they certainly wouldn't be making any money.

Girassol, for instance, an oilfield ninety miles off the coast of Angola, was discovered in 1996. The French oil company Total-FinaElf figured there could be over 700 million barrels there.[50] But the oil was cocooned under more than 4,500 feet of water,[51] over ten times more than Hibernia. The cost of building a man-made concrete island would be astronomical.

Through small incremental progress in corporate and academic research labs, the possibility of extracting oil from under thousands of feet of moving living ocean, without an elaborate system of pipes, processing facilities, and tanker terminals, was being realized. By the mid-1990s, a new oil-production model had emerged, perfect for exploiting small, remote, and deepwater oilfields: the FPSO, or floating production, storage, and offloading system.

Instead of a giant concrete-and-steel island piercing the seabed and sending oil through dozens of pipes to production facilities and ports, an FPSO could get the oil out, process it, store it, and pack it off onto tankers all from a single vessel, swishing around on the surface of the sea. No more underwater pipe jungles and extensive onshore facilities would be needed. A single gigantic vessel could serve as drilling rig, processing facility, and tanker all at once.

Perhaps most amazing of all, instead of building these marvels from scratch, the industry could simply refurbish aging oil tankers.[52] And so, FPSO construction was rapid. Generally, the oil industry took about ten years from the time they pinpointed an oil reserve to the time when they started drilling out the oil. By refurbishing an old tanker into an FPSO, they could cut that time lag by a factor of six.[53]

The technology reached its zenith in 2001, when TotalFinaElf's FPSO for Girassol chugged into Angolan waters. Oil industry insiders were positively bedazzled by it. The $2.8 billion, 343,000-ton floating rig won accolades for technological innovation from trade groups. It was big. The rig was in the deepest water ever; the platform was the largest ever; its buoys the biggest ever.[54] The Girassol FPSO would extract oil from almost two dozen wells scattered over a wide expanse of sea-floor. Over a dozen more wells were punctured to pump water and gas back into the reservoir, forcing more oil out. It could store at least 2 million barrels of oil, and so could fill up the largest oil tankers cruising the seas today, for the long trip to Europe and North America.[55] Everything would be done on board. No pipelines to shore, no processing facilities along the coast, and no tanker terminals amidst villages along the bay would be necessary.

FPSOS bypassed the painstaking courtship of traditional oil developments for a series of quickie one-nightstands. Oil extraction offshore, found via three-dimensional seismic, and sucked out by FPSO: a rapid profitable model for mining the last of the world's crude had been forged.[56]

CHAPTER SIX

Aftershocks

WHILE BIG OIL chased new frontiers in ever-more far-flung locales, its old rigs slowly rotted in its abandoned oilfields, teetering in the wake.

According to the National Research Council, it would cost nearly $10 billion to restore Alaska's North Slope to its pristine, pre-oil state, but it is exceedingly unlikely anyone will ever do it.[1] The search for oil itself disturbed plants and animals unlucky enough to trample, unknowing, upon oily graves. Between 1988 and 1998, seismic surveyors had hacked over 900,000 miles of tracks for seismic lines, opening up some secluded wild places for the very first time. Hunters and diseases followed.[2] Seismic ships sent out deafening blasts of noise that interrupted the dark, quiet waters where whales and other marine mammals clicked and squeaked to each other across the water column. Whales and dolphins were known to go quiet and veer off their ancient water trails to avoid the blasts.[3]

With oil companies developing more smaller fields and quickly depleting them, strings of "mature" drained fields litter the globe. As the fields, age their facilities require more maintenance, just as the money to be made shrinks precipitously, and so the incentive to postpone or avoid maintenance of facilities is built in.

Years after their planned obsolescence, the platforms on the North Sea's stormy seas keep chugging along. Many production platforms, towering over the water on concrete legs shoved into the seafloor, had been built in the early 1970s and were meant to last about fifteen years, the amount of time companies figured they'd need to suck the oil out and move on. But the technology of forcing the oil out of the rock keeps improving, the government's take continues to diminish, and as a result, the platforms still bob in the frigid waters, "while many of them are literally wearing out," according to the *Financial Times*.[4]

Excavating holes in the shifting sea-floor under man-made islands is extremely dangerous work, even under the best conditions on the most well-maintained rigs. In 1993, the Centers for Disease Control reported that around the world, the rate of accidental death among oil and gas workers soared above that of all other U.S. industries combined. The rate of injuries to U.S. oil and gas workers (mostly to fingers, hands, and arms) dwarfed that of any other private industry in the United States. Worse, the dangers intensified when the giant pipes and machines that crushed and twisted oil workers delved into the depths of the ocean rather than the land.[5]

On the night of July 6, 1988, as day-shift workers turned in their beds, something was leaking on the Piper Alpha, Occidental's hulking platform of 34,000 tons of steel on the North Sea. At ten o'clock that night, there was an explosion. A second explosion followed, engulfing the platform and its sleeping workers in flames and smoke. In a fury, blocks of steel, drill bits, and other equipment flew through the sky and the platform started to tilt, its metal floors reeling at perverse angles. A handful escaped the flames for a 150-foot freefall into the frigid waters below. One hundred and sixty-seven workers perished.[6] The platform, rent and torn and on fire, bubbled under the sea, 120 miles off the coast of Scotland. It was the worst accident in the history of offshore oil production, which a damning government inquiry attributed to corporate neglect. Yet, Occidental was never fined for the Piper Alpha disaster. Two workers who died on the platform were later held responsible for the explosions.[7]

Jake Molloy was on a platform a few hundred miles north when he heard the news. "We found it hard to believe, to really comprehend! To see a platform, the size of Piper, just disappear! You'd never believe that was possible!" he recalls.

≣

Jake Molloy had the physical strength and technical know-how to take on the stormy seas. Molloy grew up in Dundee, Scotland, which "should have really been the oil capital of Scotland, but Aberdeen pinched it from below our feet," he says.

Molloy is fair with droopy pale blue eyes and a laconic expression. "I worked on this guy's house . . . he worked for Chevron and he said, 'You ever thought about offshore work,' and I said, 'I'm a plumber, what am I going to do offshore?' He said, 'Well, there are maintenance jobs! In fact I think the platform is looking for a plumber, I'll put your name forward!'"

He laughs, rolling his "r's" in a rapid, sing-song burr. "I went up to the shop on Union Street, and there was a wee girl sitting behind the desk and she says, 'What size chest are you?' 'Sorry?' I say. 'You are the plumber, right? What size chest, what size boots? Right, there you are, here are a pair of overalls, some boots, and a hardhat. There's a taxi waiting downstairs, meet you at the airport.' 'Where am I going?' I asked."

The twelve-seater airplane Molloy flew on in 1980 was his first plane ride. It took him to a helicopter pad in the far north, "in the middle of nowhere." He tied his life jacket around his waist and got in, thinking he'd just work on the platforms for half a year and save some money.

Molloy joined a crew of five, for two-week shifts on the platforms, working the cranes and helicopter decks. It was hard work, followed by hard play. "We all went offshore together and went onshore together. We'd have a few beers as soon as we hit the beach. Every six months or so, we'd get a weekend away together," he remembers happily.

The workers on the North Sea platforms hailed from all over Britain. "We'd take the wives and girlfriends together for a weekend in a different part of the country where one of us lived. There was a guy from Liverpool, from Skye, from way up north. It was like family. This guy from Liverpool would often say, 'This is the guy I go to bed with six months of the year, and this is my wife!' You felt as if you were all pulled together and you had somebody you could depend on as it were."

They quickly bonded. "If somebody was leaving, you'd go and throw a bowl of custard or a cream pie or something like that [at them]. Well, it happened to me once but the silly bugger had forgotten to defrost the cake, so I ended up with a bruise! We used to organize games nights, horse racing. We set up a track in the games room, where there was table tennis and a snooker table and a darts board. Fantastic nights! It would pull everybody together. It wasn't just one crew, but the drilling crew, and the engineering crew and the catering crews. Everybody was there. Cinemas used to be a great place to go at night," he says. The camaraderie "was *brilliant*."[8]

The dangers of dilapidated rigs, neglected maintenance, and profit-driven management in the North Sea's hostile environment soon became real to Molloy. Just a month after the Piper Alpha went down, on New Years Day 1989, Molloy was enjoying a small New Year's celebration offshore. There had been some problems with a forty-by-ten-foot vessel that cooled oil and gas on the platform.

> Some of us were involved, we topped up oils, we checked pressures, and we knew there was a problem with this vessel. The vessel itself could only take about 3 bar of pressure, but outside there was a tube bundle and high pressure gas or oil comes through these tubes outside the vessel. The tubes could take something like 50 bar pressure. And everyone knew there was leak in the tubes because the pressure was building inside the vessel.

But to repair the leak, the whole platform would need to be shut down. That would have meant not fulfilling natural gas contracts in the middle of winter, so instead, production continued as the crews lined up for their New Year's Day rations. "You get a can of beer and a wee bottle of wine," Molloy recalled. Because all the workers were queued up, there was no one nearby when the cooling vessel exploded. "There was this massive blast! This vessel was like a Coke can, when you just twist it back and forward until it just tears in half. It was just like that, but this was quarter-inch thick steel plate, just ripped in half." The modest New Year's celebration had kept the workers safely inside, away from the explosion. Like Piper Alpha, incompetent workers were fingered to take the blame for the explosions.

Two months later in the ice-encased North Atlantic, a 987-foot single-hulled oil tanker called the *Valdez* filled up with Alaskan oil. What happened next would bring the problems of poor maintenance in the high-pressure oil industry to world attention.

The risk of catastrophic oil spills had steadily grown as tankers ballooned after Nasser's seizure of the Suez canal in 1956. Giant tankers, which ferry about a third of the oil Americans consume,[9] are "astonishingly" fragile, commented *Newsweek* magazine.

> Relative to their vast size, their hulls are so thin that author Noel Mostert labeled tankers 'floating balloons.' . . . Fully loaded, a typical supertanker draws up to one hundred feet of water, and it is not uncommon for one to lumber into port with less than two feet separating its keel from the sea bottom. Stopping a supertanker from cruising speed often takes more than three miles with the engines full in reverse—and while the engines are in reverse, the ship cannot be steered.[10]

For decades, oil companies resisted buttressing their balloon-like oil tankers to protect the seas from their noxious cargo, even though others transporting cargo by sea did. Since the early 1900s, military and other cargo ships had reinforced their most vulnerable parts with a second layer of steel, in double bottoms and double hulls. This would create a shell of empty space between the two layers, which cost-conscious ship owners would fill with fresh water and fuel so as to free up more space elsewhere for income-generating cargo. For giant oil tankers, the double hull would create a proportionately large gap of useless empty space, far more space than was needed for fresh water or fuel. To avoid it, oil companies assured worried government officials that their "highly sophisticated navigational equipment" onboard rendered the space-stealing double-bottoms superfluous, as shipping historian René De La Pedraja describes.[11]

With tanker costs running to $6000 a day and thirsty oil consumers to slake, oil companies pressure their tankers' captains to empty their holds of oil as rapidly as possible. They take the most direct routes possible, swerving near fragile coasts and through dangerous straits if necessary.[12] In the tropical waters of the south Pacific, thousands of cost-conscious oil tankers navigate their combustible loads between the coral heads of the Great Barrier Reef and the Aussie coast every year, even though most don't stop at coastal ports.[13] Around the frozen ports of Alaska's Prince William Sound, captains would veer off shipping lanes to bypass the floating ice, sometimes with disastrous results.

The *Valdez* was the flagship of the Exxon fleet, designed for a single purpose: to haul Alaskan oil to Panama.[14] On March 23, 1989, the oil-engorged *Valdez* hurried southward from Alaska. An iceberg appeared in its path and the rushing tanker veered off the shipping lane to avoid it. This wasn't anything new. According to the chair of the Alaska Oil Spill Commission, oil companies routinely encouraged their captains to speed towards their ports, and "if there was ice in your path . . . leave the tanker lanes and go around the ice."[15]

A device onboard—no doubt one of the many highly sophisticated ones touted by the industry—bleeped a warning signal of danger ahead, but the harried seafarers at the wheel ignored it. The device had malfunctioned before. The giant tanker continued on, silently slicing through the black, ice-chunked waters. Then, in the inky hours just after midnight came a low crushing rumble of metal on rock. The tanker had crashed into a submerged reef.

Over 250,000 barrels of oil rushed out of the hold, in one of the worst oil spills in U.S. history. The oil matted the fur and feathers of Alaska's seabirds, otters, and seals, and hundreds of thousands of some of the most hardy cold-water creatures froze to death.[16] Pictures of the gunk-covered birds horrified television viewers and newspaper readers across the planet.

The *Valdez* spill put Big Oil and the U.S. government on a collision course. The following year, Congress enacted the Oil Pollution Act, setting strict standards for the training of crews, the engineering of tankers, and the liability of oil companies for the spills their ships commit. Single-hulled tankers such as the *Valdez* would be banned from U.S. waters after 2015.[17] The *Valdez* itself, along with any other tankers that had spilled over a million gallons of oil, was banned from Alaska's Prince William Sound forever.[18]

Still, oil companies couldn't possibly avoid accidental spills, industry officials thought. "No matter how desirable it is to reach a zero accident goal," said a Shell exec in 1990, "we will never get there. Even if we operate on the basis that every accident is preventable, accidents will, unfortunately, still happen."[19]

As public opprobrium at Exxon's perceived negligence toward the environment intensified, less high-profile tragedies continued to unfold among the rotting rigs of the North Sea. In March 1992, Molloy was working as a safety rep on a platform in the North Sea. "The wind chill was twenty below. It had been so cold during the night. We came on shift at six in the morning and we couldn't get the cranes started. The cranes work on diesel, and the diesel had actually frozen," he says.[20]

> So we spent several hours trying to get the cranes working. Then somebody thought that if the diesel is frozen in the cranes perhaps we should try the lifeboats. The lifeboats run on diesel, too. We found that we couldn't get the lifeboats started. Not that anybody thought we'd have to evacuate but nonetheless we should be in a state of readiness. So we spent most of the day trying to get the platform warmed up as it were, and bring everything back up.

"But at the time there was major work going on in the field," says Molloy. "One crew had to be flown to a different rig on what is called a shuttle service. It is a helicopter, flying the guys back and forth from the platforms."

> There was a helicopter coming offshore in late afternoon with a piece of equipment; it had been deemed unsafe to fly people that day, but late in the afternoon there had been a major failure on an installation, a piece of equipment had been stuck on a helicopter and needed to be brought in. So this dinosaur of a supervisor decided to utilize this helicopter to do some shuttling.

Molloy complained that the frozen diesel, sixty-knot winds, snow, sleet, and below-freezing temperatures made the plan unsafe. "We tested the equipment and found that the equipment was indeed frozen. So we spent the next couple hours, believe it or not, this is cutting-edge technology, actually using buckets of hot water, throwing them on the pipeline to try to unfreeze the firefighting systems. Which we managed to do."

By then, the wind had dropped and Molloy's arguments had become futile. The helicopter landed on the platform. "It was about six o'clock and we were going off shift again, and the helicopter had come back to take the guys back. I went on deck and I spoke to the pilot and he said to me that he had some reservations about what he was doing but nonetheless felt he was able." One worker refused to board the helicopter, but was threatened with dismissal and so got on anyway. Molloy and the others on the platform "knocked off shift and had a meal. I went up to the cabin to get showered and changed. It was twenty past seven, I think it was, when word came in, he had gone in the sea, just twenty miles up from us." Eleven men were killed.

Commentators said that it wasn't so much that the pilot flew the helicopter into the sea as the sea's huge monster swells had swallowed the helicopter. The craft had dipped down to get lift, as usual, and was engulfed by the sea.

A year later, a friend of Molloy's ventured out one night to test the release equipment on one of the lifeboats that hung suspended on the sides of the platform. "Well, for some reason that was never explained . . . the boat free-fell ninety feet and he was inside it. He was killed on impact. The boat went underneath the platform. When the first rescue crew from the standby vessel got to him, he was dead."

Molloy's frustration with the poor maintenance of the rigs by unaccountable companies had grown incrementally since Piper Alpha. It was becoming clear that "trying to make companies accountable for their actions and failures is impossible to do," he says.

Like the coal miners before them, he and other oil workers started to organize sit-ins on the platforms for weeks at a time, forsaking their pay and building a bad reputation among the contractors. Molloy's wife and young children at home stopped getting paychecks, but he persisted nevertheless.

Meanwhile, Exxon was shelling out over $2 billion to clean up the oil they'd spilled in Alaska,[21] along with over $1 billion in damages.[22] At the pump, consumers were shunning Exxon's now-dirtier-seeming gasoline. Young engineers fled from rapidly emptying petroleum engineering departments, and oil companies started to lose a generation of experts. "The *Valdez* spill," sniffed one petroleum-engineering professor years later, "that just killed us."[23]

In an attempt to turn the tide of public opinion welling against them, the Exxon PR department targeted the friable minds of the young. In 1993, they offered free videos about the company's stellar cleanup efforts in Alaska to ten thousand science teachers across the land. Maryland teacher Susan Steele showed Exxon's video, "Scientists and the Alaska Oil Spill: The Wildlife, The Cleanup, The Outlook," to her seventh-grade class, but even the twelve-year-olds weren't biting. As Steele rewound the tape, one commented, "Mrs. Steele, we've just seen a commercial."[24]

With the potential loss of brand loyalty on the line, oil companies had to figure out some way to wash their hands of dirty oil spills. Bystanders in the shipping industry watched as the oil industry started to divorce itself from the shipping of its product. Once, the fleets of the oil companies had been the largest in the world. The *Valdez* was proudly owned by the Exxon Shipping Company; Shell emblazoned its tankers with the Shell logo. Not anymore. "The oil companies that used to operate their own ships had to insulate themselves from consumer reaction against the damage caused by ships carrying their products," explains Peter Morris of the International Commission on Shipping, an independent watchdog group. "They now contract it out. It is a ruse to conceal the ownership."[25]

The Exxon Shipping Company was axed; on its broken corpse rose a new company that carted Exxon oil: the innocuous-sounding outfit, SeaRiver Maritime. Long before the beaches off Prince William Sound were de-oiled, the *Valdez* underwent a $30 million repair job on its still-single hull, re-christened itself the SeaRiver Mediterranean, and set to work hauling oil across the Mediterranean.[26]

Other oil companies in search of anonymous outside companies to shoulder the risks of carrying vast amounts of oil around pristine coasts and waterways followed Exxon's example, and turned to the independent tanker industry.

The independent tanker business isn't an easy one. Tankers are expensive ships to build, with a price tag of at least $125 million each.[27] Operating costs, for the most part, are fixed. Registering the ship, insuring it, and other such expenses can't be avoided.[28] Legislation like the 1990 Oil Pollution Act had raised the standards for engineering and maintenance of tankers. Powerful unions and the labor standards they helped enact in North America and Europe had raised the cost of well-trained, experienced Western seafarers.

Tanker owners can coax a couple decades out of their tankers: by 2000, the average oil tanker was at least fourteen years old.[29] Most are still single-hulled.[30] Besides that, there are only two variable costs to play with: labor and maintenance. Still, even here tanker owners don't have much wiggle room.

As an influx of new contracts from publicity-fearing oil companies swept in, the pressure for tanker owners to cut corners in order to outbid competitors grew. Escaping the tough labor and safety conditions required by U.S.-and European-flagged ships, Western shipowners flocked to register their ships in Panama, Bahamas, Liberia, and other countries with notoriously lax shipping laws.[31]

Registering tankers in these "flag of convenience" (FOC) countries allowed tanker owners to hire crews from wherever in the world they liked, and to pay them whatever they decided to, without deference to the labor standards that might constrain their terrestrial counterparts. According to the European Commission, the tax breaks and lower labor costs alone saved the owners of FOC ships about $1 million per ship every year.[32]

The calculus made sense throughout the cargo-shipping industry. Today almost 55 percent of the tons of goods shipped on the world's oceans travels on FOC ships, providing a steady influx of cash for states willing to rent out their flags in exchange for looking the other

way on safety and maintenance standards. In 2003, fewer than half of
the ships that brought goods to Americans sailed under U.S. flags.[33]
Most cruise liners registered in the Bahamas and Panama.[34] Criminals
transporting Patagonian toothfish, illegal arms, and human slaves
had been flying flags of convenience for decades.[35]

But although circumventing high labor standards may have
improved bottom lines, it also added measurably to the danger of
the sea-going endeavor. Human error causes most accidents,[36] and
poorly trained, underpaid seafarers are more likely to make mistakes.
According to a lengthy investigation by the International Commission
on Shipping, with increasing pressure to cut costs, working conditions for seafarers has deteriorated dangerously. "For thousands of
today's international seafarers," writes Morris, "life at sea is modern
slavery and their workplace is a slave ship."[37]

In the fall of 2002, a subsidiary of Russian oil giant Alfa Group
hired a tanker to ferry 77,000 tons of heavy fuel oil from Latvia to
Singapore.[38]

The lineage of the *Prestige* was far from exalted. The tanker
company that owned the *Prestige* was registered in war-torn Liberia,
a popular FOC nation. The crew on the tanker had been hired out
of the Philippines. The captain hailed from Greece. The tanker
itself—a single-hulled giant built in Japan in the 1970s, whose hull
had, just a year earlier, split and been patched up[39]—was registered
in the tax-free-shipping nation of the Bahamas.[40] Apportioning
blame for what happened to this shady vessel would be next to
impossible.

On November 13, the loaded-up tanker turned into the Bay of
Biscay, a windy inlet where France and Spain curl around to meet
the Atlantic. This stormy stretch of coast, called the Coast of Death
by locals, had chewed many a ship in the past. As the *Prestige* turned

into the bay, a storm kicked up. Careening in the vicious waves, the tired tanker ruptured. Its toxic cargo started to leak out.

When the storm finally subsided, the horrified Spanish government ordered the broken, half-sunk boat out of view. Tugboats towed the dying tanker one hundred miles off the coast. The gash widened, leaving a thickening trail of oil behind it. More than three thousand tons of fuel oil had already spilled into the bay, where its dense puddles hung partially submerged, like "blobs in a lava lamp," as a U.S. government official put it.

The tanker looked like it might split in two, but the Spanish and Portuguese governments refused it access to any of its own ports, where the oil could be pumped into another ship.[41] Broken and waiting, the oily pariah listed offshore. Then, finally, on November 19, the *Prestige*'s earlier wound re-opened, splitting the tanker along the seams of its earlier repair.[42] It started to sink. Ninety percent of its oil, still in the ship's hold, slipped under the waves.

"No one seems quite sure what will happen to the oil now," opined the *New York Times* as the drama unfolded. "Optimists hope it will remain in intact containers, or solidify in the cold, deep waters even if it escapes."[43] It was thick, waxy, and might congeal, although what would happen when the *Prestige* finally hit bottom, two miles down, nobody knew.

Meanwhile, in the waters above the *Prestige*'s watery grave, the slick of oil that had already spilled out took aim at a wide stretch of coastline. Along the shore, octopus-catchers and mussel-gatherers crowded onto the blackened beaches to squint at the brown foaming waves. The wind was kicking up. It would take about a week for the *Prestige*'s spilled oil to crash onto the shore.[44]

On December 5, the *Prestige*'s oil hit the coast. Hundreds of fishers rushed out in their boats to scoop out the oil. They carried it back to the shore in thick goops, but there was nowhere to put it. Others uselessly strung blocks of polystyrene along the netting stretched across their beloved estuaries. Most gave up after a few hours, defeated by the sheer quantity of oil and the fumes pressing against their unprotected faces.[45]

This wasn't the worst of it. Slowly, oil started bubbling up from the deeps. Heavy oil was oozing out of the broken shipwreck like toothpaste out of a tube.[46] A French submarine shot footage of the sunken tanker. It was leaking 125 tons of fuel oil a day from fourteen different cracks. At this rate, the oil would keep spilling out for three years, making the *Prestige* quite possibly the very worst oil spill of all time.[47] By the fall of 2004, 64,000 tons of the *Prestige*'s spilled oil had polluted 2,600 kilometers of coastline.[48]

The *Prestige* was the fourth 1970s-era single-hulled tanker that had sunk in European waters since 1992.[49] The European Union moved to speed up the retirement of single-hulled tankers, so as in the United States, they'd be phased out entirely by 2015, over a century after the innovation had been pioneered. Most of the single-hulled tankers on the sea would have to be scrapped by then anyway.

It was a belated, inadequate technofix, critics said. Double-hulled tankers weren't sink-proof. A double-hulled chemical tanker had sunk off the French coast in 2000.[50] Plus, the double-hulled ships would be more expensive to maintain. As they aged, if market conditions remained the same, they'd be even less likely to be well-maintained. Well-trained, properly paid seafarers were many times more crucial. As Peter Morris commented, "You can have the most expensive car on the line, but if you don't know how to drive it, it won't make a difference."[51] Yet little was done to curb the FOC nations and shipowners' shady deals, nor to penalize the oil companies and other cargo owners who profited from it.

Testament to the efficacy of the oil industry's public divorce from the dirty business of shipping their products since the *Valdez*, Alfa successfully avoided any lasting association with the horrific spill, even as the oil they had loaded onto the *Prestige* continued to pollute the French and Spanish coasts. In 2003, that most green of oil

companies, B P, entered into a lucrative joint venture with Alfa with
hardly a peep from the public.[52] Not only that, just weeks before
the *Prestige* hit bottom, Exxon's re-named shipping company openly
attempted to overturn the 1990 Oil Pollution Act. The company
wants to bring the *Valdez* back to the Alaskan coast it had so despoiled,
as the tanker was losing money on its new Mediterranean route. The
company argued to the Ninth U.S. Circuit Court of Appeals that
the *Valdez* was being "wrongly singled out" by being banned from
the Sound.[53]

As the *New Statesman* put it:

> This reluctance to challenge the interests of the ship-
> ping industry—the shadiest and most rapacious on the
> planet—is typical of the feeble system of international
> maritime regulation, with flags of convenience making it
> almost impossible to enforce even such rules as there are.
> Reflect that even the shipping companies' deep involve-
> ment in terrorism and illegal immigration—the two big-
> gest current western political obsessions—has failed to
> persuade governments to regulate them adequately. Then
> ask yourself how likely they are to regulate for the sake
> of a few thousand birds or a few million prawns. . . .
>
> If we really care about global ecology, we shall use oil
> more sparingly, move it around more carefully and, as
> a result, pay through the nose for it. . . . Weep for the
> guillemots and the gulls by all means, but remember that
> oil is always dirty and that it always has a price.[54]

Ironically, though, the vast majority of the 6 million metric
tons of oil that enter the world's oceans every year comes not from
accidental spills but from chronic, routine, and deliberate ones.
More than 40 percent drips off the car-clogged roads and highways
into rivers and streams sliding into the sea. Another 30 percent
leaks in because oil tankers are so tipsy when emptied of oil. They

fill up with sea water to stabilize themselves, then pump this oil-contaminated ballast water overboard when the tanker refills with oil.[55]

Today, several thousand oil-filled monoliths ferry half a billion barrels of oil around the world every day.[56] The amount of oil shipped around on the world's oceans dwarfs any other single commodity; of the 5.9 billion tons of goods shipped on the world's oceans every year, over a quarter is crude.[57] Generally speaking, the oil industry spills more than one thousand barrels of oil for every billion barrels they transport,[58] and their evasion of public responsibility for this remains virtually unchallenged.

The oil industry's latest technique, FPSOs, will require even more tankers ferrying even more oil around the world's oceans.

At Girassol off Angola, TotalFinaElf's colossal FPSO would store 2 million barrels of oil above the deep-water corals that dotted the nearby seabed.[59] Every five days or so, a tanker would come around to the platform to fill up on a few million barrels of oil. If such a facility were anchored in American waters, it would have to unload its oil onto tankers fortified with double hulls. But it is unlikely that Angolan authorities will require any such measures.[60]

Underwater pipeline networks, although expensive and cumbersome for the oil industry to build, are much safer than transferring and conveying huge amounts of oil around on the surface of the water in tankers and other vessels, as FPSOs require, part of the reason why U.S. regulators had banned FPSOs from the Gulf of Mexico until 2002.[61]

In a single year, the hive of oil industry activity in the Gulf of Mexico emitted fully eight hundred spills of oil within ten miles of the Texas coast; over two-thirds of these spills were not from the Gulf's extensive network of underwater pipelines but from the vessels ferrying the oil to and fro.[62]

FPSOS can pitch and heave a dozen feet up and down and roll around up to 15 degrees.[63] (To put this in perspective, recall that the Ocean Ranger sank after listing between 10 and 15 degrees.) In one industry-funded study, twenty FPSOS were found to have reported more than two hundred spills of about forty-five hundred barrels each over about six years.

Potentially worse than the quantifiable risks of oil spills are the unknown risks posed by FPSOS drilling in deep waters. According to the Minerals Management Service, the arm of the U.S. Department of Interior tasked with regulating offshore oil development, the deep ocean is "so poorly understood that little more than conjecture about possible impacts are possible."[64]

Deep-sea drilling will produce even more waste than drilling in shallow water, watching environmentalists say, and what will come up the pipes from deep under the deepest seas could be much more exotic and potentially more toxic to the living water and air above it, too.[65] When oil companies drill into the rock at the bottom of the sea, they bring out more than just the oil. They also bring up large volumes of the rock itself, plus the ancient waters trapped in the rock, and any other compounds that lived inside those prehistoric sedimentary layers. They don't surgically siphon off the oil, either. They introduce new chemicals and compounds to the underworld. Mud saturated with various chemicals is shot down the holes to cool the rotating drillbit. Shattered dinosaur-era rocks, ancient water, natural gas, and chemically charged muds—now daubed with oil—spew out of the well along with the oil.

For years, rigs in the North Sea threw these contaminated wastes overboard. Today, somewhere around 300 million gallons of toxic sludge are piled in more than a hundred goopy mountains at the bottom of the North Sea. Some of these piles of waste are more than eighty feet tall, the droppings of an intestinally challenged oil predator.[66] The piles of waste contaminate the waters with barium, oil, zinc, copper, cadmium, and lead, spreading in some cases more than one hundred square kilometers from the field. Regulators fret about moving them in case the contamination spreads even further.[67] F P S O S, drilling deeper holes, will have that much more waste to dispose of; in lightly regulated regions such as the waters off the coast of West Africa, environmentalists have good reason to suspect that the uncharted pristine sea floors of the deep ocean will be similarly marred.

Puncturing the deepest sea-bottoms could also potentially disrupt methane hydrate beds, bizarre geological formations that haunt the depths.

When oil and gas seep out on land, the gas simply floats up into the atmosphere. Under the deep sea, however, the natural gas wafting out of cracks in the sea-floor starts to form hydrates, solid icelike compounds made of methane under cold, high-pressure conditions. Worms and other creatures burrow into the yellow mounds, feeding on the methane-loving bacteria that swarm on their surface.[68] If you could hold a piece of methane hydrate in your hand and light it with a match, it would explode into flames. There is fire in this ice.

Hydrates can respond quite violently to perturbations in their temperature-pressure environment. Eight thousand years ago, over a thousand cubic miles of quivering methane hydrate beds exploded with volcanic force when the seas above them got too warm. They slid almost five hundred miles off the continental slope into the Norwegian Sea, leaving behind massive craters on the sea floor. The gigantic tidal waves drowned miles of coastline.[69]

Oceanographer Jeremy Leggett was on a drilling ship when a core of methane hydrate was brought up to the surface. Out of its depth and pressure, the cylinder of dirty ice literally fizzed away in front of him. The frightened drilling engineer demanded the drilling abruptly end.[70] If they cracked through more hydrate and enough gas was released, the bubbly foam it would form at the surface would be so thick and fluffy that the boat would literally drown in it.[71]

At Girassol and other deep-water drilling sites, oil companies will obviously try to avoid the hydrates. But scientists at the National Oceanic and Atmospheric Administration are worried. "A dangerous situation can result if a small amount of friction from a drill bit is applied erroneously," the government scientists warn on their Web site. "In fact, it could start a rapid and potentially catastrophic meltdown in a hydrate bed, which could harm drilling operators and the animals who rely on hydrates for habitat and food."[72]

The consortium of oil companies banded together to innovate deepwater technology, DeepStar, had looked into the problem of methane hydrates in some detail, but their main goal was figuring out how to get the stuff out of their pipelines.[73]

Oil, lured out of its dark chambers in the earth's crust, is warm, more than 100 degrees Fahrenheit. If forced to travel through pipes drowned under thousands of feet of water, that warm oil quickly starts to cool. Soon, the chill and the burden of tons of water on the trek through the long underwater pipelines starts to vex the associated gas. The warm puffs crystallize, turning into hydrate. Soon, the gases floating along thicken into a slush of hydrate clogging the pipe. The flow of oil slows to a trickle.

It could be a major problem for deepwater oil production, especially because the same deep, cold conditions that made it more likely to happen also make it so much harder to access the pipe to unclog it.[74] At Girassol, they had insulated the pipes to prevent the hydrates from forming, but it wasn't cheap.[75]

Deepwater oil development could also disrupt the habitats of still-unknown deep-sea creatures, potentially even introducing them to new ocean territories with disastrous consequences for local species. It takes just long enough for the giant FPSOs to drain their oilfields for the swimming marine creatures in their general vicinity to incorporate the rigs into their ecosystems. Plants and animals attach themselves to platform bottoms and fish and other swimmers dart in and out of their shade. In and of itself, this isn't a bad thing. The trouble is that these mini-ecosystems are made mobile by the slow-moving FPSOs, which

then can become a vector for introducing invasive new species to the
world's seas. When the oilfields run dry and the FPSOs slowly steam
to their next drilling site, the mini-ecosystems they spawn are able to
trail alongside, thereby colonizing new stretches of ocean.

Larvae from the invasive Australian spotted jellyfish, for instance,
had found the floating oil platforms perfect nurseries and promptly
settled in. By the time the larvae had come of age, in the summer of
2000, their platforms had moved on. The now fully grown jellyfish
found themselves in the Gulf of Mexico. Voracious, the highly efficient feeders feasted on the larvae and eggs of shrimp, crab, and other
species. Fishermen and women watched as the invaders crowded out
the gentler native jellies, devouring the youngest members of the
fishery upon which their future angling success depended.[76]

What's more, the community of deep-sea creatures that FPSOS
could encounter and introduce to the world are only barely known.
Scientists do know the deep sea isn't the barren underwater desert
that regulators and the offshore industry sometimes make it out to
be. Biomass—the sum total of the mass of all the creatures living
down in the deeps—predictably declines with depth, but curiously,
diversity increases. Some oceanographers say the deep sea could hold
more biodiversity than tropical rainforests, but of course the diverse
creatures won't include iridescent blue butterflies and lianas but a
full menu of pallid worms and dark, angry-looking fish.[77]

One of the biggest predators of the deep sea, the giant sea squid
(topping sixty feet, it is the largest invertebrate on earth) had never been
seen alive until recently. For thousands of years, scientists suspected
the fantastical creatures existed only because their corpses mysteri-
ously appeared in fishermen's nets and in the stomachs of sperm whales.
Scores of intrepid missions to glimpse the creatures in their natural
habitat have failed. Then, in 2005, Japanese scientists pursued sperm
whales with a robotic camera dunked 3,000 feet underwater in hopes
of capturing the first-ever footage of a live giant squid. This time, a
26-foot-long squid wrapped two of its ten waving tentacles around the
provided bait. The creature got stuck and struggled to break free for

over four hours, leaving behind an 18-foot-long piece of tentacle. It was the first time the legendary monster had been seen alive, testifying to the chasm of knowledge about the deeps.[78]

How the giant squid, whales, and tuna—along with the rest of the deep-water gang—will respond to the new steel stranger in their midst remains to be seen. FPSO's steel tentacles, descending into the water column, would represent an evolutionary novelty as anomalous as a fifty-foot-tall furry spider leg plonked in the middle of a playground.

In the United States at least, regulators have studied the potential environmental impacts of deep sea oil drilling, but unfortunately, the studies they have had at their disposal haven't been the most rigorous. The main environmental research on oil drilling in the deep water of the Gulf of Mexico, for instance, derives from studies that are neither comprehensive nor independent. One was conducted by a researcher working for the U.S. Navy in the 1960s, another by a for-hire consulting firm with no past experience in deep sea. The results of these studies were never published in the peer-reviewed scientific literature. When marine biologists were able to review the studies, they found the works flawed in design and limited in scope.[79]

Research on the deep sea is expensive and technically difficult. Oil companies can easily charter submersible vessels to check their pipelines and fix their underwater well-heads, but for scientists to charter such subs in order to study deep-sea ecology, they have to spend up to $75,000 per day.[80] For biologists, it is an impossible sum. Applied deep-sea ecology falls outside the parameters of both the National Science Foundation (NSF) and the National Oceanic and Atmospheric Administration (NOAA), their two main funding sources. In any case, the entire NSF budget for *all* ocean sciences runs to around $300 million.[81] In contrast, the oil and gas industry spends ten times more, about $3 billion, on the research and development that catapults their rigs into the deep ocean.[82]

When companies do conduct environmental studies, they do it fast and keep costs low. "BP paid for some survey work by commercial firms," recalls biological oceanographer Bob Carney, who has conducted environmental studies for the Minerals Management Service. Carney was part of the team of oceanographers who discovered the "ice worm," a flat pink worm that nestles in underwater methane hydrates.[83] But commercial science for hire is not the same as an independent study conducted by research scientists. "These are for-profit businesses, their [scientists'] careers are built on getting work done in a timely manner at a good price," says Carney. "Academics' careers are built on writing papers that are useful in the scientific literature. Academics, such as myself, would like to ponder for five years, but BP or Shell would want the final report by next Tuesday."

The lack of solid environmental research on deep-water oil drilling won't make a big difference in the end, Carney thinks. "Oil is the camel's nose," he says. "The fact that deep oil-related studies are equivocal or irrelevant will quickly be forgotten. Proponents of exploitation will simply cite the desired conclusions and use the tally of dollars spent as 'proof' that impacts are acceptable."[84] In other words, unless the damage to the deeps is quick, catastrophic, and easily visible to terrestrial humans, nobody will really know about it.

Jake Molloy's days working on the oil rigs of the North Sea are over, he says. "There is no real maintenance" on the platforms anymore, he explains, when I meet him at his cozy office in a stone building in gray Aberdeen.[85] The refurbished flat is plastered with maps of oilfields and rigs. Molloy's new job is as head of an offshore workers' union, organizing to improve health and safety in the offshore oil industry.

"It is all reactive maintenance. It is a case of, if it's working don't touch it, know what I mean? They only carry out maintenance when the thing shuts down. So we get more platforms being run right at the very limit. . . . Everybody wants to make as much as they can, as quickly as they can, with the least amount of hassle."

"You can go to bed one night and wake up the next morning and find that the platform has been sold from under you," Molloy continues.

> That is really unacceptable practice in this day and age. If you were working in the town at the shop and went back after your shift to find that there is a new sign and a new owner, you'd be a bit shocked! You'd say, 'Well, what in bloody hell is going on around here? This company owes me!' But they can do it offshore and nobody gives a damn, because it operates out of the public eye. The only time the public really thinks about oil is when they are putting a bit of petrol in their car, you know what I mean?"

The seagulls outside Molloy's window wail mournfully. "If the price has gone up 2 pence, then they don't like oil companies; if it has gone down 2 pence then they like oil companies! They've got no idea of what's being done to deliver that petrol to the car."

"We all know there are alternatives out there," he continues. Molloy says he could tolerate wind turbines instead of oil rigs. The only trouble, he says, is that wind turbines are ugly. Behind him, his computer shimmers with its screen-saving image—a romantic sunset scene, showing an oil rig in silhouette.

CHAPTER SEVEN

The Curse of Crude

THE ACTIVITIES OF the oil industry could be just as ruinous to the people living near the oilfields as the gulls along the shipping lanes, the dolphins under the seismic ships, and the workers on board the rigs. The business of siphoning oil from countries as diverse as Algeria, Angola, Congo, Ecuador, Gabon, Iran, Iraq, Kuwait, Libya, Peru, Qatar, Saudi Arabia, and Trinidad Tobago had, ironically, sent their peoples' standards of living tumbling downward.[1]

Venezuela had a functioning democracy and the highest per-capita income on the South American continent before a massive oil boom in the 1970s. By the early 2000s, the country suffered chronic violence and a per-capita income lower than it was in 1960.[2] Saudi Arabia, the biggest oil producer in the world, ranks below Romania and Thailand on life expectancy, educational attainment, and income.[3] The average Saudi citizen has seen his annual income drop from $28,600 in 1981 to $10,430 in 2004.[4]

Analysts from relief organizations, activist groups, and even the World Bank had long ago pinpointed the cycle. Oil is struck in some remote underdeveloped country. Oil companies rush in, often driving unfair bargains with hopeful bureaucrats unpracticed at negotiating with multinational companies. As the expensive business of setting up oil infrastructure starts—the building of roads, the installation of processing facilities, terminals, pipelines, and rigs—everyone but the most elite and wealthy of the local region are shut out of the game. Once the oil starts flowing, fabulous riches flow to these elites, consolidating their power even more. Governments step up public spending for ambitious new projects, only to find that volatile oil prices send their projects, half-built, to the dustbin. Then, to make up the shortfalls, many borrow massive sums from bankers, who are only too happy to provide the extra money, as the loans are backed by black gold itself. The countries become mired in debt. Defense spending rises. If violence breaks out, government leaders easily siphon money from oil sales to fuel conflict.

Meanwhile, more sustainable activities (or at least ones not dominated by giant profit-seeking corporations) such as fishing, farming, and the like, atrophy. "It is easier to import food than to produce it if a government has the cash," Stanford's Terry Lynn Karl, an expert in oil and development, writes, "and it is far simpler to buy technological know-how than develop it." Economists call it the "Dutch disease."

Unless the population is very small and the oil deposits very large, as in Brunei or United Arab Emirates, the distortions in the economy caused by petrodollars bite hard when the price of oil falls or the oil, inevitably, starts to dry up. The local elites would have already consolidated control, and the economy would be in no shape to provide for its people.

In 2002, Shell, Total, and other oil companies extracted almost 250,000 barrels of oil from Gabon every day. Awash in petrodollars, Gabon's small urbane populace enjoys imported consumer goods, dining on tomatoes from South Africa and potatoes from France. Celebrating their oil-blessed fortunes, the Gabonese were, at one time, the world's largest per capita importer of champagne. By the late 1990s, though, Gabon's oil had started to dry up. Income from export sales started to decline.[5] By 2004, the oil hangover had started to kick in. The petro-dollars used to buy cheap imported chicken and fish from Europe were in short supply, but the Gabonese had stopped fishing and growing their own food, with just 1 percent of the country's land under cultivation. By 2004, about half of the government's income was paying the interest on foreign loans. "People used to say that Gabon was a blessed coun-try—they used to say that this oil will never dry up," said a Gabonese businessman to the BBC in October 2004. "But now I can tell you that we have lost that former dignity and we are living in poverty."[6]

In other countries, such as Angola and Sudan, petrodollars, their numbers shrouded in secrecy by corrupt government leaders and their willing partners in the oil industry, paid for wars. Over 4 million people had been displaced during Angola's civil war, while Total, ExxonMobil, and BP helped the government pull in between $3 and $5 billion in oil income every year. At least $4 billion had gone missing over the late 1990s, likely into the private accounts of elites, while the Angolan people starved.[7] It was a bloody role that had cost companies serious cash in the past. In Nigeria, sabotage of pipelines and other facilities by impoverished locals cost Shell over $1 billion in 1999.[8]

In 2005, Africa's oil provided Americans with around 15 percent of their daily oil diet. By 2015, that flow of oil is expected to double, sating 25 percent of the American oil appetite. Much of the oil comes from Nigeria's Niger delta.[9]

The 25,000 square miles of flat wetlands where the 2,600-mile Niger River splintered into hundreds of creeks, streams, and swamps before emptying into the Gulf of Guinea was one of the richest lands on earth. The mineral-intense sediments swept in the river's rush settled out as the water saturated the delta, enriching its marshy soils, which sprouted lush forests of oil palms and mangroves. Every year, one hundred inches of tropical monsoon rain would wash away some of the nutrient-rich sediments. Every year, the Niger River would replenish the land with more.

A diversity of people populated the Niger's delta, hailing from a range of different clans and ethnicities, speaking dozens of different languages. They harvested periwinkles, crabs, mussels, shrimp, and other ocean creatures swishing into salty marshes and drank the fresh water from the Niger's rivers and creeks. They planted rice, sugar cane, plantains, yams, and cassava in the fertile soil. The mangrove forests protected their fragile coast, providing the people with fruit, medicine, and materials for rope and carvings.[10]

By the time oil was found in the delta, the region had been subjugated as a resource colony for outsiders for centuries. The Portuguese had set up a bustling slave trade in the delta in the fifteenth century. Over the following centuries, slave traders kidnapped millions of the delta's inhabitants to toil on the plantations of the Americas and West Indies. They picked them off around the rivers, including a wide-mouthed one that opened into the ocean, which they called simply *Escravos*, Portuguese for "slave," for the slaves the traders bought there for fifteen brass bracelets each.[11]

In the early nineteenth century, the slave trade was abolished, but the extraction of natural wealth from the Niger Delta to the West continued. By 1856, more than two hundred European companies were shipping off 25,000 tons of the delta's palm oil every year, used to grease the steel machines in Europe's factories. Over the next century, control of the delta would change hands but its status as a resource colony for outside exploitation would remain. The British, having asserted their control over the lucrative palm-oil trade by proclaiming the Niger Delta its protectorate in 1865, left the region about a hundred years later, but only after ensuring that the delta would continue to be controlled from the outside. The British forcibly joined the culturally and geographically distinct Niger Delta to the Islamic region to its north, dubbing the conglomeration "Nigeria" in 1914.

When the British left Nigeria in 1960, they handed control over the delta to the Nigerian elites in the north of the country, who, like the colonialists before them, generally looked down on the delta's non-Muslim, tribal inhabitants. Their attempts to secede were met with a long, violent reprisal, the 1967–1970 Biafran war, which took around 2 million lives. After the war, the Nigerian government transferred all mineral rights and revenue from the delta to the federal military government. "The eastern part of the country, and particularly the Niger Delta and its inhabitants," write Nigerian journalist Ike Okonta and human rights lawyer Oronto Douglas, "have been treated as conquered territory ever since."[12]

With the delta subdued, resource extraction could continue unimpeded. When Royal Dutch Shell had struck oil in the delta in 1956, they converted the old slave ports into oil terminals, and oil companies from around the world descended on the waterlogged delta. According to the industry's burgeoning mythology, their mission was not much different from the colonial one. By their ingenuity, know-how, and bravery, they were saving the world from barbarism and darkness, providing oil for light, speed, and prosperity.

But unlike the oilfields in the arid expanses of Texas or under the choppy grey waves of the North Sea, the oil patches in the delta were situated under fragile waterways that sustained the livelihoods of thousands of people. Whether it would have been possible to develop such oilfields without massive disruption is unclear. Yet, such questions were probably not on the table. It was the Nigerian military authorities who signed the deals with Shell, Chevron, and others to develop more than two hundred oilfields in the delta's villages.[13]

What happened in the village of Okoroba is illustrative. Shell discovered oil in Okoroba in 1991, about a third of a mile away from a village precariously situated between a freshwater swamp and a saltwater marsh. The freshwater swamp provided clean water for drinking and bathing. The saltwater areas, on the other side of the village, provided nutritious, easily farmed and caught shellfish and seafood.

Into this delicate web of waterways, Shell decided to ram a canal that would be wide enough to accommodate their heavy equipment, saving the company crucial time and fuel. The dredging for the canal bulldozed a partially built hospital, coconut plantations, and ancestral graves. Six thousand people in Okoroba lost their cash crops. Piles of mud slowly silted up the life-giving waterways. Then, the saltwater contaminated the fresh waters. The fish died. The drinking water was ruined. As the oil pulsed through the pipelines that criss-crossed villagers' backyards and garden plots, it leaked out into the soil and the now brackish muddy waters.[14] The moist tropical air filled with smoke and fumes from a continuously burning plume of associated gas, constricting the lungs of the people, infesting their skin with rashes, and raining down in an acid that corroded their roofs. In Nigeria, almost 90 percent of the gas that wafted out from oil wells was burned, a perpetual bonfire that environmentalists likened to Dante's Inferno. The flares are so bright that the delta's children can't tell night from day.[15]

Similar developments transformed much of the rest of the delta. Today, the children of the Niger Delta swim in pits filled with drilling wastes, and their parents scrape together enough money to buy frozen fish, imported to the once-seafood-rich villages.

Yet, the oil itself is just beautiful: light, sweet, low in sulfur, with hardly any polluting impurities. American refineries under the firm hand of the EPA appreciated that and were willing to pay for it, too. And so, despite the growing "unrest" among the people of the delta, and the fact that Nigeria had joined OPEC, the country was "fundamentally a low-cost oil producer," as a Shell exec explained to the *Financial Times* in 1999. As such, "it is strategic to the future of the group."[16] Shell's $14 billion operation in Nigeria was "arguably Shell's largest and most complex exploration and production venture outside North America."[17]

Each oil development in the delta was actually a "joint venture" with the state-owned oil company, but the Western oil companies always operated the fields. The state oil company didn't have the expertise. The oil companies were much more powerful than the Nigerian authorities, after all. A single big oil company such as Shell could earn three times more than the entire Nigerian state in a single year. And yet, the government would have to cough up 60 percent of the cost of building and maintaining the oil facilities. If the oil industry wanted some more money for a new installation or improvement, it had only to ask, for the government had no technical ability to double-check the figures.

The ever-present possibility that the Nigerians were being boondoggled probably didn't bother the military dictators that ruled the country for many of its oil-producing years. The money required for the oil developments came out of the public treasury, while income from oil sales poured into private bank accounts. During the 1990s, Nigeria pulled in about $30 billion a year from oil sales.

About $10 billion ended up in the private bank accounts of a single military general, Sani Abacha, and his cronies,[18] with Western bankers making their fortunes investing the looted cash.[19] On the other side of the ledger, the public coffers ran up a debt of no less than $40 billion.[20]

And so, despite the billions of dollars worth of oil under their feet, the people of the Niger Delta lived in poverty and darkness. In life expectancy, education, and income, Nigeria rates among the thirty most underdeveloped countries in the world.[21] Conditions are worse in the delta. Over two-thirds of the delta's inhabitants survive hand to mouth without benefit of electricity, pipe-borne water, hospitals, decent housing, or passable roads, as even Shell's internal documents recognized. In some delta communities, up to three-quarters of the people cannot read or write.[22] The casual burning of "waste" natural gas that so ravaged the environs and the people is particularly contemptuous—if the oil companies had bothered to set up facilities to use that gas, it could provide power for not just the entire Niger Delta, but half of the African continent.[23] So complete is the theft of Nigerian oil that Nigerians themselves must import petroleum products, and often wait in days-long queues for fuel.[24]

And yet, for many years, the people of the Niger Delta could hardly resist. Years of colonial piracy and humiliation had convinced many of their inferiority. One writer from the delta, an Ogoni from Ogoniland, described the problem:

> I was teased at primary school because I was an Ogoni. . . . I grew up watching grown Ogoni men taunted by children in public. I was so ashamed of being an Ogoni that I used to beg my mother not to speak Khana [the Ogoni language] in public. I didn't know of any Ogoni man or woman who had ever done anything significant in Nigeria. . . . People said we were dirty, that we were cannibals.

It never occurred to me . . . that the gas flares in Ogoni
might be contributing to the acid rain that destroyed
the aluminium roofing of the houses in the area. I had
no idea that the incidence of oil spills in Ogoni was one
of the highest recorded in the world. Our people had
never stopped to consider that the pipelines that ran
through our villages were responsible for polluting our
environment. We rarely complained about the discrepancy between the wealth of the oil companies and the
poverty of our people.

The Niger Delta's Ken Saro-Wiwa was a successful businessman
and prolific writer who had been offered jobs at Shell and even a
post as oil minister. As a newspaper columnist, he railed against
the fact that his native Ogoniland, "which should have been as rich
as a small Gulf state, was one of the poorest corners of Africa."
Disillusioned with writing as a mode for social change in a country with 60 percent illiteracy,[25] Saro-Wiwa turned to activism.
In November 1992, Saro-Wiwa and other Ogoni activists delivered their demands directly to Shell, Chevron, and the Nigerian
authorities. They wanted compensation, an end to gas flaring, and
a place at the negotiating table. They reckoned that the Ogoni
alone—one of the hundreds of ethnic groups concentrated along
the delta—were owed at least $10 billion in unpaid royalties and
compensation for damages.[26]

Nobody noticed, not even the environmental groups in London
that Saro-Wiwa approached for support. They ushered him out the
door, "with a polite but condescending look that suggested he come
back when a few more people had been killed," as Saro-Wiwa's son
Ken Wiwa remembers it.[27]

Two months later, a massive show of popular resistance got their
attention. Saro-Wiwa led an estimated 300,000 Ogoni on a protest

march against oil exploitation in what he would later recall as the best day of his life.

In April 1993, a few months after the exhilarating march, a farmer spied Shell contractors digging up his farmlands. He had not been consulted, no environmental assessment had been done, nor had the farmer been compensated. He went out to confront the oilmen, and a curious crowd grew around him. But the Shell contractors, having been alerted to the possibility of trouble, had brought Nigerian soldiers with them. The soldiers shot at the unarmed crowd, killing a young man.

And then, with the government officials in daily contact with oil company executives, the Nigerian military unleashed another round of violence against the people of the delta. In July 1993, 132 unarmed Ogoni men, women, and children were massacred; in August, 247 more were slaughtered in an attack on the village market; in September, over a thousand were murdered.

Officials described the bloodshed as "ethnic conflict," despite the fact that experts assembled to resolve the conflict could find no evidence of any dispute between the Ogoni and their neighbors. According to interviews conducted by Human Rights Watch, Nigerian soldiers had been tricked into attacking the unarmed Ogoni by leaders who told them to expect an armed invasion from Cameroon, and to thus shoot on sight.

Shell had pulled out of Ogoniland when the violence first started, but in October, the company resolved to return. Shell and Nigerian authorities held a sham peace conference, heralding an accord that declared Ogoniland safe for a resumption of oil production. When Ogoni people nonviolently protested Shell's return, the company again called the military, and several unarmed Ogoni were killed.[28]

The campaign to crush Saro-Wiwa, however, went even deeper. Four prominent Ogoni leaders, including the brother of Saro-Wiwa's estranged wife, were killed and Saro-Wiwa framed for the murders. The accusations split the Saro-Wiwa family down the middle, Ken Wiwa writes. While Saro-Wiwa sat in jail, his wife did not visit, his children avoided writing him, and some of his nieces and nephews—whose father had been murdered—publicly questioned Saro-Wiwa's innocence.[29]

Meanwhile, a sustained campaign of rape, terror, and slaughter descended upon 126 villages in Ogoniland, under a deliberate news blackout. Nigeria's Colonel Paul Okuntimo called for "ruthless military operations," in order that the oil industry's "smooth economic activities" could continue.[30] Okuntimo had been trained in 204 ways to kill people, he bragged, and looked forward to showcasing the breadth of his repertoire.

Soldiers under Okuntimo told Human Rights Watch that "the idea was to go into villages, shooting in the air, and then when people ran, to grab some as prisoners. The orders were to shoot on sight able-bodied men, if they ran," one said, adding that "the Ogonis, they lost many people." The soldiers raped Ogoni women and girls of all ages. "First they beat me on my back with the butts of their guns," one woman told Human Rights Watch. "One kicked me in the lower abdomen. Then they raped me," she said. "They covered my mouth but I still tried to scream. . . . I was screaming until I couldn't scream anymore. The breath finished from inside me."[31]

The oil companies provided logistical support. "To do this," Okuntimo later admitted to London's *Sunday Times,* "we needed resources, and Shell provided these." No fewer than thirty villages were razed altogether.

While the slaughter was going on, Ken Saro-Wiwa's brother met with Shell Nigeria's C E O Brian Anderson, pleading with him to use his connections with the government to end the carnage. Anderson agreed—as long as the Ogoni issued a press release stating that no environmental damage had been done in the area and called off the campaign against Shell. Wiwa refused. Anderson issued a cold statement, asserting that "a large multinational company such as Shell cannot and must not interfere with the affairs of any sovereign state." Two days later, on November 10, 1995, Ken Saro-Wiwa and eight other Ogoni were hanged.[32]

Ken Wiwa describes how his father's execution haunted him. "I couldn't even bring myself to say the word 'hang,'" he writes. "I would flinch whenever I heard it. You'd be surprised how often it comes up in conversation—hang on, hang up, hang around, hang the consequences."[33]

After Ken Saro-Wiwa's execution, South African president Nelson Mandela called upon the United States to impose sanctions against Nigeria. The U.S. government said it "strongly condemned" Saro-Wiwa's hanging, but continued to buy Nigeria's sweet oil. Whether anyone in Washington, DC, consciously noticed or not, a deal had been struck. Nobel-prize-winning novelist Nadine Gordimer spelled it out in the editorial pages of the *New York Times* in 1997: "to buy Nigeria's oil under the conditions that prevail," as the United States did, she wrote, "is to buy oil in exchange for blood. Other people's blood; the exaction of the death penalty on Nigerians."[34]

With lucrative markets firmly anchored in place, Nigerian authorities continued their campaign against dissent unhindered. In late 1998, activists in the Ijo community launched a campaign to extinguish the gas flares polluting their atmosphere. The Nigerian military responded with two warships and 15,000 soldiers, and more than 200 villagers were killed. In other confrontations, Chevron provided helicopters and called in the navy against unarmed protesters, resulting in more deaths.[35]

The PR game, however, did change after Saro-Wiwa's execution. Oil companies still would not admit to any *obligation* to compensate locals for the disruption their activities caused or to negotiate with them on future developments. But many erstwhile silent executives found their voices in order to complain about the corruption and

irresponsibility of their partners in the Nigerian government. Some
started to devote modest sums to help "develop" the delta.

Extracting even small concessions from the oil companies, though,
generally entailed a struggle. Chevron had turned the old slave port
of Escravos into a prolific oil terminal, protected by gates and guards
from the villagers that surrounded it. Embankments sheltered the
Chevron facilities from the encroaching waters pouring out of the
creeks they had widened. American oilmen flew helicopters in and
out of the terminal, venturing out only to wander down the short
path the company had paved to the bar, where they were soothed
by local girls turned prostitutes.

Outside the terminal, there were no paved roads and no telephones. The villagers' shacks had no indoor plumbing. The village
of Ugborodo didn't even have a gas station. The rising waters of the
creek that Chevron had widened were slowly washing away the village
cemetery. "Before Chevron came to this land many years ago, we the
people used to kill fish and crayfish," remembers one local woman.
"We could kill shrimps and big fishes in the creeks." But all that was
gone.[36] When men and boys protested conditions in the delta, they
set off a chain of violence. In the village of Ugborodo, the women
decided to get organized. First they sent a letter to Chevron officials,
to which they received, to their indignation, no response at all.

In July 2002, hundreds of women hijacked a boat and occupied
Chevron's Escravos facility. Once inside the facility, they saw air-
conditioners, telephones, microwave ovens, and fresh fruits and veg-
etables. "When we got in there, it was really like paradise," said one.
"I saw America there," another added. Clearly, Felicia Atsepoyi said,
"They achieved something from this community for forty years."

The women stayed put, trapping more than seven hundred Chevron staff in the facility and blocking the arrival of helicopters, planes,
and boats that might bring fresh supplies to the oil workers. If Chevron didn't listen, the unarmed singing protesters said, they would
humiliate the men in the worst way possible. The women would
take their clothes off. Stunned security staff didn't know what to

do. "Chevron ha[d] used armed forces to quell similar protests and takeovers," wrote journalist Isioma Daniel, "but its armed security men had never received any training on how to contain an invading army of women singing solidarity songs."

It took ten days for Chevron to agree to some of their demands. The company would share some of its plentiful electricity and clean water, and might build a few buildings amidst the rubble of the lands they had devastated. They would even, perhaps, start to construct a new place for the villagers to live, once the flooding they had unleashed submerged the village entirely.[37]

Environmentalists who encountered internal company documents about such community development projects, write Okonta and Douglas, found that the execs "had no sympathy for the plight of the Niger Delta communities, generally saw them as indolent, and also regarded the whole exercise as a waste of time."[38]

One aid group traveled to the delta to examine Shell's development program. "The region," they reported in 2004, "is now a veritable graveyard of projects, including water systems that do not work, health centres that have never opened and schools where no lesson has ever been taught."[39]

American consumers might have objected to this state of affairs, had they known the gasoline they poured into their tanks was streaked with the blood of Nigerian villagers. Yet most reports from the Niger Delta that reached the warm lit homes of the West described a familiar, if vaguely troubling, conflict that had little to do with them. The oil companies "have been plagued by ethnic violence," the BBC moaned.[40] They face "many security problems," the *Financial Times* confirmed.[41] "Nearly everywhere, the oil firms run the gauntlet of community protests, acts of sabotage, compensation claims, demands for protection money and the kidnapping of workers for ransom," Reuters news service complained.[42]

Most news reports failed to describe oil companies' environmental devastation and the military's years of violence against dissent, generally trotting out the oil industry's explanation for the mayhem, involving mercenary troublemakers and the envy of badly trained villagers. It was hard for the news media to know who to believe, after all. The welter of ethnic groups among the oil installations and the mix of organized activism and ad hoc vigilantism complicated the entirely conflicting claims of the oil companies and the people. "The competing claims . . . are virtually impossible to verify," complained the *New York Times*.[43] The news reports and corporate press releases left it to the reader to determine why the troubled impoverished Africans of the delta kept complaining, lashing out at each other and the generous oil companies that graced their lands. Many no doubt relied on old imperialistic standards involving mindless savagery in Africa's heart of darkness.

For the United States government, Nigeria's crude continued to be a flow of oil worth safeguarding. In April 2003, Shell once again publicly warned that "criminal elements" were targeting its facilities. First, President Olusegun Obasanjo responded, on cue, with a call for "firm action by security forces" to quell the "civil unrest."[44] Then, the U.S. government promptly donated seven patrol ships to assist the Nigerian navy.[45]

The curse of crude similarly struck the people of Colombia. Oil explorers had discovered recoverable oil in Colombia in 1905. It wasn't a lot, but more could probably be found in the foothills of the eastern mountains, they thought. There, oil was seeping to the surface. Extracting Andean oil, however, would have to wait until Colombia's infrastructure improved, as workers would have to build miles-long pipelines able to withstand landslides and floods along the Andes' summits and valleys in order to do it.[46]

Between 1914, when the United States plowed a canal through Panama, significantly easing Colombia's isolation from world markets, and World War II, Colombia transformed itself into a viable resource colony for the West. By the 1920s, Colombia was the second largest coffee producer in the world. Banana plantations run by the United Fruit Company sprouted across the region. Rainforests were cleared for rubber plantations to feed American tire manufacturers. Money started to pour into the government's coffers, not least a $25 million indemnity from the United States for its capture of Panama.

As the Colombian government consolidated its power, strengthened on its new earnings, it sent forth its soldiers to suppress any troubles in goods-producing areas. On one day in 1928, when an American manager of a banana plantation got word that his workers were planning to strike, he contacted the Colombian president about the "extremely grave and dangerous" situation. The president dispatched the army, who, "infuse[d]" with a "spirit of conquest," as historians Frank Safford and Marco Palacios write, unleashed a massacre, a pattern that was to become familiar.[47] The bloodbath on the banana plantation was later enshrined in world literature by Nobel Prize-winning Colombian writer Gabriel García Márquez in his 1970 novel *One Hundred Years of Solitude*.

In 1943, a fungal disease decimated Colombia's banana plantations. Then, with Europe embroiled in World War II, coffee exports foundered. According to Safford and Palacios, Colombia tumbled into a "vicious circle of export depressions–fiscal crises–civil wars."[48]

La Violencia, as it came to be known, raged from the mid-1940s to the 1960s, a generalized civil war between supporters of the Liberal and Conservative parties that relentlessly vied for power in the capital. In what historian James D. Henderson called a "perverse bloodletting," machete-wielding gangs murdered peasants throughout the rugged remote land.[49] Some estimate that up to 400,000 died.

Under cover of the ongoing violence, gangs eked out a decent business, stealing coffee from abandoned farms and cattle from abandoned ranches.[50] Intrepid oil explorers searched for more oil. In the early 1960s, Texaco and Gulf found the Orito oilfield, a modest yield of around 200 million barrels of oil, lying close to the border with Ecuador, and valiantly built a pipeline across the lofty peaks to the Pacific, while the blood of Colombians still flowed down the mountainsides.[51]

In the late 1950s, the warring parties agreed to a period of bipartisan rule. But by then, Colombians had adapted to life under siege. In their remote communities far from a sometimes hostile government that seemed to have neither will nor power to protect them, they organized private armies and vigilante self-defense groups. In the early 1960s, some of these aligned themselves with the Communist Party and Cuban revolutionaries, proclaiming their ambitions for political revolution in Colombia.

The United States, firmly in the grip of anti-Communist, anti-hippie fervor, nourished the Colombian military with aid to fight the nascent revolutionaries. As the 1970s rolled around, *Fuerzas Armadas Revolucionarias de Colombia* (FARC) and *Ejército de Liberación Nacional* (ELN), along with others, emerged as full-fledged, armed guerrilla groups. The aid-engorged Colombian military's violent reprisals had effectively hardened their resolve, and the guerrillas would go on to bully Colombians for decades.[52] Under pressure from the United States, Mexico had successfully stanched its drug trade, which promptly transplanted itself in the fertile ground of strife-ridden Colombia. By 1975, Colombia supplied the United States with 70 percent of its imported marijuana.[53] As the drug business sustained peasant communities, they were zealously guarded by private paramilitary armies, which became in some parts of the country, "de facto governments."

With the Colombian government effectively occupied with the fight against the guerrillas, Colombian drug traffickers soon expanded into even more lucrative narcotics to feed the growing ranks of U.S. drug users: cocaine and heroin.[54]

If U.S. policies and the desires of its consumers sparked Colombia's drug trade and guerrilla insurrection, it was oil that would help keep the conflagration fueled for years.

In 1983, Occidental Petroleum discovered a true *El Dorado*: 1 billion barrels of recoverable oil in the Caño Limón oilfield near the Venezuelan border. In the black gold rush that followed, a 483-mile pipeline across the Andes mountains was built in less than three years[55] as the populations around the oilfields tripled.[56] This was the "hottest . . . action to hit Latin America in years," *Oil & Gas Journal* reported. The oil finds would "revolutionize Colombia's economy," the magazine wrote.[57] By 1986, Colombia had flipped from being a net importer of crude to a net exporter, sending more oil to the United States than Norway's North Sea fields.[58] Two years later, oil companies drilled no fewer than eighty exploratory wells, searching for more oil. In 1988, BP found the Cusiana oilfield, to date the last giant oilfield discovered in Colombia, holding 1.5 billion barrels of oil.

By then, the fire of Colombia's civil strife had overwhelmed much of the country; homicide had become the leading cause of death for adult men in Colombia, and the second leading cause of deaths overall.[59]

For the military, guerrillas, and paramilitary groups locked in hostilities, oil provided an ideally vulnerable asset to harness in service of their cause. Paramilitary groups funded themselves by selling gasoline stolen from illegal taps on the pipelines. By the late 1990s, using extortions and kidnapping, guerrillas raked in

$140 million a year from the oil patch, a sum rivaling the amount they were pulling in from their alliances with drug traffickers.[60] The ELN bombed the Caño Limón pipeline no fewer than five hundred times between 1984 and 2003. One such explosion aimed at the pipeline sent a fifty-meter fireball hurtling toward a village, slaughtering seventy people as they slept in their beds.

The government, in response, intensified its war against the rebels, "militarizing these [oil-rich] areas and terrorizing the local population, whom they presume to be guerrilla supporters," as advocates from the North American Congress on Latin America reported.[61]

Oil companies help foot the bill, paying a "war tax" of $1 per barrel to help the government pay the military and police to guard the oilfields. Occidental has also allegedly paid guerrillas directly. According to an embassy official who spoke to activists from Witness for Peace, "Occidental gave [the guerrillas] between $1 and $5 million so that they would not blow up the pipeline during construction."[62]

As analysts at the Washington Office on Latin America conclude, Colombian crude "provides revenues that enhance the armed actors' ability to participate in the war; the war in turn, provides them with opportunities for profit."[63] It's a positive war economy that shows no signs of abating as long as the crude keeps flowing.

Sometimes, oil companies conspired directly with the Colombian military to subdue guerrillas, catching innocent civilians in the cross-fire. Occidental, for instance, had hired contractors to fly over the company's pipelines, looking out for guerrillas. In December 1998, they did much more than that.

This time, they took a Colombian air force officer with them. They weren't just looking for guerrillas; they were helping the air force pinpoint where to drop a United States-made cluster bomb on them. When they flubbed the job, fingering a village instead of a rebel stronghold, the Colombian pilots dropped a bomb on the village of Santo Domingo, killing eighteen unarmed villagers.

One man lost three relatives that day, as the *Los Angeles Times* reported:

> His mother, who had been tending the family store at the front of their home, was killed by flying shrapnel. His fourteen-year-old cousin was killed after running outside and waving in an effort to alert the airmen that there were civilians below. His twenty-five-year-old sister died en route to a hospital. His blind father survived wounds to both shoulders.

In 2000, Occidental's president testified before Congress in favor of a multibillion military aid package to Colombia; Texaco, Occidental, and BP all lobbied for the aid package, although it ostensibly was meant for the fight against drug trafficking, not guerrillas in the oil patch. By the end of the year, 85,000 gallons of pesticide had been sprayed on Colombian coca fields, sickening locals and livestock for miles around. The amount of coca under cultivation rose, nevertheless, by almost 25 percent.[64]

The drug war foundering, the Bush administration made its aims more explicit in 2003. Bush earmarked over $100 million for U.S. forces to train Colombians on how to better protect the oil industry's pipelines. In his 2004 budget proposal, the Bush administration requested another $147 million to station eight hundred soldiers along the precious pipe.

One villager who lost his father and cousin in the Santo Domingo massacre couldn't understand it. "I would ask the United States, 'Why do you want to train more people to kill peasants?'"[65]

The answer was simple, according to the U.S. ambassador in Colombia. Big Oil's pipelines and the golden liquid they carried were "important to the future of . . . petroleum supplies and the confidence of our investors."[66]

The International Labor Rights Fund (I L R F) and human rights lawyers filed a suit against Occidental for their role in the Santo Domingo massacre in 2003. But it was unclear whether the U.S. government would allow it to move forward. When the I L R F had helped villagers from the Indonesian province of Aceh sue Exxon-Mobil for hiring Indonesian soldiers to brutally violate them, the State Department squelched the case, warning the court that the case couldn't be heard because it would "risk a potentially serious adverse impact on significant interests of the United States."

By 2004, B P and Occidental together were pumping out 70 percent of Colombia's daily oil flow. Despite the terror, the kidnappings, and extortions, according to a B P spokesperson, Colombia's oil still provides "a good return" and "is a solid, robust investment." Plus, he added, "there are still sites to be found."[67]

Conservatively projecting from World Bank figures, activists at Catholic Relief Services calculated that between 2003 and 2013, over $200 billion in oil revenues will be deposited into the slim bank accounts of sub-Saharan African countries, where oil companies have targeted new oil. The World Bank planned to foot some of the bill of building the new oil infrastructure that would help siphon West African oil, despite its own analysts telling it that bankrolling oil projects in poor countries "did more harm than good," as the *New York Times* reported.[68] In Equatorial Guinea, for example, ExxonMobil, ChevronTexaco, Total, and others rushed to buy up oil licenses, the Texan oilmen descending upon the nation's capital, Malabo, aboard flights conveniently routed direct from Houston. "The hopes of people watching new pipelines built through their communities or seeing the impressive installation of offshore platforms can be palpably felt," writes Karl. "They believe that oil will bring

jobs, food, schools, healthcare, agricultural support, and housing."
Yet revelations in the news media suggested that the pernicious
cycle had already begun: in 2003 Equatorial Guinea's president had
deposited over $300 million in oil income in a private bank account
in Washington, DC.[69] A 2004 U.S. congressional inquiry revealed
that oil companies had been paying the president and his relatives
millions of dollars, depositing the funds directly into their personal
bank accounts.[70]

Tiny São Tomé, which the U.S. State Department deemed "the only
stable democracy in West Africa" descended into oil-boom-induced
chaos by July 2003, as military leaders unsuccessfully attempted to
overthrow the democratically elected president, explaining that
"at the bottom of [the coup attempt] was oil."[71] In January 2006,
an experimental agreement between the World Bank and Chad to
devote oil income to poverty reduction failed, when Chad's parliament voted to overturn the agreement and spend its oil money on
the military or however else the Chadian leadership deemed fit,
without oversight.[72]

After West African oil starts to dry up, the next black gold rush
will most likely occur in some other impoverished region. Having
scoured and depleted much of the West's oil endowment, the U.S.
oil industry, between 2002 and 2022, planned to spend the biggest
portion of its exploration budget searching for oil in developing
countries.[73]

Oil execs are, by and large, unrepentant about the fallout their
activities will have on local people living under despotic regimes
empowered by petrodollars. As *Forbes* magazine noted, "if you are
running a big oil company, you either deal with the despots or watch
your company liquidate itself."[74]

"You kinda have to go where the oil is," added ExxonMobil's Lee
Raymond.[75]

CHAPTER EIGHT

Carbon Perils

For hundreds of millions of years, the carbon that had filtered down deep into the earth's crust lay dormant, locked in its silent caves and tunnels beneath tons of rock. Then, in just a blink of time, humans expelled over half of it back to the circulating winds and currents at the surface of the planet.

The first glimmers of what this might do to the climate had been predicted over a century ago. In 1883, in an explosion heard over two thousand miles away, the Indonesian volcano Krakatau erupted, projecting ash, dust, and carbon dioxide six miles out into the atmosphere. Over 35,000 people died under tidal waves and a two-hundred-foot-thick layer of ash smothered area islands. The sun's rays didn't penetrate the thick cloud of dust for over two days.

On the other side of the planet, the chemist Svante Arrhenius was studying for his doctorate. The eruption set him to thinking. He theorized that the rapidly growing factories spouting carbon and other pollutants into the air might not be so different from Krakatau's explosive release in its climate-changing impacts. He called it the "hothouse" effect.

Carbon dioxide in the atmosphere, along with methane and water vapor, absorbs the heat that radiates from the sun-warmed ground and seas, enmeshing the planet in a warming protective blanket. Water vapor is more abundant and methane absorbs more heat, but carbon dioxide is arguably a more dynamic player. It can linger in the atmosphere for centuries.[1] A doubling of the atmosphere's carbon dioxide levels, Arrhenius wrote in an 1896 paper, would increase the planet's average temperature by five to six degrees Celsius.

The wooly Swede wasn't too worried about it. The global warming would "allow our descendants, even if they only be those of a distant future, to live under a warmer sky and in a less harsh environment than we were granted."[2]

During the 1980s, humans released 5.5 billion tons of carbon dioxide into the air every year, primarily from the global combustion of oil, natural gas, and coal.[3] Every single car buzzing around hauled a 5-pound sack of carbon out its tailpipe every 20 miles or so. Once dug up from its underground tomb and sapped of the energy that bonds them hydrogens, the on-the-loose carbons link up with heavier oxygen atoms and make their escape into the air. The 5-pound bag of carbon balloons into a 19-pound bubble of carbon dioxide gas. Every barrel of oil burned sends up 800-odd pounds more.[4]

The forests suck in about 1.4 billion tons of the excess carbon. The oceans slowly take up another 1.7 billion tons. But at least 3 billion tons of extra carbon are not absorbed by the increasingly denuded land or the oceans. They linger in the atmosphere, catching the sun's reradiated heat as the centuries tick on.[5]

By the early 1980s, Arrhenius' hothouse effect was discernable. There hadn't been so much carbon dioxide in the atmosphere for perhaps as long as 20 million years.[6]

Peruvian fishermen had named the warm ocean current that visited their shores after baby Jesus, the boy child or *el niño* in Spanish, because it always seemed to appear around Christmas. Usually, the fish stocks died down for a bit while El Niño lingered, but it didn't matter much as the hardworking fishers wanted a break for the holidays anyway.[7] The warm patch would generally pay annual visits to the shorelines of Peru and Ecuador for about three to six years in a row. After that, cool currents rushed in, an opposite phenomenon later named La Niña. The natural fluctuation between El Niño and La Niña had probably been going on for millennia, influencing the trade winds, jet stream, and storm tracks that shaped the planet's climate.[8]

In the winter of 1982 to 1983, El Niño torched the seas by four degrees Celsius. About two thousand people died in the droughts, floods, fires, and storms that followed, resulting in over $13 billion in damages.[9] Afterward, El Niño storms became more frequent and intense, and a host of other disturbing changes were noted.

In 1987, marine biologists, oceanographers, and other experts gathered in the Virgin Islands to discuss a mysterious new scourge that had befallen the Caribbean's coral reefs. Across the region that year, the usually colorful coral reefs had started to turn white.

For their lush colors, coral polyps, small anemone-like creatures, rely on tiny plant-like creatures called zooxanthellae that live in their tissues. The photosynthesizing zooxanthellae provide the polyp with both food and energy. Their humble partnership allows both to thrive in clear, calm tropical waters where most other creatures would be hard pressed to find a meal. This relationship also allows the polyp to grow in great colonies, building their limestone skeletons one atop the other, arduously creating the world's coral reefs. Giant reefs provide oases in clear, underwater nutrient deserts, attracting teams of diverse species of fish and marine mammals. Their massive skeletal walls protect coastlines from erosion and provide calm waters that many fish species use as nurseries for their young.

But the coral polyps had expelled their zooxanthellae, without whom they turned white or bleached. Pockets of "uncommonly hot water" noted one coral expert, may have been to blame. If the strange warmth persisted and the polyps and zooxanthellae didn't partner up again, within a few weeks the polyps would die of starvation.

Luckily, most of the Caribbean's corals survived 1987's summer heat. But, the coral experts agreed, when the rainforests of the sea collectively blanch, it could be a "signal of change, a signal worth looking into," as one told the *New York Times*.[10]

Over the past hundred years, the Pacific ocean warmed by almost four-fifths of a degree Celsius;[11] and the land by about half a degree Celsius. The Arctic sea ice thinned by 40 percent. The warmer temperatures and drip of melting ice off the continents have expanded the volume of the sea, the newly enlarged waters overflowing into freshwater reservoirs, drowning miles of coastline. The global sea level rose between ten and twenty centimeters during the past century.[12]

These changes could be less than half of the effects expected from the carbon dioxide emissions of the last two centuries, as they likely are the consequences of emissions from long ago.[13] Worse, changes in the climate could trigger other changes, which might intensify the initial effects. The pressure would build and slowly a giant switch could be flicked. Things might change rapidly after that.

For instance, warmer seas (or a drop in sea level) could melt methane hydrates, triggering massive meltdowns that could rapidly release billions of tons of methane into the air.[14] Because the methane in the hydrates is so concentrated—a single crystal holds 160 times more methane than a similar volume of pure methane gas—even relatively small meltdowns could release tons of heat-trapping methane into the atmosphere. Fifteen thousand years ago, meltdowns shot the global temperature up by ten degrees Celsius, an abrupt finale to the last ice age.[15]

Wide bands of carbon-sucking forests, fine-tuned to thrive within a precise range of climatic conditions, could rapidly collapse. Although some animals might flee on foot and wing northward to escape the encroaching hot, dry weather, many species of trees can't spread more than a few hundred feet in a year. If current rates of warming continue, they will have to move about two miles a year to stay within their climate comfort-zones. Whole forests might be left rooted to inhospitable spots, depleting the planet's capacity to absorb extra carbon in the air.[16] As the carbon locked in their decomposing carcasses is released into the air, the planet's forests could switch from being a net carbon absorber to a net contributor.

According to computer models, even if humans stopped burning fossil fuels tomorrow, the sea may keep rising and the ice sheets continue melting for hundreds, even thousands of years. By 2100, the sea level could rise by as much as eighty-eight centimeters over its 1990 levels. The temperature of the planet could rise between 1.4 and 5.8 degrees Celsius, a dire prediction given that a shift of just a few degrees spells the difference between a green, habitable planet and one enveloped in snow and ice.[17]

Human civilizations had arisen during an unusually stable period in the planet's climate, which the earth had enjoyed since the end of the last ice age ten thousand years ago. Before, brutally rapid changes in the climate, probably triggered by the switching on and off of ocean currents, had most likely been a merciless constant in Earth's long history. That period of climatic stability, it appeared, was coming to a close.[18]

The news about human-induced climate change trickled down into the heart of the oil industry, where, at London's premier training ground for oil and mining companies, the Royal School of Mines, gangly, curly-haired oceanographer Jeremy Leggett recounted the legends of oil strikes to his enrapt students. Surrounded by superstars of the oil world, Leggett helped train hundreds of petroleum engineers and geologists. One of Leggett's colleagues had found an oilfield in Pakistan. "When the well had hit oil, he threw an impromptu champagne party for half the faculty in a luxury Kensington hotel. Lectures were cancelled for days afterwards," Leggett recalled.

Leggett had fallen in love with the search for crude. Money was part of the appeal. Leggett's lucrative academic career at the Royal

School of Mines sent him jet-setting across the globe, enjoying the finest sashimi in Japan and the best Bordeaux in France, attempting to pinpoint where the seas of long ago had left their rich oily sediments.

There was "something primeval" about the oil business, he said. It was the "hunter's thrill" of stalking oil, on foot and with tools and weapons, the deep penetration of the earth, the huge machines, and the "fascinating engines." The oil industry "hunts, and kills, with sophisticated toys," he said. "I was one happy camper," he remembered.[19]

But by 1988, the evidence of climate change had "become impossible to ignore," he says. "I felt my sense of mission, future and professional identity eroding with every new report I read."

One day he decided he wanted out.

> And there I stood, that day, giving my lecture on the giant offshore California oilfield, once again teaching the students new tricks in the search for oil, as though concerns about the global environment . . . were somehow just a sideshow. Until then, my entire professional life had been dedicated to training people like these to go forth and find fossil fuels, to add carbon as heat-trapping carbon dioxide and methane to the atmosphere. To quite literally fuel a threat to the future, and risk bequeathing their children an uninhabitable world. It had to stop.

In 1989, he left the Royal School of Mines and joined Greenpeace.[20]

The following year, the Intergovernmental Panel on Climate Change (IPCC), a group of hundreds of climate scientists from around the world convened by the United Nations General Assembly, met to hash out their first scientific assessment report. Greenpeace sent Leggett to observe the report's final drafting. He wasn't the only advocate in the audience. Whatever credo the panel laboriously hammered out would be one that shaped potentially economy-transforming policies in legislative chambers across the planet. The IPCC meetings were full of Leggett's former colleagues, oil industry public relations staff and oil ministry officials from oil-producing countries.

The industry's future dealings in carbon were in peril. "These companies, some of which have existed for a hundred years, are essentially about extracting petroleum," commented one industry consultant. "And in a world where you don't extract petroleum any-more, the first order of expectation is that you're dead."[21] Whereas earlier environmental concerns had restricted the way the industry conducted its business, this growing concern about carbon dioxide in the atmosphere attacked the very notion of a petroleum industry, confronting, for the first time, the value of the product itself. Not only did the petroleum industry emit over 87 million tons of carbon into the atmosphere in the United States alone,[22] it relied on bil-lions of other people buying its products and emitting hundreds of millions of tons more.

If government leaders decided to clamp down on machines that exhaled carbon into the air, investors might properly decide to stop anteing up for oil companies. Consumers would shun the pump. Bright-eyed graduates would stop applying for jobs. The entire industry could collapse.

The oil industry pinpointed the high-level, international climate talks as its public enemy number one. Each report that the IPCC scientists wrote up had to be approved by government delegates. Leggett watched as oil industry consultants and the oil-producing countries "chipped away at the draft, watering down the sense of alarm in the wording, beefing up the aura of uncertainty," Leggett says. The point was to "wear the scientists down with diplomatic gutter tactics, if possible to derail the meeting procedurally, but certainly to reduce the impact of the product."

Despite the fossil fuel industry's efforts, the IPCC's conclusions in its 1990 scientific assessment report were critical, if not yet damning: they concluded firstly that global warming was indeed occurring and secondly, that human activities were causing it. But, the IPCC added, they would need more time to be truly certain.[23]

International negotiations kicked off to enact some kind of agreement based on the IPCC's 1990 findings. Fossil-fuel lobbyists were dispatched to circulate the industry's arguments: that "stabilizing carbon dioxide emissions would have little environmental benefit," and "the benefits of increased carbon dioxide have been ignored and the warming exaggerated," as Leggett described.

An OPEC official making the rounds at the climate talks openly admitted that OPEC wanted to scuttle the looming agreement. "My motives are selfish," he told Leggett. "We don't want this convention. There's nothing in it for us."[24]

By 1992, the much-harangued international talks rendered an international agreement, the UN Framework on Climate Change (UNFCC). As Leggett described it,

> It was a masterpiece of circumlocution, mentioning the possibility of developed countries stabilizing emissions by the end of the decade, but at an unspecified level, and merely as an "aim," not as a legally binding commitment. It allowed the Europeans and Japanese to claim that the "spirit" of the convention as negotiated meant committing—as they all had, unilaterally—to a freeze in carbon dioxide emissions by the year 2000. The Bush Administration meanwhile could claim to Congress that they had committed to nothing.[25]

Signatories did agree to continue meeting to negotiate something a bit more binding. By then, Democrats Bill Clinton and Al Gore had taken the White House. Environmentalists were hopeful that the United States might surprise the international community with a bold pledge to cut back or at least stabilize its emissions.

Meanwhile, the rising waters of the mighty Pacific threatened to swallow its islands whole.

More than thirty thousand islands peek out of the Pacific Ocean, but many are barely land, snatching the tops of volcanoes and the corals that formed around them for tiny patches of solid ground.[26] In what historians call one of the most amazing feats of maritime navigation in human history, thousands of years ago seafarers had set off from the Chinese mainland into the vast, featureless, and uncharted Pacific, miraculously finding Polynesia's specks of habitable ground.[27]

Tuvalu, for instance, is a series of coral atolls and islands comprising ten square miles of land stretching across 350 miles of ocean. Most jut just a few feet above sea level. On their white sands sprout willowy coconut trees. People survive on Tuvalu's little bit of paradise fishing, raising pigs, and growing taro, bananas, cassava, and coconuts in the island's sandy soils. They practically live in the lagoon and ocean that encircle them. A reporter from the *Guardian* described their ocean-drenched life:

> Men and women stand neck-deep in the sea, eating fish and bits of coconut, or periodically raising pans they are silently scrubbing beneath the surface of the water. At midday, a father and son heave four pigs into the lagoon for slicing up; the pigs' slashed-open bellies turn the water red and their entrails drift off on the ocean. At dusk, islanders gather on motorbikes to watch the sunset from the low concrete jetties jutting out into the lagoon. Children slide down algae-covered boat ramps into the water and a man clutches a fish the size of a dog to his chest.

During the Second World War, American troops arrived to build a landing strip on one of Tuvalu's islands. The soldiers scratched into the thin soils, leaving behind pits (some as big as 300 feet by 50 feet, and 10 feet deep) that destroyed about one-third of the island's arable land. After the war, the islanders took to using the pits as garbage bins.

The sea provided food and livelihoods, but money came from elsewhere. In the early days of the Internet, Tuvalu had acquired the Internet domain extension ".tv." Leasing the rights to the domain netted tiny Tuvalu a $50 million deal with the American company dotTV—not bad for a country with an annual GNP, before the dotTV deal, of $8 million a year. They even sold postage stamps showing a smiling Tuvaluan woman with flowers in her hair, gazing up at the South Pacific sky, and the giant ".tv" emblazoned across it.

All might have seemed sun-soaked and placid yet there was something more than clever Internet domain names floating in the South Pacific sky.

Tuvaluans were used to weathering one or two serious cyclones every decade. Over the 1990s, the islanders confronted no fewer than seven major cyclones. Each storm took another bite of Tuvalu's hard-won ground, each high tide digesting another slice, rendering the land thinner, saltier, and less nurturing. In 1992, as the UNFCC made its lackluster debut, Tuvalu's prime minister announced that the island nation was the "world's first victim of climate change" and started forming a plan to evacuate.[28]

He left his watery island for Washington, DC, where with Jeremy Leggett's help, he tried to bring the plight of his drowning island to the attention of the people whose fuming machines, he was convinced, had caused the problem.[29]

The Clinton White House rebuffed Tuvalu's prime minister but in April 1993, President Clinton announced that the United States would stabilize its greenhouse-gas emissions at 1990 levels within seven years. He didn't say how the country would do it, nor did he explain what the United States planned to do after the year 2000. Still, it was progress.[30]

The oil industry stepped up its attack on the IPCC science that underlay Clinton's alarming move, exploiting and extending its influence in academia. Like any good defendant on trial, the oil industry trained and showcased its own roster of expert witnesses, renegade scientists willing to counter the consensus-driven, peer-reviewed science of the IPCC.

Because oil companies had already infiltrated the ivory tower, shaping the priorities and directions of fields ranging from geology to engineering and astrophysics, this tactic was both highly effective and easily achieved.

In 1993, Sallie Baliunas, a Harvard astrophysicist who studied how changes in the sun's magnetic cycle correlated with changes in the star's brightness, published a paper stating that the sun had grown between 0.1 and 0.7 percent brighter since 1700—sufficient extra brightness at the medium- to high-end of the estimate to account for all of the observed global warming of the last century.[31] It was just a correlation, Baliunas admitted, but the natural variation had to be taken into account when dusting for the human fingerprint on climate change.

The implications of Baliunas' research fell on receptive ears in the oil industry. In 1994, Exxon and other corporations whisked Baliunas on a media tour.[32] To her Harvard audiences, Baliunas was coy: "I am addressing scientific issues. Economic, political, and environmental considerations are quite another story," she said.[33] Yet, a couple of years after her Exxon tour, as federal funding for research in astronomy dried up, Baliunas publicly called for the government to encourage greater corporate underwriting of scientific research.[34] Baliunas would go on to join a parade of scientists, who under fossil-fuel industry largesse, would bring the uncertainties, contradictions, and unknowns about climate change to the broader public.

The temperature was rising, and fossil fuel combustion added to the heat-trapping carbon dioxide in the atmosphere: these were observable facts that couldn't be seriously disputed. Yet climatologists had found the connection between the two—that burning oil changed the climate—notoriously difficult to prove. Industry-funded scientists took pains to expose this soft underbelly of climate science.

The American Petroleum Institute, a trade organization representing the American oil and gas industry, launched a campaign in which "victory will be achieved when average citizens understand . . . uncertainties in climate science." The institute proclaimed that those promoting cuts in greenhouse gas emissions "on the basis of extant science appear to be out of touch with reality."[35]

The industry-friendly academics offered a range of arguments to counter the IPCC's doomsday scenarios. Perhaps ancient astronomical processes altered the climate in ways that had little to do with human activities on the planet's surface. The sun dimmed and brightened over time, as NASA's satellites confirmed in the 1980s, possibly because the earth itself wobbles on its long orbit around the star. These tiny wobbles could alter the amount of sunlight coming to earth enough to trigger and melt ice ages. (In fact, the IPCC did take the influence of solar variation into account in their reports and still concluded that burning fossil fuels had changed the climate.[36] Baliunas herself admitted, "It may be that it's a coincidence that these two things have changed together."[37])

What would happen after the planet started to stew was even more difficult to predict. Who was to say that the new warm weather wouldn't be a good thing? Indeed, over a century ago when scientists had first detected carbon dioxide's role in warming the globe, they rejoiced. Fewer people would freeze to death. It would be easier to grow crops. "Global change is inevitable," allowed Thomas Gale Moore of the conservative Hoover Institute, but "warmer is better."[38] "Warming is definitely better than cooling. It is certainly better for agriculture and therefore for basic human existence," added industry darling S. Fred Singer, a professor emeritus of environmental science from the University of Virginia, who traveled the world promoting his anti-IPCC opinions on the coal industry's tab.[39]

Then again, perhaps the planet wouldn't warm, the trend in the air offset by any number of other unpredictable changes. The whispery thin ozone layer hovering high above the planet had been punctured and the hole could cool the planet. Forests could temporarily store carbon dioxide, keeping it out of the atmosphere and so help mitigate the warming effects of heightened levels of carbon dioxide. When they were gone, the denuded plains, blanketed with winter's white snow, would reflect rather than absorb radiated heat and so would cool things down.[40] Nobody could accurately predict the behavior of the fly-by-night clouds: the wispy ones could trap the earth's reradiated heat, contributing to global warming, but the dark ones could block incoming sunlight and effect a cooling.

Although their arguments, promulgated in scientific papers, op-eds, and magazine features, were sometimes arcane, industry-allied scientists contradicting IPCC science served a vital purpose, creating in the public mind the appearance of an actual scientific controversy. The news media helped, by pitting this small minority of contrarian scientists against the much larger majority who stood by the IPCC consensus, as if both sides were equal. If the scientists themselves couldn't agree on whether the climate was changing or what it meant, why should citizens commit themselves to doing anything about it?

Many in the oil industry truly believed that climate change was an "overhyped nonproblem," as Leggett described it. Exxon's top scientific advisor felt certain that "most of the recoverable oil and gas would be burnt, and that it would have no noticeable effect on the climate," Leggett says. A Texaco spokesperson pinned his hopes on future technology: centuries would pass before researchers settled the science, and by then, the problem might be moot: "someone discovers the gene that eats the carbon dioxide or something." Others confessed that the planet probably was warming, but felt it wouldn't be a major disruption. A prominent coal industry spokesperson wondered, "What's wrong with a bit of sea-level rise? It is merely changing land use—where there were cows there will be fish." A contrarian spirit, he asked the *Washington Post*: "How many people were following Moses when he started? And there was only one guy saying the earth was round in the beginning. It's nothing to be ashamed of."

One day, a Ford representative revealed how he understood his role in warming the planet. "You know, the more I look, the more it is just as it says in the Bible," he said.[41] Ford Motor Company's John Schiller believed that the earth is not 6 billion years old but only 10,000 years old.

According to Schiller, climate change is part of the planetary devastation foretold in the Book of Daniel, according to which a one-world government, led by an Antichrist, would eventually take over. It isn't worth worrying about because it has all been prophesied, and according to the prophecies, the Antichrist won't rule for long. In this particular worldview, environmentalists agitating for controls on greenhouse gas emissions collaborated, whether knowingly or not, with the Antichrist himself, as Leggett later noted in his book, *The Carbon War*.[42]

Although certainly an outlandish belief, if the last century of scientific evidence is to be believed, it is by no means an unusual one. Polls suggest that nearly one-half of all Americans believe that both humans and the planet sprang into being around ten thousand years ago.[43] Critics debate whether these are genuine beliefs or evidence of poor science education, but either way, the widespread incomprehension of the planet's geological history doesn't bode well for public understanding of the science behind climate change.

Even unsentimental industry scientists hewed to the doubts expressed by their colleagues, although for different reasons. Most of the scientific expertise in the oil industry tends towards the geological disciplines. For geologists, a million years is nothing; the events they study occurred on scales of hundreds of millions and billions of years. In geological time, the climate has changed many times before. For some industry geologists, nongeologist humans are simply myopic, absurdly viewing the changing climate in terms of their own miniscule human time-scales.

"I myself am not particularly convinced by this climate story," petroleum geologist Colin Campbell said.

> I think the science is extraordinarily weak. I know in a geological sense there's been huge epochs of global warming in the past, and the degree to which this one is due to Man's activities—it almost certainly is to some degree, but. . . [w]e live in Europe in a very vulnerable place because the Gulf Stream comes rushing across the Atlantic. There's a current down the Davis Strait, west of Greenland, and in times of warming the meltwaters deflect the Gulf Stream. It's like blowing at the base of a flame, a relatively small lateral push on this current shifts this Gulf Stream a few degrees, and this has an astronomical effect on the climate of Europe. So if we observe great climate fluctuations in Europe it's not to say they're all man-made. It's a vulnerable climatic condition because we're so dependent on the Gulf Stream. And I mean after all, Aleric the Goth managed to sack Rome because the Rhine froze in 406, and I wouldn't imagine this fellow was wanting to move south for any particular reason except that it got kind of tough at home, you know.[44]

Had, say, biologists been the scientific experts at oil companies, at least some sectors of the industry might have been more easily convinced of the potential dangers of climate change. Ecologists study the fragile balance eked out in niche ecosystems and how seemingly tiny variations can have broad devastating effects. In the language of ecology, extinction is real, final, and heartbreaking. Under geology's macroscope, extinctions happen all the time.

≣

While Baliunas and other industry-sponsored experts made
their rounds on the lecture circuit, evidence of irreversible climate change mounted. Warm winters and retreating sea ice had
stalled the pumping of heavy cold waters into the deep seas off
Greenland.

This was disquieting news. Ocean circulation is one of the key
regulators of the planet's climate, as the seas absorb more than half
of the heat the sun provides to the planet, distributing it around
the globe.

Many factors drive ocean circulation, but one of the most important ones is the "thermohaline circulation." In just a handful of patches
of ocean, cold seas freeze into ice, leaving behind masses of dense
salty water. Being salt-laden and thus heavier, these waters drop
down to the depths, as far as four kilometers down. Warm surface
waters rush in to replace the cold, salty sinking waters. In this way,
the cold saline waters of the north slip southward, while above, the
warm waters of the tropics rush northward. It is a thousand-year-old
circulation that regulates weather on land, and originates in just four
regions of the planet, including the waters around an alternatively
freezing and melting tongue of ice off the east coast of Greenland.[45]
The news came out in 1995 that this vital pump had been stilled.[46]
The dense salty water mass has thinned to the point that it only drives
surface water down a single kilometer.

Late that year the IPCC announced that "the balance of evidence"
indicated a "discernable human influence on the global climate system." International pressure for a treaty requiring legally binding
cuts in greenhouse gas emissions intensified. The showdown would
come at the third annual review of the UNFCC in Kyoto, Japan,
scheduled for 1997.

≣

This time, indusstry execs focused on a principle that had been long agreed upon: that Western countries, not developing ones, would pay for any new low-carbon economic infrastructure. "This is a wealth-transfer scheme between developed and developing nations," railed ExxonMobil's Bob B. Peterson. "And it's been couched and clothed in some kind of environmental movement. That's the dumbest-assed thing I've heard in a long time."[47]

Robert Priddle, as the former executive director of the International Energy Agency, advised government leaders from twenty-six oil-consuming nations around the world on how to control oil markets. He delivered his clipped assertions with all the smooth certainty of the British elites who steered the empire decades before him. For him, unrestrained consumption of finite stores of petroleum make eminent sense; the real problem for the climate is that poor Third World people keep burning carbon-sucking trees down.

After delivering a twenty-minute soliloquy on the inevitability and necessity of the world's continuing consumption of oil and gas for a gathering of oil executives, Priddle projected an image upon the screen behind him, showing a wrinkled brown woman, hunched under her basket of twigs, presumably gathered for the small fire that would cook her meager meal. He frowned. "This," he admonished, pointing his finger at the woman, "is unsustainable!" Environmentalists who pointed their fingers at the oil industry often misrepresented the facts, he sniffed, describing himself as "appalled."

Priddle and other oil-industry insiders often deflected blame for climate change by painting overpopulation and deforestation in developing countries as the real sources of the problem. Every year, nearly sixty thousand square miles of tropical forest disappear from Latin America, Africa, and Asia. According to the IPCC, the destruction of the world's forests, among other land use changes, accounts for between 10 and 30 percent of global carbon dioxide emissions, as decomposing and burning trees bequeathed their carbon back to the air and disappeared, never to absorb carbon again.[48]

Yet, the equation between population growth and deforestation wasn't so simple. India's rate of deforestation had declined since 1980, despite the relentless forward march of its population. The pressure to chop down the forests came from more than just hordes of locals.[49]

Logging companies, cattle ranchers, and other industries felled large chunks of the world's rainforests to produce luxury items for consumers in the industrialized world. The paper industry boils and presses 40 percent of all the world's harvested wood to turn it into paper, two-thirds of which is consumed by Europeans, Americans, and Japanese.[50] Every year the United States imports about 300 million pounds of beef from cows raised in Central America, each quarter pound of that beef requiring the clearing of 55 square feet of rainforest, releasing 500 pounds of carbon into the air.[51] The oil and gas industry itself posed grave threats to rainforests around the world. A single oil project in Ecuador, for instance, resulted in the loss of almost 8,000 square miles of rainforest.[52]

In fact, according to the IPCC, local people excessively harvested wood for fuel only in a few African countries. In other places, when local people chopped down trees to use as fuel or building materials, they often reduced overall carbon dioxide emissions. If they hadn't used wood, the logic goes, they would have used energy-intensive cement, steel, oil, or coal instead, combusting a lot more carbon.

In July 1997, just months ahead of the climate talks in Kyoto, Congress passed a nonbinding resolution, by 95 to 0, urging then-President Clinton not to sign any international agreement that didn't require developing countries to cut emissions as well.[53] Meanwhile, oil execs bolstered the resolve of developing countries to disown the climate treaty. "It would be tragic indeed if the people of this region were deprived of the opportunity for continued prosperity by misguided restrictions and regulations," Exxon's Lee Raymond argued to the Asian government officials gathered at the World Petroleum Congress in Beijing in 1997. The science was "far from airtight" and any regulations to rein in the problem would be "administered by a vast international bureaucracy responsible to no one."[54]

In the final hours of the Kyoto conference, the clause describing how developing countries would participate in Kyoto's mandates was stricken from the protocol. President Clinton signed the doomed Kyoto Protocol, in full knowledge that without any mandates regarding developing countries' emissions, the Senate would never ratify it.

"The alliance between oil and auto companies is one of the most powerful alliances in the world," admitted the head of the UN environmental program. "It can paralyse governments."[55] It did. The treaty that finally emerged from Kyoto had been so watered down that it called for the year 2012 to see a cut in carbon emissions equal to just 5.2 percent less than 1990 levels; if loopholes were exploited, the 2012 carbon emissions could be as little as 3 percent lower.[56]

In the United States, carbon indulgence reigned. A week after Clinton signed the protocol, the EPA exempted SUVs and pickup trucks from its new air-quality regulations. The biggest of the light trucks would be allowed to emit more than five times more smog-causing gases than cars; the smaller light trucks would be allowed over three times more emissions than cars. American drivers, frightened by the increasingly unsafe roads dominated by SUVs and light trucks, and egged on by automakers' advertising that subtly and not-so-subtly suggested that cars were less safe than SUVs, stood in line to buy the giant gas-guzzlers.[57]

In Europe, where consumers were considerably more worried about the changing climate, oil companies assuaged fears with clever PR. British Petroleum, for instance, embarked on a $200 million rebranding effort, throwing out its old corporate logo, a green and yellow shield, for a "green, yellow, and white sunburst that seemed to suggest a warm and fuzzy feeling about the earth," as the *New York Times* put it. They shortened the company name to simply "BP," and the new slogan for the outfit that produced several billions of barrels of oil and gas every year was, slyly, "Beyond Petroleum."[58] The gas stations that B P refitted with solar panels sold more gasoline, too.[59]

In 1998, the mysterious scourge of 1987 returned with a vengeance. This time, the corals didn't survive. Warming seas killed 16 percent of the corals in the world's tropical oceans. Almost half of the corals in the Indian Ocean died. Between 60 and 95 percent of the Great Barrier Reef's corals bleached; 5 percent died.[60]

"Once the corals have died," commented one distressed reef activist, "the combined effects of changes in ocean chemistry, increased cyclones from climate change, and more species that bore into corals predominating, means that eventually the reef will collapse." The coral reefs of the world could wash ashore as rubble, a loss as devastating to life in the ocean as the loss of rainforests for terrestrial ecosystems. More fisheries would fold, as the open seas washed over broken reefs, disturbing once-calm nursery waters. Erosion would devastate coastlines.[61]

Some coral experts, like Ove Hoegh-Guldberg, a sunburned diver whose retreating hairline gave him the look of a creature more marine than terrestrial, watched these underwater genocides unfold in slow motion. He'd get the N O A A reports of approaching warm weather and know, with a sinking feeling, that about a month later he'd watch the reefs off the Australian beaches outside his offices start to pale.

The irony—that Guldberg's cherished reefs could themselves turn to oil after sinking deep into the seabed—was something the loquacious scientist preferred to keep to himself. While the American public dithered about why the climate was changing, and U.S. leaders stood jowl to jowl with oilmen, Guldberg, with an arrogant certainty, knew who was responsible, openly deriding oil execs as "idiots" and their rationales as "crap."[62]

By 2002, the industry coalition formed to disrupt the Kyoto talks disbanded. It had "served its purpose," as its ghostly Web site put it. Within a year, more than 750 billion tons of carbon would infuse the air,[63] compared to about 580 billion tons of carbon in the pre-industrial atmosphere. Some of Tuvalu's islands shrank to just half their original size, the water-logged garbage in the pits dug by American soldiers decades ago overflowing practically into islanders' homes.[64] Planners at the Pentagon envisioned a world of "endemic warfare," drowned cities, and a frozen Europe in a secret report on abrupt climate change.[65]

The crisis for the industry had effectively ended. BP retreated from its rebranded persona, by way of explanation noting to its investors that "the impact of the Kyoto agreements on global energy (and fossil fuel) demand is expected to be small."[66] In the new post-Kyoto environment, ExxonMobil along with a consortium of oil and other companies openly greenwashed their corporate grant to Stanford, dubbing the $20 million, ten-year program the "Global Climate and Energy Project," despite the fact that it would be led by a petroleum engineer and revolve around technofixes to enable decades of continued oil drilling.[67] Even Jeremy Leggett decided it was time to move on, starting up what would become the biggest solar power company in Britain.[68]

Former oilman President George W. Bush defended his retreat from Kyoto. He called it a "plan" that involved "cuts," but this was essentially linguistic trickery. Instead of reducing greenhouse gas emissions, the Bush plan would reduce greenhouse gas *intensity,* that is, the amount of greenhouse gases emitted per dollar of GDP. Polluting industries would be free to keep expanding, but would be asked to aim to use a bit less carbon to do it.[69] Bush advocated cuts in greenhouse gas intensity of a whopping 18 percent from present levels. In fact, according to the World Resources Institute, the U.S. greenhouse gas intensity *had already fallen* by almost 17 percent over the preceding decade. Bush's plan was, therefore, essentially no different from business-as-usual.[70] Environmentalists saw through the ruse but for those not following the arcane twists and turns of the climate change talks, it may have sounded soothingly bold.[71]

In fact, in some cases, Bush's plan was even worse than the status quo.

Inspired by Bush's challenge, the electric power companies, who together emitted 40 percent of the United States' carbon dioxide, pledged to reduce their greenhouse gas intensity by up to 5 percent—2 percentage points less than what the Department of Energy had predicted even without the benefit of the Bush plan.[72] While the signatories of the Kyoto Protocol would be cutting their emissions levels to 3 to 5 percent below 1990 levels by 2012, the Bush scheme would allow U.S. emissions to rise by up to 28 percent over the same period.[73]

In December 2005, U.S. negotiators stormed out of international climate talks once again. This time, they agreed to return to the table to discuss a post-Kyoto future only after winning a stipulation from the other delegates: not to discuss anything that might require the country to cut its emissions.[74]

CHAPTER NINE

Running on Empty

B‍Y THE EARLY 2000s, it seemed clear that escalating oil consumption would surpass available oil supplies before long. The ever-growing American thirst for oil, the cars taking over Beijing's bicycle paths and India's decrepit, cow-clogged roads, the growing hordes of global elites eager to mimic the high style of the petrolife were projected to send oil and gas demand marching forward by around 2 percent every year, zooming to nearly 120 million barrels a day by 2025, over 50 percent more than the amount the world consumed in 2001 and nearly six times the amount the world consumed in 1960.[1]

Providing enough oil to meet growing world demand, the president of London's Institute of Petroleum, Dr. Pierre Jungels, told industry officials in 2003, would require $1 trillion in capital investment, plus "the work of some 350,000 engineers and scientists and advances in technology at least as great as those of the last 30 years." It seemed to Jungels practically insurmountable. "The industry faces huge challenges to find and produce the hydrocarbons required over a twenty-year horizon," he said. "Even if technical, financial, human resource and political issues can be resolved, there is no escaping the fact that the industry needs to . . . manage the transition . . . when the hydrocarbon inventory is depleting fast whilst demand keeps on growing."[2]

Faced with such doom-and-gloom scenarios, many looked to oil giant Saudi Arabia for relief, believing that Saudi's mighty wells would easily pour forth extra crude from its bountiful reserves. All one had to do was to twist the taps. But signs appeared indicating that even Saudi Arabia's much vaunted "surplus capacity" could be more mythical than real. Saudi Arabia's Ghawar oilfield, providing 60 percent of the country's total oil output had started to spurt increasing volumes of water. By 2003, Ghawar was producing 1 million barrels of water along with its nearly 4.5 million barrels of oil, analysts noted.[3] According to Department of Energy insiders, all of Saudi Arabia's oilfields were pumping large amounts of water.[4] Small amounts of water generally infuse the oil that wells unearth, but the wells are dug so that they can siphon the oil beneath the buoyant water floating on top. When large amounts of water come flowing out of an oil well, it generally means that the oil is nearly gone.

The modest discoveries of new oil would be of little help. The top five oil companies, ExxonMobil, BP, Shell, TotalFinaElf and ChevronTexaco, had spent $110 billion looking for new oil between 1999 and 2001, but for all that money only pumped out 500,000 more barrels of oil or oil equivalent every day. "These are extraordinary sums merely to keep production flat," energy investment banker Matt Simmons wrote.[5] New oil finds in places like Angola and Gabon added just under 4 billion barrels to the planet's known reserves of oil. Although gargantuan for the lucky oil companies that happened upon them, the world's oil-hungry machines could burn through that much in less than three months. Industry analysts estimated that production from oil and gas fields would continue to decline at an average rate of 3 to 5 percent every year.[6]

The dreaded peak in the world's production of oil, that point when about half of the reserves are gone, approaches.

Former Shell geologist Kenneth Deffeyes retired from teaching at Princeton in 1998 with plans to buy a small oil well. He figured that world oil production would be peaking in a few years, so the investment would be well worthwhile. "But nobody believed it! People who were well informed, had money to invest, they were spectacularly uninterested," he recalls. Shocked at their complacency, Deffeyes spent six months applying Hubbert's calculations to world oil production. When he reached his result, he knew better than to confine the news to industry insiders. In 2001, he released *Hubbert's Peak: The Impending World Oil Shortage*, defiantly stating that the world's oil production would peak within a few years. "An unprecedented crisis is just over the horizon," he warned. "There will be chaos in the oil industry, in governments, and in national economies. Even if governments and industries were to recognize the problem, it is too late to reverse the trend. Oil production is going to shrink."[7]

Never mind the oil spills, the various asthma epidemics, the perils of blasting carbon into the air—here was a threat that could actually arrest the march of Big Oil.

As demand starts to outstrip declining supplies, the oil market has entered a period of volatile oil prices. Cautious consumers, especially in industries, will reasonably be expected to start shopping around for energy sources with prices around which they can shape their budgets. Prudent ones have already started to shun oil-burning machines, opting instead for more expensive electric ones so as to avoid enslavement to the unpredictable costs of oil. Oil companies themselves have become less willing to invest in expensive projects, lacking any ability to predict what their future, oil-price-dependent income might be. By 2003, energy consultants had noticed some of the biggest companies' cold feet when it came to pricey new investments. The fear alone of wildly fluctuating prices froze them stock-still.[8]

At the same time, investments in new oil, found in ever deeper, ever more hostile climes, are increasingly risky in and of themselves. New oil today requires billions of dollars and years of planning, making each investment increasingly precious, and even garden-variety sabotage ever more deadly. A mere two-year delay fighting with environmentalists, fending off lawsuits, or negotiating with upset locals can send a project tumbling into the red.[9]

In 1999, Goldman Sachs summed up the situation. The oil business, they said, is a "dying industry."[10]

As the realities of depletion dawn on the world's biggest oil companies, one by one they have readjusted their outlooks for the future, dumping their "growth" strategies in favor of "capital discipline" and the "delivery of superior financial returns," according to analysts from *International Petroleum Finance*.[11] As Susan Cunningham, a senior vice president of an independent oil company explained, "the reservoirs are getting smaller and smaller and it is more difficult to find that smaller reservoir."[12] In 2003, BP, Shell, and ChevronTexaco announced they planned to abandon their annual ritual of forecasting the next year's oil production. They had missed growth targets for 2002 and apparently decided that the future was too uncertain to even attempt to predict.

"Their actions speak a lot more than their words," comments petroleum geologist Colin Campbell, who has written extensively about world oil production. "If they had this great faith in growing production for years to come, why do they not invest in new refineries? There are very few new refineries being built. Why do they merge? They merge because there is not room for them all. It's a contracting business."[13] The industry hasn't built a new refinery in its biggest market, the United States, since 1976. Even when oil prices surge, companies aren't pushing up their drilling activity; there just isn't enough left to find so they aren't bothering, as Cunningham admitted in an industry trade journal:

> The price is high and rig costs are pretty reasonable for the price so we should be drilling. It comes down to the shareholder because what is missing is the volume we are getting from the drill bit. . . . You can't just keep on drilling for smaller things at higher costs. You are getting less per

well because you have less pressure to support it. You do
have to replace your reserves, but you can't replace them
at any cost and some companies have been doing that.[14]

And yet, despite all the signals that the earth had bled most of its
best oil already, government officials and industry analysts continued
to argue that there was no need to start planning a less oily future.
In early 2005, with the price of a barrel of oil poised to top $50 a
barrel and nearly every major magazine planning wildly speculative
features on the end of the oil age, the Department of Energy issued
its annual energy forecast, blithely stating that oil drillers would
easily sate increasing demand over the next twenty years. By 2025,
the agency reported, the world would be swimming in cheap oil:
nearly 24 billion barrels snaking the planet in pipelines and tankers,
costing just $30 each.[14]

It isn't difficult to keep up the appearance of abundant oil. After all,
nobody really knows how much oil is down in the rocky reservoirs
until every last drop has been drained and the wells run dry. Whatever anyone says about the size of a reservoir of oil before that point
is essentially just a guess.

The size of oil reserves is generally calculated by reservoir
engineers employed by oil companies. It is an exercise equal parts
hope and manipulation. After pinpointing a reserve, companies
drill several "appraisal wells," chasms opened up into the reserve
to judge how rich and thick those oily rocks really are. Steel arms
dive into the deep holes to pluck bits of rock for the geologists
to mull over in the lab. Yet even with the most sensitive statistical tests and the most advanced petrochemistry, what the oily
samples on the lab table reveal about the formations under the
ground is limited. "The geology, which controls the amount of
oil in the reservoir, is liable to change between our information

points, our wells," admitted Robert Stoneley, a Royal School of
Mines petroleum geologist. "Until we have actually produced all
of the oil that we ever shall, we are involved with a greater or less
degree of uncertainty."[16]

Essentially, the size of the reservoir is estimated using a formula
that multiplies several different factors together, each of which is
itself an educated guess. Different estimates for the variables render
"wildly different answers" on the size of the reserve, according to
Stoneley. To make statistical sense of it all, each factor used in
estimating a reserve can be given a range of figures and the formula
crunched through in all of the various combinations fifty to one
hundred times. The result is a range of possible answers for the
size of the reserve, within which, it is hoped the truthful one hides.
This range, again, can be evaluated statistically, rendering a series
of guesses, each with its own statistical probability of being true
(their "P" factor) attached like a price tag. The reservoir engineer
then chooses one, gracing it with a banner emblazoned "proven."
But which one?

Deffeyes put it this way:

> Shell was interviewing three potential employees: a
> geologist, a geophysicist, and a petroleum reservoir-
> estimation engineer. The test question asked was "What
> is two times two?" The geologist mumbles for a while and
> announces that it is probably more than three, maybe less
> than five. The geophysicist punches it into his calculator
> and announces 3.999. When the reservoir engineer is
> asked, he jumps up, locks the door, closes the shades,
> unplugs the phone, and whispers, "What do you want
> it to be?"[17]

To complicate matters further, industry's estimates on the size
of their oil assets change over time. For financial and regulatory
reasons, oil companies sometimes prefer to low-ball their public

estimate of reserves when they first find a new oil deposit.[18] Then, the numbers are slowly refined as it becomes clearer just how much oil is really buried underfoot. The proclaimed size of the reserve depends, also, on how much money industry is willing to spend on extracting the oil.

And so, despite the fact that the rate of discovery of new oil has been falling since the 1960s, every year the industry releases new, ever-larger estimates of their reserves, providing an illusion of growth. The bigger numbers do not result from discoveries of new oil, but from the fact that oilfields already found actually hold a bit more oil than the company had initially reported. Between 1946 and 1989, for example, the estimated number of barrels of oil in U.S. oilfields kept climbing, but it wasn't because more oil was being found. Up to 80 percent of all of those added barrels came from improved estimates of old oilfields.[19]

"Companies and countries are often deliberately vague about the likelihood of the reserves they report," notes Campbell, "preferring instead to publicize whichever figure . . . best suits them." There is no standard, no audit by independent outsiders to temper whatever political or financial incentives companies may have in presenting a more or less optimistic spin on their numbers.

In the United States, the Securities and Exchange Commission requires that companies bestow their estimates with the moniker "proven" only when such numbers have at least a 90 percent chance of being true. But conservative estimates are not so common elsewhere. The former Soviet Union, for example, for years promoted "wildly optimistic figures" (those with less than a 20 percent chance of being true) as "proven" estimates of reserves, Campbell says.

When, in the late 1980s six OPEC countries reported that their oil reserves, even while being drained, had abruptly ballooned by 287 billion barrels, it was only the worst example of statistics-bending. In 1997, fifty-nine countries claimed that their oil reserves, despite being continually siphoned off, hadn't changed in size one iota from the previous year. They were sucking as fast as they could but the glass stayed full.[20] Iraq's reported reserves magically remained an even 100 billion barrels for over a decade. In 2004, Shell announced that it had overestimated the size of its oil and gas reserves by 3.9 billion barrels. In 2006, word leaked out from Kuwait's national oil company that its oil reserves amounted to just 48 billion barrels, not the whopping 99 billion barrels as officially figures have it. According to the leaked information, reported by *Petroleum Intelligence Weekly*, of those 48 billion barrels, only 24 billion had been proven to exist.[21] As Deffeyes puts it, "'reserves' exist in the eye of the beholder."[22]

Nevertheless, these flawed reserves estimates are collected by trade journals such as *Oil & Gas Journal,* which publish them uncritically, passing them down to government agencies such as the Department of Energy and the International Energy Agency for their widely disseminated reports on the state of the oil market.[23] With the imprimatur of government and international agencies behind them, the unadulterated oil-industry numbers float down into journals, newspapers, and books and the soft politicized estimates harden into brittle facts.

By this time, the probability figures, the "P" numbers, are long gone, even though it wouldn't be particularly difficult to standardize their use. As Stoneley points out, even weather forecasters specify whether there's a 10 or 50 percent chance of rain in the afternoon.

It isn't just the corporate reservoir engineers and OPEC oil ministers who play the reserves number game. Even the esteemed U.S. Geological Survey (USGS) participates.

In 2000, the USGS released a 32,000-page report on the world's petroleum assets,[24] methodically assessing the "undiscovered potential" for the world's petroleum basins. The intrepid USGS scientists assessed each basin for the range of volumes of "undis-covered" oil it might hold. The usual way to affix a number to this intrinsically unknowable amount is to consider how probable the formation of an oil trap was in a given area. Several conditions had to be met and each can be assigned a likelihood, all of which can be multiplied together to give an overall probability of a certain amount of oil patiently waiting to be discovered. "This figure is extremely imprecise and may be not much more than a guess,"[25] Stoneley points out, but the USGS pushed forward, ranking its results in terms of probability. The average of the not-very-prob-able amounts (those with a 5 percent chance of being accurate) and the quite-probable amounts (those with a 95 percent chance of being accurate) render a mean value, the average probability of finding a certain amount of oil. These amounts of undiscovered oil, each having an average probability of existing, were then added together.

The USGS's presentation was authoritative but the numbers were at least as speculative as those of Shell's managers and Iraqi oil ministers. In the case of Greenland, for instance, the government geologists had determined there was a 95 percent chance of finding just a single barrel of oil. Given the lack of industry interest in the region, such a tepid assessment could be considered a fair reflection of conventional wisdom. But, ever-optimistic, the USGS noted that there was, indeed, in the farthest reaches of probability, a 5 percent chance of finding vast amounts of oil. The precise amount they predicted could be discovered was no less than 111.8 billion barrels, just 2 million barrels short of Iraq's 112 billion barrels of proven reserves.[26]

"You might as well say that there is a 5 percent chance that I am a frog," Campbell retorted.[27] Yet the USGS used their fanciful 5 percent figure, averaged with the 95 percent figure, to suggest that 47.1 billion barrels of oil could be found in Greenland. "Can we really give much credence to the suggestion that this remote place, that has so far failed to attract the interest of the industry, holds almost as much, or more, than the North Sea, the largest new province to be found since the Second World War?" Campbell asked. "Could this be pseudo-science at its best?"[28]

Worse, Greenland's chimerical 47 billion barrels were summed together with other such whimsical figures to render a startling conclusion. The USGS had pinpointed 649 billion barrels of undiscovered oil,[29] 20 percent more than their previous estimate for non-U.S. reserves. USGS representatives were ordered off to international conferences to spread the word.[30] It made an impression. Never mind the skyrocketing rate of consumption of oil and the increasingly fruitless search for new oilfields. The world was awash in oil. Reviewing the USGS report, *Scientific American* concluded: "There's gobs of oil out there."[31]

When government agencies, such as the Energy Information Administration (EIA), the Department of Energy's number-crunching department, are tasked with making public predictions of future oil demand, they use the USGS report, along with the flawed numbers from the *Oil & Gas Journal* to report that there will be plenty of oil to go around. According to the EIA, by 2025 the oil industry would find another 76 billion barrels in the United States alone. In other words, the EIA is betting that an oil reserve the size of Venezuela's is hiding somewhere in the most explored country in the world. Ample graphs and charts, using the numbers from the USGS assessment and the *Oil & Gas Journal* estimates, provide a commanding illustration of just how.[32]

When confronted with such absurdities, Campbell professes exasperation. "Really it is a huge job to track all of these moves and counter moves which would test the skills of Sherlock Holmes," he says.[33] "Probably the most rewarding tactic," Deffeyes suggested, "would be to locate the EIA's drug dealers. They seem to be selling some really potent stuff."[34]

The obscurity of the world's oil supply slowed the impetus for change and masked the governments' ugly grabs for the increasingly limited resource. These were obviously policy objectives dear to the heart of any sitting government. Yet without lead time to prepare, it would be the blissfully ignorant, oil-sated public that would suffer when their plush carpet of oil was rudely pulled out from underneath them.

That is not to say that more reliable information isn't available. Campbell had seen the real numbers. He spent three decades exploring for oil in Trinidad, Colombia, Papua, Ecuador, and Norway for major oil companies including Texaco, B P, and Amoco, and over a decade consulting for governments and major oil companies.

"The information could be provided without particular technical challenge," Campbell says.[35] Instead, inside information on the true size of the reserves is classified, proprietary data. "The 'technical' values . . . are confidential for most countries," noted oil-industry analyst Jean Laherrere, and there is a "huge discrepancy" between those internal numbers and the "'political' values of the reserves" that *Oil & Gas Journal* and other official outlets hawk.[36]

Private firms buy the "technical," more realistic data for their corporate and governmental clients. Petroconsultants, a private firm in Geneva that later merged into I H S Energy Group, is widely believed to own one of the largest, most accurate, private databases on the size of the world's oil reserves. They don't publish their figures in journals or databases, of course. Access comes at a prohibitive price, sold to intelligence agencies and industry insiders.[37]

Using Petroconsultants' and other technical data, industry insiders such as Campbell, Deffeyes, and other petroleum geologists have analyzed the rate at which we are eating into the global oil supply. According to their analyses, the oil industry will produce less than 80 million barrels a day in 2010, falling to 70 million barrels a day by 2020.[38] Deffeyes predicted the peak in world oil production had already passed, in the year 2000. Only time would tell whether he was correct. Campbell predicted the peak would come in 2010. Either way, they say, it is coming—not in twenty years or thirty years or more—but within the next decade.

It would be reasonable to expect that along with higher-ups at oil companies, savvy government leaders are conversant in the "technical" reserves data provided by outfits such as IHS Energy. After all, in the United States, many government leaders have deep roots in the oil industry. (According to a long-standing rumor, Deffeyes notes, the U.S. Central Intelligence Agency is IHS Energy's biggest customer.[39])

And yet, there's little evident attempt to rein in profligate fuel use, perhaps most notably in the U.S. Defense Department, that instrument of U.S. global might. The U.S. military consumes about 85 million barrels of oil a year, making it the biggest single consumer of fuel in the country and perhaps the world.[40] According to an interdisciplinary panel convened by the Defense Science Board (DSB), cheap oil has distorted the American military into a handful of super-killing steel monsters, with the majority of the forces devoted to the logistics of simply feeding and fueling them. The Army employed sixty thousand soldiers solely for the purpose of providing petroleum, oil, and lubricants to its war machines, which have themselves become increasingly fuel-heavy. The sixty-eight-ton Abrams tank, for instance, burns through a gallon of fuel for every half mile. With its inefficient, 1960s-era engine, the Abrams tank burns twelve gallons of fuel an hour *just idling*.[41]

So much time and money is spent fueling the American fighting machines that, according to the head of the Army Materiel Command, a gallon of fuel delivered to the U.S. military in action can ultimately cost up to $400 a gallon. Indeed, 70 percent of the weight of all the soldiers, vehicles, and weapons of the entire U.S. Army is pure fuel.[42]

When given a choice between a gas-guzzling, high-maintenance machine and a lighter, more efficient one, the military generally chooses the former, analysts have found. The B-52 bomber is a good example. These fighter planes guzzle more than three thousand gallons of fuel an hour, using engines designed in the 1960s. New engine models could improve the B-52's fuel efficiency by 33 percent, propelling them so far that they wouldn't require expensive mid-air refueling, making possible the scrapping of fifty-five tanker platforms. Taking all that into account, the new engines could save the military over $1 billion. Yet the Air Force refuses to do it. According to its calculations, in which fuel costs less than a buck a gallon and delivery is free, the new engine isn't worth the investment.[43]

Evidently, the military's fuel-distended belly isn't something that the Defense Department considers a big problem. As of 2001, the computer program that today's high-tech, surgically striking military uses to calculate its fuel efficiency hadn't been updated since 1972. The computer language it is written in, FORTAN, is so old and seldom used it is practically extinct.[44]

As the DSB panel noted, there are two ways to satisfy the U.S. military's ravenous oil appetite: "to make platforms and systems more efficient so they require less logistics," they reported, "or acquire more logistics assets." If the military's wanton oil consumption and casual disregard for fuel efficiency is any indication, the top brass have decided to simply capture access to more oil.

Generally speaking, the U.S. market, by its sheer size, can count on crushing any competitors for oil should it become scarce. Americans demanded over 20 million barrels a day in 2004; Japan and China, the next two largest consumers, have markets around one-quarter

the size: in 2004, China required just 6.68 million barrels a day and
Japan just 5.28 million barrels a day.[45] By 2025, the U.S. market will
still be three times bigger than its nearest rival, but there'll be significantly less oil to go around. Its nearest rival will be much closer
in terms of market size and is an unfriendly, historically hostile
country: China. China depleted the majority of its own oil by 1993
and was even having trouble keeping its coal fires burning by the
early twenty-first century.[46]

China's prodigious coal production (involving some 5 million
coal miners toiling in about 75,000 coal mines[47]) provides about
70 percent of the country's energy.[48] But the massive reserves are
dwindling. The looming coal shortage is "one of the greatest hidden
dangers in China's future," a Chinese coal industry spokesperson
warned China's parliament in 2003. Chinese officials decreed that
Xilutian, the country's largest strip coal mine, after nearly a century
of operation rendering over 250 million tons of coal, would be closed
down in 2007. The three giant mountains of slag that had been dug
out of the mine would somehow be turned into a "forest park."[49]

With coal-deprived Chinese on the prowl for scarce energy supplies, the already tight market will get even tighter in coming years.
Big oil companies are already lining up to feed China's engines, primarily with new oil developments in Russia. The Russian government
plans to pipe oil from the windswept island of Sakhalin, floating in
the Bering Sea between Russia and Alaska, direct to thirsty oil consumers in China. ExxonMobil, Shell, BP, and others have descended
upon the former Czarist penal colony to help them do it.[50] Shell is
likewise building "a formidable presence" in north Asia, according
to *Petroleum Economist*. The company's expanding assets in China are
"gravitating towards the centre of its investment strategy."[51] In March
2002, BP committed up to $20 billion in oil assets in Russia, mak-
ing it the third largest company operating there, in order to service
China's major emerging market.[52] By 2004, oil-hungry Chinese leaders would set off on whirlwind tours of oil hotspots such as Algeria
and Gabon, staking their claim to the world's crude.

China's rising roar for oil echoes in the halls of the White House. In May 2001, not long after George W. Bush ascended from the Texan oilfields to the White House, the administration issued an energy policy report, underlining the U.S. need to corral the world's remaining oil supplies for itself.[53] The Bush administration, as was *de rigeur* since the 1970s, called its mission "energy security." But for former oilmen like Bush and Vice President Dick Cheney, the equation of "energy" with "oil" couldn't have been more transparent. The United States must "explore for energy," Cheney asserted. Clearly, the former CEO of Halliburton was not suggesting his colleagues go hunting for sunlight to shine on solar PV panels.[54]

After the devastating attacks on New York and Washington on September 11, 2001, it appeared that in the public mind, the government could do no wrong. "I really think this period is analogous to 1945–1947 in that the events started shifting the tectonic plates in international politics," said former Chevron board member and national security advisor Condoleezza Rice. The oil tanker that Chevron had named after Rice had been renamed after she moved to Washington, DC, in 2000, but the strength of her commitment to the petrolife remains clear. "It's important to try to seize on that and position American interests and institutions before they harden again," she said.[55]

Early in his first term, President George Bush met with the Canadian prime minister to hash out Canada's role in supplying Americans with oil and gas. After September 11, 2001, the two governments, suitably enjoined to finally solve the West's Middle Eastern problem, fingered what they deemed a "secure and strategic source of hydrocarbons": the oil sands of Alberta, Canada.

Across the bleak landscape of northeastern Alberta, over millions of years, a giant oilfield had risen from its grave. Freed from its rocky tomb, the oilfield's light molecules of oil and gas evaporated, leaving behind a thick, tarry sludge to bask in the thin northern sun. The sludge gummed up with the Albertan sand.

If the oil lingering in these sands, called "tar sands" or "oil sands," could be recovered, Alberta could provide 300 billion barrels of oil, more than the proven reserves of Saudi Arabia, awed industry groups said. Beyond those 300 billion potentially recoverable barrels lie a whopping 2.5 trillion more. Alberta, in other words, held more oil in its tar sands than the entire world endowment of conventional oil.[56] It isn't the only such deposit, either. Another giant deposit of tar sands sits in the Orinoco belt in Venezuela, buried deep underground.[57]

In the 1980s, the cost of extracting oil from tar sands ran to around $30 a barrel,[58] obviously a losing proposition when each barrel of oil fetches between $20 and $25 in the marketplace. Saudi Arabian oil, in contrast, costs just $2 a barrel to extract.[59] The tar sands lay fallow for years until the Canadian government started to aggressively subsidize their development. In 1995, the Canadian federal government announced that whichever oil companies braved the Albertan winter to rescue the stranded oil sands could write off 100 percent of their expenses,[60] the government forgoing the lion's share of its royalty until the industry started to earn a profit.[61]

A few years later, an armada of oil companies muscled in to Alberta's tar sands, selling off their assets in other parts of Canada to focus on the sludgy bitumen in the north.[62] Shell and Chevron committed to a mine, pipeline, and new refinery to process the tar sands into crude, at a cost of over $2.6 billion.[63] It was Shell Canada's biggest investment in a single project ever.[64] A host of smaller companies as well as outfits from Japan, China, Israel, and Korea buzzed around the suddenly sweeter tar sands play.

The trouble is, Alberta's tar sands are nothing like conventional crude oil, which is why trade magazines and government agencies historically haven't taken tar sands into account when tallying up the world's reserves of crude. Thick and tarry, tar sands oil can't be conveniently bundled off down a pipeline to the refinery. It must be treated first, with natural gas and other petroleum products, in order to flow. Not just with a little bit either; the tar sands require over five times more of these precious petroleum products than regular heavy crude.

Even when begrudgingly flowing, the oil is heavier than most refineries can handle. New refineries must be built or revamped in order to process it, and all they may be able to turn out is road asphalt or boiler fuel. Alternatively, yet more fuel can be burned to heat tar-sands oil into a synthetic crude oil.[65]

For each barrel of tar-sands oil, no less than two tons of sand and clay must be mined, using the widely reviled methods pioneered by the coal industry: forest-killing open-pit mining. With all the eviscerating procedures and additional treatment the tar sands require, extracting oil from the sands sucks up two-thirds of the energy they ultimately render,[66] poisoning the atmosphere with carbon in the process. Producing a single barrel of oil from tar sands emits no less than six times more carbon dioxide than producing a barrel of conventional oil.[67]

By 2002, over $10 billion had been invested in Alberta's oil sands, and the industry planned to squeeze out more than 3 million barrels a day by 2012.[68] By then, a handful of companies that had been mining the tar sands, using the world's biggest shovels and trucks, had depleted most of the shallow deposits. Companies turned to the deeper deposits, more than six hundred feet down. Open-pit mining wouldn't do, but they could drill holes and shoot steam down, to push the oily sands out.[69] The new technique, "steam assisted gravity drainage," sent the price of producing a barrel of tar sands plummeting down to around $5 to $7 a barrel.[70] It also required vast amounts of precious fresh water, which after being contaminated with chemicals is pumped into giant festering lakes of waste water.[71]

The oil-sands industry gorges on a quarter of Alberta's scarce fresh water—each barrel of oil needing six barrels of water to flush it out[72]—and burns up to a fifth of the entire nation's natural gas supply.[73] According to a leaked report from a Canadian environmental agency, the pollutants from the expanding tar-sands operations will result in enough acid rain to destroy much of the region's majestic forests as well.[74]

Most oil-sands projects have gone over budget by 15 to 20 percent and worse,[75] suffering sporadic sabotage from livid locals.[76] But it doesn't matter, analysts say. Government subsidies have drained the projects of financial risk. "Even if this project goes 20 percent or 30 percent over budget," a big oil company like Shell "will still have effectively zero debt on its balance sheet," an energy analyst told *Petroleum Economist*.[77]

In 2003, to the glee of the Canadian oil and gas industry, the U.S. Energy Information Administration added some 180 billion barrels of oil from the Alberta tar sands to its tally of "conventional" oil reserves, catapulting Canada's reserves above those of Iraq's and second only to Saudi Arabia's.[77] Provided they could stave off the shivering farmers and their thirsty livestock, the North American governments remained supportive, and with the price of oil high, the oil industry could potentially stay in business extracting oil from tar sands for centuries. "There's no environmental minister on earth who can stop the oil from coming out of the sand," Canada's environment minister said in the fall of 2005. "The money is too big."[78]

Alberta's oil, being politically safe, might relieve some of the pressure of the United States' dependence on Middle Eastern oil, but greater quantities of crude would be required for Bush and Cheney's sought-after energy independence.

One such flow of oil could have been from the Caspian Sea. But in 2002, disappointing news started to emerge from the ancient oil territories around Baku, precipitating even more aggressive stampedes for oil.

During the mid-1990s, seismic data had revealed a giant geological structure under the northern Caspian Sea, a monolith stretching two hundred miles long and fifty miles wide. If it were full of oil, it could be the largest oilfield in the world.[80] "The Caspian may well be the Persian Gulf of the twenty-first century," *Offshore* magazine reported in March 1996.[81]

Over in the State Department, ears were pricked. In 1997, the State Department had informed Congress that the Caspian held almost 200 billion barrels of oil.[82] The message was not lost on the senators. "You can picture back in the think tanks of America, and the foreign service departments and the military planners, all of these people seeing this great gem sitting out there in the Caspian, and their interest shifted to how to get the damn stuff out," recalls Campbell. "Since they are obviously not geologists, it was sort of taken as an assumption that it was there, and the problem would be to export it and bring it onto world markets."

State leaders in the impoverished region jockeyed for position. The Caspian Sea was landlocked, bordered by a gallery of countries and peoples who nursed age-old feuds with each other: Russia, Iran, Kazakhstan, Turkmenistan, and Azerbaijan.

Struggles emerged over the sea itself. Was it a lake or was it a sea? Before 1991, only two countries bordered the Caspian: Iran and the Soviet Union. Under international law, resources in lakes are generally shared between bordering countries. This suited the Soviet Union and Iran, as all they wanted to get out of the Caspian were its wandering sturgeon and caviar. Calling the Caspian a lake and divvying up the roving delicacies was easier than hoping that the fish swam and laid their eggs on one side of the Caspian rather than the other.

Oil, however, is a much more stationary resource. After the Soviet Union broke up, Iran insisted on keeping the lake definition, but some of the new bristling countries bordering the Caspian wanted to classify the water as a sea. It was salty, after all, and had been called a sea for ages. Also, if the Caspian were reclassified a sea, under 1980s-era UN conventions, it would be sliced like a pie, with each bordering country getting a single piece. Envisioning the slicing of the Caspian cake in their minds, the various countries vied for the tastiest morsels.[83]

More pressing questions followed. Which way would the biggest pipelines with their precious cargo run? Which countries would net the windfalls of transit fees, and which wouldn't? The problem of transport had already triggered violent conflict. When the Russians had decided to pump early Caspian oil through their leaky pipelines running through Grozny, the capital of Chechnya, they had set off six long years of bloody war and repression. The prize was even bigger now, and so was the brewing fight. Oil companies foresaw ferrying $21 million worth of crude oil and gas out of the Caspian Sea through pipelines every single day.[84]

The easiest cheapest route for a pipeline would be to pipe the oil through Russia or Georgia to the Black Sea, or through Iran to the Persian Gulf.[85] Western companies were unlikely to build pipelines through Iran, in as much as the country was still under U.S. sanctions.[86] The Russian route appeared most promising, and could make use of existing Soviet-era pipes. These were notoriously leaky, dripping oil into the frozen ground, which thawed into great standing lakes of oil (the biggest was eleven kilometers long and two meters deep) during the summers.[87]

But the United States objected. Never mind the leaky pipelines, the United States did not want any of this precious new oil to go through any potentially hostile territories like Russia. The cherished cargo, instead, should travel a longer and more expensive route, through Georgia and U.S. ally Turkey, government analysts insisted.

In the late 1990s, the United States started pouring money into the region to prepare the ground, feting the new leaders of the Caspian states at lavish White House diplomatic events.[88] The pipeline the United States wanted would cost around $3 billion. BP said it couldn't be done without "free public money," signing on to build the line after the U.S., U.K., Japanese, and Turkish governments agreed to subsidize the project. President Clinton traveled to Istanbul in 1999 to sign a deal for the pipeline that would carry Caspian oil into Turkey, where it could be loaded onto tankers in the

Mediterranean.[89] U.S. military bases sprouted across Central Asia, an iron embrace that tightened considerably with the 2001 invasion of Afghanistan, a violent and unsuccessful attempt to capture the wily Saudi terrorist Osama bin Ladin.

But then the other shoe fell. Something was going wrong in the oil patch. In 2001, BP and Statoil had gotten enough bad news. They pulled out. By late 2002, the oil industry had drilled three wells on the most promising Caspian oilfield, Kashagan, the hoped-for 200-billion-barrel savior. What they found was that "far from it being a single huge structure containing 200 billion barrels as they had hoped," recalls Campbell, "it is made up of different individual reefs, very deep, high sulfur, and the latest estimates are it's only got between 9 and 13 billion barrels!"[90] Of the dreamed-of 200 billion barrels, just one-twentieth might materialize. The Caspian would be no substitute for the Middle East.

The pipeline, however, proceeded apace. The people along the pipeline route, impoverished by war and years of neglect, their oil-rich land lacking even in the refineries that would provide them jobs, would most likely end up seeing their most lucrative resource pumped right out from under their noses with little to show for it. They braced themselves for an earthquake, as the sturgeon-rich Caspian was prone to them. Locals feared, too, greater contamination of the air with "sour gas," natural gas mixed with oil and deadly hydrogen sulfide, which was already being released by many fields in the region.[91]

One can only imagine how the news of the Caspian oil crash was greeted by the oilmen sitting in the Oval Office in the spring of 2002. It wasn't long afterward that Iraq, that treasure-chest of unexplored oil riches, fell under their gaze.

Only 17 of 80 discovered oilfields in Iraq have been developed; only 2,300 wells drilled, less than 1 percent of the number of wells drilled in Texas alone, according to the EIA. Iraq's vast Western Desert is virtually virgin territory; modern oil hunters had never subjected these oil lands to the reach and scrutiny of their directional drills and three-dimensional seismic surveys.[92]

Unlike the rest of his colleagues in OPEC who had been chastened by their fall from grace after the 1973 oil embargo, Iraqi President Saddam Hussein was still willing to use Iraqi oil as a weapon to punish his enemies, not least the United States. In September 2000, Hussein announced that Iraq would no longer accept U.S. dollars for its oil, only euros. In April 2002, from the seat of his starving country, weakened by years of sanctions, Hussein withheld all Iraqi oil from the market, in another attempt to punish Israel's allies.[93] It wasn't just the West that met with the leader's opprobrium. Hussein impetuously ripped up a deal with a Russian oil company after Russian president Vladimir Putin supported sanctions against Iraq.[94]

Hussein had bigger plans. In February 2003, he claimed Iraq would double its oil production to 6 million barrels a day by 2012, perhaps even 10 million barrels a day, if sanctions were lifted.[95] In anticipation, the Iraqis were planning to drill more than four hundred new wells, and had already inked some deals to get the job done. The rub was that the oilmen who would drill those wells would not be working for ExxonMobil or ChevronTexaco, but Russian, French, and Chinese companies.[96]

Then, seemingly out of nowhere, in the spring of 2003, the United States invaded Iraq on a flimsy pretext, purporting to rid the broken country of destructive weapons.

It may have been a mistake when *USA Today* reported on Operation Iraqi Liberation (OIL) in a March 26, 2003 story, but the oily ramifications of what came to be known as Operation Iraqi Freedom were clear nevertheless.[97] As American killing machines advanced in the Iraqi desert, long lines of five-thousand-gallon tanker trucks trailed behind, stopping to refuel at military bases aptly named after Shell and ExxonMobil. "The forward bases are normally refueling points," a Pentagon spokesperson said. "They're basically gas stations in the desert."[98] Hundreds of airborne oil tankers refueled the Air Force's fuel-hungry bombers, the newest ones pumping more than six hundred gallons a minute while hovering in mid-air. B-2 bombers flew nonstop from Missouri to Afghanistan and back, replenished a dozen times in mid-air by the flying oil tankers, many of which could themselves be refueled in mid-air.[99]

Burning over 2 million barrels of oil every week, the U.S. forces crushed the Hussein regime within weeks.[100]

Enraged Iraqis and others resisted the U.S. occupation that followed, felling more than five hundred U.S. soldiers between the fall of the Hussein regime and early 2004, torching pipelines and blowing up cars. Much ink was spilled detailing the U.S. concern for the Iraqi people, yet weeks after the war ended, many still lacked drinking water and electricity. They didn't even have gasoline. Lines at the local gas stations stretched for miles and took days to inch forward. Schoolchildren waited for buses that never came. The sick died waiting for gas to fuel the cars that might take them to the hospital.[101]

The flow of oil from Iraq's two giant, aging oilfields, Kirkuk in the north, discovered in 1927 and Rumaila in the south, discovered in 1953, comprised about two-thirds of Iraq's daily oil production before the invasion, but reservoir engineers who descended upon them after the smoke cleared found grave damage. Forced to produce oil while deprived of modern technologies, the reserves had been overpumped and flooded with water, outdated techniques frowned upon by the modern oil industry. Water seeped into Kirkuk's oil deposits, and hundreds of thousands of barrels of oil were being injected *into* Kirkuk's wells in order to maintain pressure. In the south, oil experts convened by the United Nations say, less than half of the hypothetically recoverable oil could ultimately be pumped out. If the United States tried to pump more oil out of these damaged fields, they could be destroyed irrevocably, some experts said.[102]

Despite extreme provocation, the Iraqi regime declined to use the much-feared weapons of mass destruction that the United States had warned about, and indeed after the regime fell, none were ever found, casting doubts on whether they ever existed at all. Still, pesky Hussein was gone and the contracts that Iraq had negotiated with the Chinese and the Russians were unilaterally declared null and void.[103]

Immediately, the U.S. occupying forces instructed Iraq's oil ministers not to make a move without their permission,[104] installing former Shell C E O Phillip Carroll to help lead Iraqi oil development, despite an abundance of highly trained, efficient oil technocrats from Iraq itself.[105] Before new oil could be pinpointed and extracted, a massive investment to rebuild the country's oil infrastructure would have to be made, one that would net billions for Big Oil and its contractors. Halliburton alone would take home at least $3 billion in reconstruction contracts.[106] Oil companies demurely pointed out how expensive and time-consuming such contracts would be for them. But given the length of time and amount of money they'd spend elsewhere, for less oil in more hostile places, it was a bit of a stretch. To put it in perspective, ExxonMobil spent close to thirty years negotiating access to a mere billion barrels in war-torn Chad; the industry was spending almost $40 billion to develop oil in Kazakhstan, despite the trouble they'd face in piping it out.[107] In Iraq, the industry might have to spend several billion dollars to get the country's oil infrastructure stabilized, but in the end, the prize would be access to the second largest proven conventional oil reserves in the world. Most, like Shell, aimed to "establish a material and enduring presence in the country," as Shell exec Gavin Graham said in April 2005.[108]

The U.S. regime in Iraq promptly set about twisting the spigots off for their enemies and on for their friends. For a country that considered using oil as a weapon anathema, when given the opportunity it quickly jumped at it. U.S. soldiers cut off a pipeline carrying two hundred thousand barrels of Iraqi oil daily to Syria, in one fell swoop bleeding Syria of up to $1 billion a year.[109] Discussions on how to rebuild a pipeline to pump cheap Iraqi oil to U.S. ally Israel kicked off.[110]

President Bush meanwhile set off on a whirlwind tour of Africa, the first time a president had visited the continent in his first term. That summer of 2003, the administration toyed with the notion of sending troops to storm Liberia. "African oil has become of national strategic interest to us," explained one U.S. official. "The stability of West Africa"—home to the West's new *El Dorado*—"is important to U.S. interests," added national security advisor Condoleezza Rice.[111]

The Bush administration continued to promise the American public that sales of Iraqi oil, not their taxes, would pay for Iraq's $100 billion reconstruction.[112] But by November 2003, dogged by sabotage, United States-occupied Iraq was producing just 1.9 million barrels a day, well under the 3.5 million barrels the country proffered daily before 1990.[113] The flow of Iraqi oil reached 2.5 million barrels a day a year later, but once again fell to just over 2 million by the summer of 2005.[114] As the occupation of Iraq dragged on, the U.S. administration started to sow the ground for what they considered the next step for the world's last super-power: decades of unending war, Vice President Cheney told a crowd in Los Angeles in January 2004, under the guise of a generations-long "war on terrorism."[115]

In 2004, China, instead of using 7 percent more oil than it had the year before, as it had been doing for the past few years, used a bit more oil. That year, China consumed 325 million barrels more oil than it had the year before, an increase of 15 percent over the previous year. With the world sucking down oil nearly as fast as it could be supplied, the extra consumption from China sent the entire system into pandemonium.

Until the industry somehow brought more hydrocarbons online, any minor disruption in the flow of oil could now be expected to lead to regional scarcities and skyrocketing prices. A series of devastating hurricanes in the Gulf of Mexico, shutting down more than 25 percent of the U.S. refining capacity did the trick, pushing oil prices to $70 a barrel.[116] American consumers accustomed to $1.50/gallon gas were shocked by prices topping $3 at the pump. The lines at the pumps lengthened, and magazine editors readied their speculative features on the end of the oil age.

The oil industry was in for an earful from politicians who complained that greedy oil barons were depriving voters of their birthright to cheap oil. Hauled before a Senate hearing in late 2005, oil execs from ExxonMobil, Shell, BP, Chevron, and ConocoPhillips were scolded by camera-conscious senators. Build new refineries! they yelled. Drill deeper, harder, longer! they demanded. "The oil companies owe the country an explanation," fumed senator Pete Domenici.[117] But the industry execs had heard it all before. Despite record-breaking profits, maybe they would and maybe they wouldn't. "We don't want to build capacity without demand," explained Saudi Arabia's oil minister Ali al-Naimi, later.[118]

Saudi Arabia was the only answer to the problem, according to the International Energy Agency. Every other producing country already had the taps full on. And so, the kingdom would just have to increase its 10.5 million barrels of daily oil production to 18 million barrels a day by 2030, the agency announced. According to Fatih Birol, chief economist of the IEA, it didn't matter whether there was enough oil in the ground to bring up. "Mr. Birol said the issue was whether investments were made, not whether reserves existed," the New York Times reported.[119]

President Bush met with Saudi Arabia's Prince Abdullah for "a straight answer" on how much oil the kingdom could cough up. Triumphantly, in April 2005, the president extracted an assurance from the Saudi oil minister that the kingdom would, indeed, ramp up its oil flow. According to the minister, the kingdom had no fewer than 200 billion barrels of as-yet-undiscovered reserves.

That view sounded optimistic to some, who wondered how the minister could be so sure about the as-yet-to-be-discovered 200 billion barrel goldmine. The truth later tumbled out from Saudi Aramco's former head of exploration Edward O. Price. According to Price, the source of the fantastic sum was none other than the U.S. Geological Survey's notorious 2000 report.[120]

CHAPTER TEN

Challengers, Old and New

SOLAR POWER'S POTENTIAL is vast. Generally, a typical square foot of land in the United States receives, absolutely free for the taking, about nineteen kilocalories of sunlight an hour.[1] If applied to all the available roofs in even a cloudy country like Britain, solar panels could generate more electricity than the entire nation consumes in a year.[2] Indeed, covering just 0.4 per cent of the globe with 15 percent efficient solar panels could supply enough electricity for the entire planet's primary energy needs.[3] Where the sun doesn't shine, the wind generally blows, and its power per square foot is about the same.[4] Oil companies know this. "All the world's energy could be achieved by solar many thousands of times over," a Shell official said in 1995.[5]

Despite the promise of renewable energies, less than 3 percent of the world's energy needs are met by solar and wind power, according to the International Energy Agency. Because the overall investment in solar and wind energy remains so small, the technologies themselves are expensive compared to mature, well-subsidized fossil fuels. Today, according to calculations cited by ExxonMobil, it costs about $100 to $200 to transform sunlight into the amount of energy in a $25 barrel of oil.[6]

Technological improvements rein in the price of renewable energies, but such investments must play catch-up with the R&D blitz for fossil fuels. In the United States, scientists researching and developing new photovoltaic technologies manage with about $50 to $75 million a year,[7] a fraction of the $3 billion their colleagues working in oil and gas research labs enjoy.[8]

To date, the oil companies have not considered it in their interest to pursue renewable energies with a fraction of the zeal they lavish on their quest for oil. Some have invested, modestly, in renewable energies. In the small pond that constitutes the renewable energy market, giant oil companies can make large ripples. BP's solar division makes it the second biggest solar company in the world. Shell is one of the world's ten biggest wind farm owners.[9] But according to the *Economist,* such ventures should be seen not as genuine entrepreneurial ventures but rather as hedging bets "should the transition to clean energy happen unexpectedly soon."[10]

Big companies such as BP and Shell could easily make solar energy affordable to today's consumers, triggering a switch away from fossil fuels. As Saudi Arabia's oil minister warned his OPEC colleagues decades ago, "if we force western countries to invest heavily in finding alternative sources of energy, they will. This will take them no more than seven to ten years."[11] Today, a single large manufacturing plant for solar cells—one capable of producing one hundred megawatts of solar panels a year—would make the price of solar PV cells competitive with coal. Such a plant would cost less than a "single leg of a deep-water drilling rig," says Jeremy Leggett.[12] And yet, such a plant remains a dream. In 2004, the biggest solar-cell plant churns out just twenty-five megawatts worth of solar panels a year.[13]

Relative to the days when farmers scooped oil floating atop blackened rivers, bleeding crude from the Earth's crust today has become an energy-intensive affair, requiring massive amounts of concrete, steel, earth-eviscerating machines, and armies of workers. Although industry managers affix price tags on the effort, subtracting the cost from the projected windfall of cash from the barrels of oil that might be unearthed, they don't analyze the amount of limited energy resources their activities consume relative to the amount they provide.

Obviously society, as a whole, must invest in energy sources that provide more energy than they consume, or it will soon enough run out of energy altogether. Mining the iron, firing it into steel, crushing stone into concrete, building the rigs, feeding the workers: all of these things require vast amounts of energy, whether the oil company pays for these costs directly or not.

When the biggest and shallowest oilfields were first tapped, oil's net energy, the amount of energy it provided compared to the amount of energy its extraction required, was around 100 to 1 or better. By the 1970s, with oilfields becoming smaller, deeper, and more remote, (and thus requiring more energy to get at) the net energy of oil dropped. By the 1970s, it was around 23 to 1 and falling.

Hydropower provides the next best return, at 11 to 1; coal 9 to 1; and nuclear power a 4 to 1 return.

Still, these energy "profits" dwarf those of more abundant energy sources like sunlight and wind. Fossil fuels concentrate sunlight; the difference in what they pack is many times greater than the difference between wine and grape juice. According to energy analysts, direct solar energy can perhaps provide 1.9 units of energy for every one it consumes in its production and manufacture. Wind energy hovers around the same return.[14] Silicon for solar panels and aluminum for windmills abound in the Earth's crust, but it takes energy to mine and process these into energy-catching contraptions, and even the best solar panels can't convert more than 30 percent of the sunlight that falls on them into electricity.[15]

This reality forms the bedrock of a deep disdain for energy sources that don't rely on giant shovels and holes in the ground, even among the more thoughtful people associated with the oil industry. Kenneth Deffeyes writes, with some finality, that neither solar nor wind energy can be an "immediate, large-scale solution to the energy problem."[16] Oil execs who presumably have some conflicts of interest on the topic are more direct. Oil companies might be expected to address some environmental impacts of their business, but "that does not mean we should accept facile suggestions about moving rapidly away from using fossil fuels to rely on renewable forms of energy," asserted Shell's chairman Philip Watts in June 2003. BP's Lord John Brown concurred: "There is still no source of alternative or renewable energy that can be supplied commercially to meet mass energy needs."[17]

ExxonMobil's Rex Tillerson could barely bring himself to say the words "renewable energy." "We expect *so-called renewables* such as wind and solar to grow rapidly," he said, "although primarily due to government incentives not market economics."[18] Tillerson's boss is even more forthright. Renewable energy is "a complete waste of money," he told the *Economist*.[19]

It may be that price and energy analyses alone will never fairly measure the value of harnessing solar, wind, and other renewable energy sources. In one way or another, society pays the bills for the ravages of climate change, smog, gas flaring, and oil spills; the disrupted lives of people, animals, and ecosystems around oil facilities; and the violence, war, and corruption spawned by profit-seeking oil companies and their allied state interests. It is unlikely that renewable energies would impose anywhere near the same penalties. Sun, wind, silicon, aluminum: these resources are distributed more or less equally around the planet. A society run on renewable energy might be much less lavish, much more provincial, and far less elaborate, as G N P wouldn't keep marching forward, and complex, energy-intensive industrial factories might come screeching to a stop—but a slow-growing society might also be a lot longer lasting and equitable.

If recent energy initiatives are any indication, the energy future being written today by those leading the most energy-hungry country in the world, from presidents and governors to major automakers and oil companies, will consist not of solar panels and wind farms, but hydrogen fuel cells, coal mines, nuclear power plants, and ethanol. Each, in its way, is promoted with alluring double-speak about its efficiency, cleanliness, and sustainability. Yet each, in its way, will likely ensure continued consumption of oil and growing emissions of carbon dioxide into the air.

Hydrogen fuel cells produce electricity from hydrogen and oxygen, leaving behind a drip of pure water. The fuel cell harnesses hydrogen's powerful attraction to other elements, turning it into electricity, then releases the hydrogen to bond with oxygen, forming H_2O. Hydrogen is plentiful; in fact, it is the most abundant element in the universe. But, the properties of hydrogen that make it so appealing as an energy carrier also make it exceedingly difficult to capture. It is vanishingly rare as a free element. If not locked up in hydrocarbons or water, hydrogen atoms are so light they can rapidly escape out of the atmosphere and into the blackness beyond. To exploit the energy of hydrogen's attraction to other elements, energy must first be expended prying hydrogen out of the different hydrogen compounds found on earth. Hydrogen can be extracted from water using renewable energy sources, or from "reforming" natural gas. It can also be extracted from other hydrocarbons, including gasoline.

Enthusiasm for a "hydrogen economy" has been building since the late 1990s. In 1999, Iceland announced its plan to become the world's first hydrogen society.[20] A few years later, the European Commission announced a $2 billion scheme to enable a hydrogen-powered Europe, in order to meet the region's environmental commitments under the Kyoto Protocol.[21] In Iceland, buses fill up at stations where the country's plentiful geothermal and hydroelectric power zaps water into hydrogen and oxygen.[22] The European Union similarly planned to make hydrogen using renewable energy sources.[23]

These inroads into oil markets filled environmentalists with hope for a carbon-free future. The oil industry may well collapse, some said. "The commercial implications of a transition to hydrogen as the world's major energy currency will be staggering," wrote the Worldwatch Institute in 2001, "putting the $2 trillion energy industry through its greatest tumult since the early days of Standard Oil and Rockefeller."[24]

The hydrogen fuel-cell car promised a future full of zooming vehicles but no more smog, no more noisy highways, and no more carbon-spewing tailpipes. Filling stations would provide a jet of hydrogen to feed the fuel-cells, their floors stained not with black grease but distilled water.

Hydrogen-powered cars would be many times more efficient than internal-combustion-engine cars, too. Only about 16 percent of the energy in gasoline can be put to work turning the wheels of an internal-combustion-engine car. The newest fuel-cell cars could convert 42 percent of the hydrogen-oxygen attraction into wheel-turning power.[25]

But where would all the hydrogen come from? Misperceptions abounded. "We can now look forward to running our automobiles on water," enthused a California congressperson.[26] Not exactly. Hydrogen fuel-cell cars might zip around dripping pure water, but the hydrogen-extracting factories in the distance could be just as dirty as the stinkiest coal-burning power plant.

The oil and petrochemicals industry has been producing hydrogen for decades, extracting it from petroleum to make fertilizers, diesel, and other products. In 1997, Chrysler unveiled its own hydrogen fuel-cell car, one that extracted hydrogen from gasoline.[27] Instead of being burned, the gasoline would be vaporized and infused with steam inside the car, "reforming" it into carbon dioxide and hydrogen. Then-President Bill Clinton hailed the gasoline-to-hydrogen technology as a "dramatic breakthrough." The oil companies could keep producing and refining oil and piping it to gas stations. The pump at the filling station would still pour gasoline into cars. The only difference would be what happened to the gasoline once it got into the car.[28]

The whole complicated procedure was a messy one that would emit over three-quarters as much carbon dioxide as a regular gasoline combustion engine, a far cry from the zero-emissions transport that environmentalists envisioned, or even the interim natural-gas-to-hydrogen system many consider both clean and practical.[29] In addition, it would require just as much if not more gasoline consumption. "Though a more expensive and slightly dirtier route than the others that have been proposed," commented the *Economist* drily, "this could make sense in an America wedded to keeping petrol cheaper than bottled water."[30]

In 2001, Toyota, Nissan, and Renault announced their commitment to gasoline-to-hydrogen cars. BP and Shell opened hydrogen divisions in their companies.[31] Shell and General Motors announced they'd invest up to $1 billion to develop a "hydrogen economy" in 2003. President Bush earmarked nearly $2 billion to develop hydrogen fuel cells, and California governor Arnold Schwarzenegger vowed to build a $100 million "hydrogen highway" studded with over 200 hydrogen filling stations by 2010.[32] "When you add it all up and talk about the sales of everybody that's involved and all those kinds of vehicles we've talked about, you're talking in the trillions," GM's CEO told a 60 *Minutes* crew excitedly.[33]

Much of Bush's billion-dollar R&D commitment would flow, via an industry-government project called the FreedomCAR initiative, straight into the research departments of GM, Ford, and Chrysler.[34]

What precisely was the point? many wondered. The gasoline-hydrogen fuel-cell cars that the big automakers favored had the same fuel efficiency and emissions as the new, highly efficient electric-gasoline hybrid cars, which were cheaper to manufacture and already on the market to boot.[35] "Talk of a hydrogen revolution is no more than an elaborate piece of window dressing and will never result in the new clean fuel economy that many people hope for," opined the *Engineer* magazine in 2003.

Many believe that hydrogen is being used to distract public attention from more immediate changes that could have a greater effect on carbon emissions but are less palatable to business. Environmental groups also claim that car and petrochemical firms promote the hydrogen option because they know that it would be many decades before a workable system could ever be contemplated.[36]

Disappointed critics took to dubbing hydrogen fuel-cells "fool cells."[37] Undaunted, Shell opened its first hydrogen filling station in November 2004, on Benning Road in Washington, DC.[38]

President Bush had another plan for showing how the hydrogen economy might work: by mining more coal. In 2003, Bush announced a $1 billion grant for companies to build a high-tech new facility, called "Futuregen," that could produce hydrogen without emitting any greenhouse gases. The facility, strangely enough, would use coal,[39] despite the fact that carbon-packed coal only holds about 5 percent hydrogen, as opposed to the much richer hydrogen content in methane or water.

Turning coal into hydrogen gas isn't a particularly futuristic application, the plant's name notwithstanding. The chemicals industry routinely does so to make ammonia and other feedstocks. The twinkling innovation in the project is that the carbon dioxide released by the process would be "sequestered."[40] Generally carbon dioxide emissions from coal "gasification" float out the smokestack along with other pollutants. Under the Futuregen plan, those emissions would be trapped and closeted somewhere.

ExxonMobil's grantees at Stanford, among others, plugged away at figuring out how to stash the excess carbon dioxide. Some could be pumped into aging oil wells to help pump out more oil. More could be stored in abandoned coal mines and other geological formations, but these may not provide enough space, so the deep ocean might provide a final resting place.[41]

With all the renewed attention, the coal industry was jubilant. "King coal is back!" thundered the headlines in the coal-industry trade press. By 2003, ninety new coal plants were in the works.[42] "The second coal age is beginning," agreed a researcher at the National Energy Technology Laboratory, a government lab well-funded by the Bush administration. "The issue is not whether this is a good idea or not, because it will happen no matter what," he added.[43]

The coal industry had helped put George W. Bush in the White House. The head of West Virginia's Coal Association called Bush's beneficence to the industry "payback." The president is "appreciative," he said. "He knows if not for us, he wouldn't be president."[44]

But even a rejuvenated King Coal could scarcely eclipse oil. Coal companies burn oil to mine coal. Right now, the worker-deprived coal companies use giant oil-burning machines to mine coal, lopping the tops off mountains and turning alpine villages into wastelands. Their machines burn as much as one hundred gallons of diesel an hour.[45]

Another initiative that appeared, in Orwellian fashion, to promote renewable energy was the push to ramp up ethanol production. In his 2003 energy bill, which passed in 2005, President Bush aimed to double ethanol use to at least 5 billion gallons a year by 2012.

Ethanol, an alcohol made from fermented grain, "doesn't require the Defense Department to protect it, and doesn't pollute the atmosphere," as one ethanol advocate put it. By requiring that drivers fill up with ethanol rather than gasoline, the new rule would reduce oil consumption by 250,000 barrels a day by 2012, advocates said.[46]

Corn farmers and giant agricultural conglomerates such as Archer Daniels Midland have been touting ethanol as a renewable and secure alternative to foreign oil since the 1970s. If ethanol took off as a fuel, midwestern farmers could stop growing corn merely for cows, sheep, and soda syrup. Instead, in a world in which over 800 million went hungry every night, they could grow corn to feed Americans' cars, "creating a new market for local corn and some added income from the processing," as the *Washington Post* described.[47]

But the oil industry hasn't been so keen on the farmers' fermented corn. Although they can ship gasoline from their refineries to their gas stations through pipelines, they can't do the same with ethanol. Moisture seeps into the pipelines along the welded seams. This isn't a problem with gasoline, because the water can easily be drained off at the end of the pipeline. But it is a problem with ethanol. Ethanol blends with water, emulsifying into an inseparable brew. If it became necessary to ship ethanol from its midwestern cradle to gas stations across the country, special tankers would have to be built and pipelines updated, all at extra cost.

In 1997, when the first ethanol-burning cars were unveiled, about 0.03 percent of all the gas stations in the country supplied ethanol-based fuels, which cost more to burn than gasoline anyway. Drivers filled their more efficient, ethanol-burning cars with less efficient gasoline instead. Eventually, automakers stopped promoting the ethanol-burning capability in their dual-fuel vehicles, mentioning it only in passing, deep within the fine print of owners' manuals. According to a 2001 study by the Department of Transportation, so unavailable was the fuel and so poorly marketed was the capability that most drivers of the ethanol-burning cars didn't even know their vehicles could burn anything other than gasoline.

Automakers kept building the ethanol-burning cars anyway. GM, Ford, and Chrysler manufactured 1.9 million ethanol-burning cars by 2001. As *New York Times* auto reporter Keith Bradsher explains it, the auto industry could use the dual-fuel vehicles' higher ethanol fuel efficiency, rather than the lower gasoline fuel efficiency that the cars actually achieved on the road, when calculating the average fuel efficiency of their fleets. The ethanol-burning cars, in other words, allowed the car industry to sell more gas-guzzling s u v s while still meeting their average fuel efficiency requirements. According to Bradsher, "by making possible the sale of more gas-guzzlers, the dual-fuel vehicles had actually increased American gasoline consumption by 473 million gallons in 2000."[48]

Not only that, but growing enough corn to ferment into ethanol requires nearly as much fossil fuels as the stuff's use replaces, as a University of California study revealed. American drivers might save 250,000 barrels of oil a day by using ethanol instead, but corn farmers and processors would need to burn 214,000 barrels of oil a day in order to provide enough ethanol for them.[49]

Should the auto and oil industries have their way, ethanol, like hydrogen fuel cells, would scarcely make a dent in Americans' consumption of crude. "The promotion of ethanol in the United States has been so tied up in federal pork and corporate welfare," opined the *Los Angeles Times* in early 2006, "that it's hard to see it as anything but a boondoggle."[50]

While the oil industry swatted away the pests challenging its primacy—hydrogen fuel cells, coal, ethanol—they groomed their own royal successor: methane-rich natural gas. Although it would require major investments and risks, the oil industry appears to view natural gas, its hitherto neglected stepchild, as its key growth industry during the long slide down oil's decline.

"There is an obvious consensus," according to reporters at the *Petroleum Economist,* "that natural gas will assume increased importance in the world's energy mix over the next thirty years." Shell hoped that demand for natural gas would outshine that of oil by 2025.[51] Half of the $8 billion investment b p earmarked for alternative and renewable energy in 2006 would go not to renewable solar, wind, or wave power, but to natural gas, using it to produce hydrogen and electricity. With its record earnings of 2004 and 2005, ExxonMobil launched its single largest investment in a new project ever: a $7 billion project to turn natural gas into diesel, the *New York Times* reported in 2006.[53] The next two decades, Shell's chairman Philip Watts said, are a "window of opportunity" for the oil industry to shift their customers from shrinking oil supplies to relatively more abundant natural gas.

Natural gas is generally found with oil, but unlike oil, it is difficult to get the stuff to market to sell. Gas can't be shipped in conventional tankers because even small quantities expand to fill the whole tank. It takes years to build the specially coated, high-pressure pipelines needed to transport gas into factories or homes, and if such a market isn't nearby, the investment isn't worthwhile. For years, the natural gas found in association with oil in remote fields has essentially been considered a waste product.[54]

The solution has been to simply burn the stuff, flare it.

But with many countries cracking down on the dirty, wasteful practice, the price of oil on the rise, and others gearing up for Kyoto-imposed carbon cuts, the natural gas market has started to look more interesting. Many newly discovered deposits of fossil fuels hold little oil but swarm with gas. And so, industry researchers have aggressively studied how to compress or cool natural gas so it can be transported and sold.[55]

Of course, an expensive new infrastructure would have to be built to provide more gas for Western consumers, including special tankers and specialized ports and processing facilities. The gas would have to be cooled to negative 260 degrees Fahrenheit—nearly absolute zero—to render it liquid before it can be shipped.[56] Over the last decade, however, the economies of scale have improved and the cost of shipping liquefied natural gas has dropped by more than 25 percent, analysts say.[57] With a veritable boom in liquefied natural gas plants, "there is no shortage of supply potential," said Watts. In 2006, the CEO of Dow Chemical would set off on a public campaign to urge

Congress to build dozens of terminals for liquefied natural gas. In 2005, only 4 such terminals existed. "We need 20 to 30 times as many," he said. "I want Congress to declare a national emergency."[58]

The disruptions of a stepped-up trade in natural gas will likely be just as severe as those of oil's. Natural gas supplies in major markets such as the United States have already started to decline. In 1998, the Texas gas industry had to drill four thousand new wells in order to keep natural gas production steady; the following year, they had to drill sixty-four hundred new wells to do the same. In the Gulf of Mexico, the number of drilling rigs looking for gas shot up by 40 percent between 1996 and 2000, but produced virtually the same amount of gas.[59] The United States increasingly relies on natural gas from Canada, but soon they'll have to start competing with the tar-sands industry for it. Between 1998 and 2007, after drilling more than a hundred thousand wells, Canadian natural gas production was expected to essentially remain flat, analysts said.[60]

In the Rocky Mountain region today, natural gas wells sprout like weeds. Nature-loving retirees "bought their five, ten, twenty acres of southwestern Colorado," comments a local lawyer, "and all of a sud-den, boom! They've got a gas well 150 feet from their back porch."[61] The Bush administration announced in 2004 a $1 billion subsidy for oil and gas companies prepared to continue drilling for natural gas in the depths of the Gulf of Mexico. "With demand for natural gas rising as more American families and businesses choose this clean-burning fuel," U.S. Interior Secretary Gale Norton explained, "we must provide incentives for development of known resources that are harder to reach."[62]

The battle to pry open foreign lands for natural-gas drillers is not far behind. As with oil, the biggest remaining natural gas fields lay under places such as Nigeria, Angola, Venezuela, and Indone-sia. "We're on the verge of discovering that natural gas is almost as important as oil for our energy supplies," commented one energy analyst. "Once we wake up to this, we'll have to deal with the geopolitical implications of importing natural gas from some of the more unsavory parts of the world," she added.[63]

As with oil, unconventional sources of natural gas such as methane hydrates enticed. "The magnitude of this previously unknown global storehouse of methane is truly staggering," shocked Department of Energy analysts reported. The Department of Energy, ever hopeful, anticipated that methane hydrates would be providing natural gas to consumers by 2015.[64] In the spring of 2003, independent oil company Anadarko drilled three thousand feet down into the Alaskan perma-frost to extract methane hydrates, in one of many multimillion-dollar experiments funded by the energy department.[65] The Navy, too, puzzled over how to turn those deepwater hydrates into underwater gas stations for their submarines cruising the depths.[66]

Setting aside the palpable threats to the climate and to local people and habitats should a drilling accident set off a hydrate meltdown, mining methane hydrates would be disastrously disruptive to the sea-floor, oceanographers say. Many schemes to capture the underwater hydrates resemble strip-mining. "Go out with a vessel, put a great big tent over the sea floor, inject antifreeze under the sea floor and poof, all the gas is trapped under the tent . . . and then you would move along," explains oceanographer Robert S. Carney.[67]

Key to the industry's sales pitch about natural gas is that it is a "clean" alternative to crude. Methane, packing just a single carbon atom for four hydrogen atoms in its molecules, is much less carbon-intensive than oil, and so burning it emits less carbon dioxide into the air. "It has virtually no contaminants," said Chevron's chief operating officer, referring to liquid fuel made from natural gas. "It exceeds all anticipated regulations anywhere in the world."[68] In a carbon-constrained world, added one Japanese official at 2003's World Gas Conference in Japan, "shifting to natural gas, with its low environmental impact, is a powerful way forward."[69]

But intensified natural gas use could actually be as bad or worse for the climate as combusting crude.

Because methane sucks up so much more heat than carbon dioxide, if even small amounts leak into the air—unburned—they could intensify global warming by twenty-three times more than an equivalent amount of carbon dioxide. As Jeremy Leggett points out, "just a 3 percent leakage of gas from the production, transportation, distribution, and use of gas and you would lose the advantages of its lower carbon intensity with respect to oil. At twice that, you were not even beating coal."[70]

Already, by the late 1990s, about 2.3 percent of the natural gas the industry produced leaked out of valves, old pipes and other porous infrastructure, floating straight into the smothering mesh of greenhouse gases sizzling the planet.[71] By 2010, the International Energy Agency predicted, the amount of methane wafting out of the oil and gas industry's leaky pipelines would be as effective at warming the planet, over a century's time, as the burning of over 3.8 billion barrels of oil.[72]

After the price of oil reached $50 in 2004, American consumers and the press that caters to them renewed their flagging interest in energy efficiency and renewable energy. President Bush's Energy Policy Act of 2005, the first energy legislation to pass in over a decade, handed out tax credits to those who bought more efficient vehicles, appliances, and buildings. When the price of oil spiked after Hurricane Katrina in 2005, the president himself gestured toward energy restraint by ordering the White House staff to nightly turn off their humming copiers and computers.[73] But if the American energy appetite could indeed be suppressed, the Energy Policy Act was no plan to keep it that way for long. The two most sure-fire ways of cutting oil consumption—forcing automakers to increase the average fuel economy of their fleets and taxing gasoline—were conspicuously absent from the table. Indeed, the most far-reaching of the new laws aimed not to restrain consumption but rather to ratchet up the energy supply in the long-term.[74]

Over the coming years, state governments would find their authority to ban L N G plants and offshore drilling weakened. The oil and gas industry would find itself free from various environmental regulations that have hampered its exploration and drilling activities in the United States, and enjoy $1.7 billion in tax breaks plus $1.5 billion in subsidies for ultra-deep drilling. The coal industry would enjoy $3 billion in tax credits and $6 billion in new incentives, plus federal loans for at least 16 new coal-fired power plants. The nuclear industry would enjoy $6 billion in new subsidies.[75]

CONCLUSION

Death Throes

THE END OF oil's story is still being written, but it is clear that the conclusion nears.

Much will depend on how a thousand other stories end. In Montreal in 2005, representatives from one hundred and fifty nations announce they will begin the messy business of negotiating mandatory cuts in their post-2012 carbon emissions. Will the talks finally throttle the tailpipe?[1] Elsewhere, reluctant government regulators brood over the latest scientific findings that around a third of the species in three of the most biologically diverse places in the world may be condemned to climate-change-induced extinction within fifty years.[2] Will these losses be enough to change their minds? In Colombia, some Indian tribes succeed in protecting their lands from industry's oily explorations, but then the state-run oil company plans to continue. Will the tribes' threat of mass suicide deter the drills again?[3]

The signs are ambiguous, to say the least. In 2006, the world's biggest carmaker, General Motors, announces plans to shrink its capacity to build cars and BP's solar division reports its first few years of profit. Meanwhile up north in Canada, officials giddily sign proclamations announcing their intentions to step up tar-sands production.[4] In Beijing, a new law requires that 15 percent of the country's energy be supplied by renewables by 2020,[5] while across India, workers pour tar on 40,000 miles of new highway.[6] In London, people are penalized for driving their cars,[7] while in Beijing and Shanghai, erstwhile bicyclists press up against the sparkling glass of GM and BMW's new showrooms. Will they buy? Will the Chinese leadership allow the hordes of invading automakers in?[8]

Around the world, people resist the petrolife, practicing less consumptive ways of feeding, transporting, and sheltering themselves, the vast majority under the strictures of deprivation, others by choosing new ways and rediscovering old ones. The end of the story of oil will depend on them, too, and how they fare against Big Oil's bulldozer, for there is still time before the ancient liquid vanishes for people to realize, as Kenneth Deffeyes put it, that "crude oil is much too valuable to be burned as a fuel." Perhaps a new era of sporadic supply interruptions and volatile prices coupled with an influx of better technology to harness solar, wind, and other renewable energies will start to slowly persuade people not to opt for oil. Worries about climate change might restrain the quest for new oil and gas, with declining oil production easing the inequities it so frequently triggers. Perhaps there might be enough oil left, in other words, to mine aluminum and silicon for windmills and solar panels before the drills, shovels, and clouds of carbon dioxide render earth uninhabitable.

Whatever happens, when the oil is gone, in one hundred or two hundred years, it will be gone forever. Today's humans won't wait for 100 million years for more crude. But whether society shifts to an energy-constrained way of living, finds some astounding new source of energy, or crashes after baking the planet to an unlivable crisp, one thing is for certain. Underfoot, the powerful black liquid will accumulate again. The shallow seas will rain down their sediments and the shifting plates will trap them in their rocky pores, perhaps more than once before the sun burns out in 7 billion years.

Twisting and turning in its tunnels underground, will it call out, once again, to the imperfect beings traversing the surface, whoever they may be? What will they do? Will they be our descendants? Will they remember?

Where is the World's Oil and How Much is Left?

COUNTRY	REMAINING OIL RESERVES[1] (billions of barrels)	AMOUNT OF OIL DRAINED TO DATE[2] (billions of barrels)	PEAK YEAR OF OIL PRODUCTION[3]
Saudi Arabia	262	97	2008
Iraq	112	28	2017
Abu Dhabi	98	19	2011
Kuwait	96	32	2015
Iran	90	56	1974
Venezuela	78	47	1970
Russia	60	127	1987
United States	30	172	1971
Libya	29	23	1970
Nigeria	24	23	2006
China	18	30	2003
Qatar	15	7	2000
Mexico	13	31	2003
Norway	10	17	2001
Kazakhstan	9	6	2033
Algeria	9	13	1978
Brazil	8	5	1986
Canada	7	19	1973

1 *BP statistical review of world energy 2003.* Does not include shale oil and tar sands.

2 Association for Study of Peak Oil, "World Summary, Regular Oil Production," May 15, 2004. Does not include shale oil, tar sands, oil from polar regions, bitumen, extra-heavy oil, liquids extracted from gasfields, or oil under more than 500 meters of water.

3 Association for Study of Peak Oil, "World Summary, Regular Oil Production," May 15, 2004.

COUNTRY	REMAINING OIL RESERVES[1] (billions of barrels)	AMOUNT OF OIL DRAINED TO DATE[2] (billions of barrels)	PEAK YEAR OF OIL PRODUCTION[3]
Oman	5	7	2001
Angola	5	5	1998
Indonesia	5	20	1977
United Kingdom	5	20	1999
Ecuador	5	3	2004
India	5	6	1997
Yemen	4	2	1999
Egypt	4	9	1995
Australia	3	6	2000
Malaysia	3	6	2003
Argentina	3	9	1998
Syria	2	4	1995
Gabon	2	3	1996
Colombia	2	6	1999
Congo	1	2	2001
Brunei	1	3	1978

TABLE TWO

Who Owns Rights to the World's Oil?

	OIL RESERVES[4] (billions of barrels)
Saudi Arabia	259
Iraq	115
Kuwait	96
Iran	90
Abu Dhabi	87
Venezuela	77
Libya	36
Nigeria	24
Lukoil	19
Mexico	17
Qatar	15
Yukos	14
ExxonMobil	12
China	11
Royal Dutch Shell	10
ChevronTexaco	9
BP	8
TotalFinaElf	7
Malaysia	3

---

4 From Hoover's Company Capsule Database: World Companies, 2004. Royal
Dutch Shell reserves from Hoover's Company Capsule Database: World Companies, 2003. Iraq, Libya, Qatar, and Nigeria reserves from Energy Information
Administration, Country Analysis Briefs. ExxonMobil reserves from Exxon-
Mobil Web site at http://www.exxonmobil.com/corporate/files/corporate/
ARfinancial2003.pdf . ChevronTexaco reserves from ChevronTexaco Web site,
at http://www.chevrontexaco.com/investor/annual/2003/financials/operating.
asp , BP reserves from BP Web site, at http://www.bp.com/investor_centre/
info/intro.asp . TotalFinalElf reserves from Total Web site at http://www.
totalfinaelf.com/ho/en/profile/keyfigur/index.htm .

Who Earns the Most Money from Selling the World's Oil?

	2004 INCOME[5] (billions of dollars)
BP	285
Royal Dutch Shell	265
ExxonMobil	263
Chevron	143
Total	166
Saudi Arabia	116
Venezuela[6]	42
Mexico	70
China	41
Kuwait[7]	28
Malaysia[8]	26
Abu Dhabi[9]	17
Iran[10]	16
Lukoil[11]	34
Yukos[12]	11
Qatar	N/A
Libya	N/A
Nigeria	N/A

5 From Hoover's Company Records In-depth Records, January 3, 2006, unless otherwise noted.

6 Data from 2002.

7 Data from 2001.

8 From 2006 Nelson's Public Company Profiles, Petronas Dagangan Berhad.

9 Data from 2001.

10 Data from 2002.

11 From Lukoil Analyst DataBook, 2005, available at http://www.lukoil.com/materials/doc/DataBook/DBP/LUK_DataBook%202005_E_ConsolAccounts&FinRatios.pdf.

12 Data from 2002.

Who Consumes the World's Oil?

	2004 OIL CONSUMPTION PER CAPITA[13] (gallons/day)		2004 OIL CONSUMPTION PER CAPITA[13] (gallons/day)
Belgium & Luxembourg	3.04	France	1.38
Canada	2.92	Italy	1.37
United States	2.90	Portugal	1.35
Iceland	2.70	Germany	1.34
Netherlands	2.60	United Kingdom	1.24
South Korea	2.00	Iran	0.93
Norway	1.91	Venezuela	0.92
Republic of Ireland	1.90	Malaysia	0.85
Hong Kong SAR China	1.86	Turkmenistan	0.84
Australia	1.81	Czech Republic	0.83
Finland	1.81	Russian Federation	0.76
Japan	1.74	Mexico	0.76
Spain	1.63	Lithuania	0.64
New Zealand	1.62	Belarus	0.64
Taiwan	1.62	Chile	0.61
Greece	1.57	Thailand	0.60
Sweden	1.50	Hungary	0.58
Switzerland	1.50	Slovakia	0.58
Austria	1.47	Bulgaria	0.53
Denmark	1.47	Poland	0.50

13 Calculated from *BP Statistical Review of World Energy 2005* and United Nations Population Fund, *State of World Population 2004*. Population data on Iceland and Taiwan from *CIA World Factbook*. Does not include major exporters.

	2004 OIL CONSUMPTION PER CAPITA[13] (gallons/day)		2004 OIL CONSUMPTION PER CAPITA[13] (gallons/day)
South Africa	0.49	Peru	0.23
Ecuador	0.44	Indonesia	0.22
Brazil	0.43	China	0.21
Argentina	0.42	Colombia	0.21
Romania	0.40	Uzbekistan	0.19
Turkey	0.40	Philippines	0.17
Egypt	0.32	India	0.10
Algeria	0.31	Pakistan	0.08
Ukraine	0.30	Bangladesh	0.02

Top Oil Consumers, 2004

	TOP OIL CONSUMERS, 2004[14] (thousands of barrels/day)
United States	20,517
China	6,684
Japan	5,288
Germany	2,625
India	2,555
South Korea	2,280
Canada	2,206
France	1,975
Mexico	1,896
Italy	1,871
Brazil	1,830
United Kingdom	1,756
Spain	1,593
Netherlands	1,003
Thailand	909
Taiwan	877
Australia	858
Belgium & Luxembourg	779
Singapore	748
Turkey	688

14 *BP Statistical Review of World Energy 2004*. Excludes major exporters.

Top Oil Consumers, 2025 projected

	TOP OIL CONSUMERS, 2025 PROJECTED[8] (thousands of barrels/day)
United States	28,300
China	12,800
former Soviet Union	6,400
Japan	5,800
India	5,300
Brazil	3,800
Mexico	3,500
Germany	3,300
South Korea	2,900
Canada	2,800
France	2,200
Italy	2,200
United Kingdom	2,200
Eastern Europe	2,100
Australia/New Zealand	1,700
Turkey	1,100
Netherlands	1,000

---

8 Energy Information Administration, *International Energy Outlook 2004,* Table A4: World oil consumption by region, reference case, 1990–2025.

Notes

Preface

1 Ryszard Kapuscinski, *Shah of Shahs* (New York: Harcourt, 1983), pp. 34–35.

Introduction

1 Jon P. Davidson et al., *Exploring Earth: An Introduction to Physical Geology*, 2nd ed. (Upper Saddle River, NJ: Prentice-Hall, 2002), pp. 4–5.

2 Ibid., pp. 190–191.

3 Ibid., p. 9.

4 Charles F. Conaway, *The Petroleum Industry: A Nontechnical Guide* (Tulsa, OK: PennWell, 1999), p. 7.

5 M. Grant Gross, *Oceanography: A View of Earth*, 6th ed. (Englewood Cliffs, NJ: Prentice-Hall, 1993), p. 329.

6 Ibid., pp. 310–311, 325.

7 Ibid., pp. 314–315.

8 Davidson et al., *Exploring Earth*, p. 389.

9 Gross, *Oceanography*, p. 314.

10 Davidson et al., *Exploring Earth*, p. 389.

11 NASA Earth Observatory, "The Carbon Cycle," http://earthobservatory.nasa.gov/Library/CarbonCycle/.

12 A gigaton equals 1 billion tons.

13 *Microsoft Encarta Encyclopedia 2002*, s.v. "Carbon Cycle (ecology)."

14 NASA Earth Observatory, "The Carbon Cycle."

15 Ibid.

16 Jeremy Leggett, *The Carbon War: Global Warming and the End of the Oil Era* (New York: Routledge, 2001), pp. 45–46.

17 *Microsoft Encarta Encyclopedia 2002*, s.v. "Carbon Cycle (ecology)."

18 NASA Earth Observatory, "The Carbon Cycle."

19 Kenneth S. Deffeyes, *Hubbert's Peak: The Impending World Oil Shortage* (Princeton, NJ: Princeton University Press, 2001), p. 18.

20 Ibid., p. 36.

21 Ibid., p. 16.

22 Robert Stoneley, *An Introduction to Petroleum Exploration for Non-Geologists* (Oxford, UK: Oxford University Press, 1995), p. 31.

23 Deffeyes, *Hubbert's Peak*, pp. 17–21.

24 Conaway, *The Petroleum Industry*, pp. 24–25.

25 *Microsoft Encarta Encyclopedia 2002*, s.v. "Carbon Cycle (ecology)."

26 A barrel of oil contains forty-two gallons.

27 NASA Earth Observatory, "The Carbon Cycle."

28 Deffeyes, *Hubbert's Peak*, p. 169.

29 Daniel Yergin, *The Prize: The Epic Quest for Oil, Money, and Power* (New York: Simon & Schuster, 1991), p. 716.

30 Deffeyes, *Hubbert's Peak*, pp. 169–170. Also, Kenneth S. Deffeyes, interview by the author, December 28, 2002.

31 Greenpeace Australia Pacific, "Shale Oil: A Risky Business," http://www.greenpeace.org.au/climate/shale_oil/risky.html.

32 Stoneley, *An Introduction to Petroleum Exploration for Non-Geologists*, p. 37.

33 Conaway, *The Petroleum Industry*, pp. 31, 33.

34 Ibid., pp. 26–27.

35 Stoneley, *An Introduction to Petroleum Exploration for Non-Geologists*, pp. 37–43.

36 Conaway, *The Petroleum Industry*, p. 33.

37 Davidson et al., *Exploring Earth*, pp. 496–497.

38 Deffeyes, *Hubbert's Peak*, p. 167.

39 Kenneth S. Deffeyes, interview by the author, December 28, 2002.

40 *Microsoft Encarta Encyclopedia 2002*, s.v. "Tethys (mythology)."

41 Gross, *Oceanography*, p. 179.

42 Michael Benton, "Dinosaur Summer," in Stephen Jay Gould, ed., *The Book of Life* (London: Ebury Hutchinson, 1993), pp. 127–128, 140–141.

43 Davidson et al., *Exploring Earth*, p. 494.

44 Gross, *Oceanography*, pp. 64–65.

45 Davidson et al., *Exploring Earth*, p. 494.

46 Stoneley, *An Introduction to Petroleum Exploration for Non-Geologists*, pp. 29–30.

47 G. W. O'Brien, "Influence of Hydrocarbon Migration and Seepage on Benthic Communities in the Timor Sea, Australia," *APPEA Journal* 42 (2002), pp. 1–12.

48 Peter Andrews and Christopher Singer, "The Primates' Progress," in *The Book of Life* (see note 42), p. 232.

49 R. J. Forbes, "Chemical, Culinary, and Cosmetic Arts," in C. Singer et al., eds., *A History of Technology, Volume I: From Early Times to the Fall of Ancient Empires* (London: Oxford University Press, 1954), pp. 250–253.

50 "No precise recipe for making it exists, but the main ingredients were sulphur, pich, nitre, and petroleum, which were boiled together." C. Messenger, "Weapons and Armour," in I. McNeil, ed., *An Encyclopaedia of the History of Technology* (London: Routledge, 1990), p. 971.

51 A. R. Hall, "A Note on Military Pyrotechnics," in C. Singer et al., eds., *A History of Technology Volume II: The Mediterranean Civilizations and the Middle Ages c 700 BC to c AD 1500* (London: Oxford University Press, 1956), pp. 374–377.

52 *Microsoft Encarta Encyclopedia 2002*, s.v. "Zoroastrianism."

53 David Price, "Energy and Human Evolution," *Population and Environment*, March 1995, pp. 301–319.

Chapter One

1 Barbara Freese, *Coal: A Human History* (Cambridge, MA: Perseus Publishing, 2003), pp. 27–57.

2 Charles A. S. Hall, Cutler J. Cleveland, and Robert Kaufmann, *Energy and Resource Quality: The Ecology of the Economic Process* (New York: Wiley, 1986).

3 Freese, *Coal*, p. 60, citing Robert Galloway, *Annals of Coal Mining and the Coal Trade* (Devon, UK: David and Charles, 1971), p. 80.

4 Frederick Engels, *Conditions of the Working Class in England* (London: Panther, 1969).

5 Freese, *Coal*, pp. 51–67, 78, 82, 98, 233–234.

6 Lilian Pizzichini, "The Big Smoke: London's Killer Fogs Inspired Artists and Provided Novelists with the Perfect Emblem of a Sinful City," *New Statesman*, December 9, 2002, p. 36.

7 Marshall Brain, "How Gasoline Works," HowStuffWorks, http://science. howstuffworks.com/gasoline.htm.

8 Anthracite coal releases 7,200–8,300 kilocalories/kilogram. Humans are 20 percent efficient at turning food energy into work energy; an average diet would be 3,000 kilocalories, rendering 600 kilocalories of work energy per human per day. Hall et al., *Energy and Resource Quality*, pp. 106, 229.

9 Daniel Yergin, *The Prize: The Epic Quest for Oil, Money, and Power* (New York: Simon & Schuster, 1991), pp. 20, 27, 30–33, 42, 52, 55, 58–59, 72–73, 84–85, 135–140.

10 Craig C. Freudenrich, "How Oil Refining Works," HowStuffWorks, http://science.howstuffworks.com/oil-refining.htm.

11 Yergin, *The Prize*, pp. 22–23.

12 R. J. Forbes, "Petroleum," in C. Singer et al., eds., *A History of Technology Volume III: The Late Nineteenth Century c1850 to c1900* (London: Oxford University Press, 1958), p. 113.

13 Yergin, *The Prize*, p. 55.

14 Ibid., p. 97.

15 Robert Silverberg, *Light for the World: Edison and the Power Industry* (Princeton, NJ: Van Nostrand, 1967), pp. 1–6.

16 Yergin, *The Prize*, pp. 39, 79.

17 Hall et al., *Energy and Resource Quality*, p. 23.

18 Jean-Pierre Bardou, Jean-Jacques Chanaron, Patrick Fridenson, and James M. Laux, *The Automobile Revolution: The Impact of an Industry*, trans. James M. Laux (Chapel Hill, NC: University of North Carolina Press, 1982), pp. 5–6.

19 Ibid.

20 Kenneth T. Jackson, *Crabgrass Frontier: The Suburbanization of the United States* (New York: Oxford University Press, 1985), p. 158.

21 Hall et al., *Energy and Resource Quality*, pp. 23, 103.

22 Bardou et al., *The Automobile Revolution*, p. 13.

23 Yergin, *The Prize*, pp. 84–85.

24 Bardou et al., *The Automobile Revolution*, p. 13.

25 Jackson, *Crabgrass Frontier*, p. 160.

26 Gale E. Christianson, *Greenhouse: The Two-Hundred-Year Story of Global Warming* (New York: Penguin, 1999), p. 135.

27 Yergin, *The Prize*, p. 110.

28 Ibid., pp. 155–156.

29 Michael Klare, *Resource Wars: The New Landscape of Global Conflict* (New York: Henry Holt, 2001), pp. 30–31.

30 Lee Mertz, "Origins of the Interstate," Department of Transportation, Federal Highway Administration, http://www.fhwa.dot.gov/infrastructure/origin.htm.

31 *Microsoft Encarta Encyclopedia 2002*; Stephen B. Goddard, *Getting There: The Epic Struggle Between Road and Rail in the American Century* (New York: Basic Books, 1994), excerpted at http://stephongoddard.com/.

32 Yergin, *The Prize*, p. 183.

33 Jim Klein and Martha Olson, "Taken for a Ride," PBS documentary transcript, August 1996.

34 David James St. Clair, *The Motorization of American Cities* (New York: Praeger, 1986), p. 16.

35 Peter H. Spitz, *Petrochemicals: The Rise of an Industry* (New York: Wiley, 1988), p. 235.

36 Penny Sparke, ed., *The Plastics Age: From Modernity to Post-Modernity* (London: Victoria & Albert Museum, 1990), pp. 17–21.

37 Spitz, *Petrochemicals*, pp. 246–247.

38 Ibid., p. xiii.

39 Sparke, ed., *The Plastics Age*, p. 50.

40 Spitz, *Petrochemicals*, p. 153.

41 "WWII Wrecks Haunt Pacific Atolls with Toxic Cargoes," PR Newswire, November 1, 2002.

42 Yergin, *The Prize*, pp. 358–361.

43 Spitz, *Petrochemicals*, pp. 153–154.

44 Yergin, *The Prize*, pp. 395, 400–401.

45 Klein and Olson, "Taken for a Ride"; Cecilia Rasmussen, "Did Auto, Oil Conspiracy Put the Brakes on Trolleys?" *Los Angeles Times*, March 23, 2003, p. 4.

46 Hall et al., *Energy and Resource Quality*, p. 255.

47 Paul Raeburn, "The Moth That Failed," *New York Times*, August 25, 2002, p. 12.

48 Pizzichini, "The Big Smoke"; John E. Thornes and Gemma Metherell, "The Big Smoke: One Hundred Years Ago, Thick Smogs Regularly Brought London to a Standstill," *Geographical* (September 2002), p. 20.

49 Freese, *Coal*, pp. 160–168.

50 Ibid., p. 144.

Chapter Two

1 Molly O'Meara Sheehan, "City Limits: Putting the Brakes on Sprawl," Worldwatch paper 156, June 2001, p. 13.

2   Kenneth T. Jackson, *Crabgrass Frontier: The Suburbanization of the United States* (New York: Oxford University Press, 1985), p. 162.

3   The Nobel committee commemorated Haber's achievement despite his disturbing wartime activities. Haber committed himself to the German war effort in 1914. Under his direction, on April 22, 1915, the Germans released 168 tons of chlorine gas on French troops. The greenish-yellow mist smothered ten thousand within ten minutes, and a week later Haber was on his way to the Eastern Front to launch gas attacks there. Just days later, his devastated wife committed suicide. But Haber was unapologetic. To his way of thinking, chemical weapons were no crueler than steel missiles.

4   Vaclav Smil, *Enriching the Earth: Fritz Haber, Carl Bosch, and the Transformation of World Food Production* (Cambridge, MA: MIT Press, 2001), pp. xiii–xvii, 113; Reginald H. Garrett and Charles M. Grisham, *Biochemistry*, 2nd ed. (New York: Harcourt Brace College, 1999), p. 853.

5   American Plastics Council, "History of Plastics," http://www.americanplasticscouncil.org/benefits/about_plastics/history.html.

6   Penny Sparke, ed., *The Plastics Age: From Modernity to Post-Modernity* (London: Victoria & Albert Museum, 1990), p. 31.

7   Kenneth S. Deffeyes, *Hubbert's Peak: The Impending World Oil Shortage* (Princeton, NJ: Princeton University Press, 2001) pp. 2–3; Kenneth S. Deffeyes, interview by the author, December 28, 2002.

8   Dilip Hiro, *The Middle East* (Englewood Cliffs, NJ: Prentice-Hall, 1996), p. 16.

9   Daniel Yergin, *The Prize: The Epic Quest for Oil, Money, and Power* (New York: Simon & Schuster, 1991), p. 451.

10 Peter Mansfield, *Nasser's Egypt* (Baltimore: Penguin, 1965), pp. 130–131.

11 Yergin, *The Prize*, pp. 479–481.

12 P. J. Vatikiotis, *Nasser and His Generation* (London: Croom Helm, 1978), p. 235.

13 Yergin, *The Prize*, pp. 479–480, 497.

14 Ibid., pp. 521–523.

15 Energy Information Administration, "Non-OPEC Fact Sheet," June 2002, http://www.eia.doe.gov/cabs/nonopec.html.

16 Yergin, *The Prize*, p. 433.

17 Energy Information Administration, Table 11.10, "World Petroleum Consumption, 1960–2001 (Million Barrels per Day)," http://www.eia.doe.gov/aer/txt/ptb1110.html.

18 Deffeyes, *Hubbert's Peak*, p. 41.

19 Matthew R. Simmons, "The World's Giant Oilfields: How Many Exist? How Much Do They Produce? How Fast Are They Declining?" (Simmons & Company International, December 18, 2001), p. 19.

20 Deffeyes, *Hubbert's Peak*, p. 16.

21 Charles F. Conaway, *The Petroleum Industry: A Nontechnical Guide* (Tulsa, OK: PennWell, 1999), p. 41.

22 Mark Chapin et al., "Integrated Seismic and Subsurface Characterization of Bonga Field, Offshore Nigeria," *Leading Edge*, November 2002, p. 1125.

23 Deffeyes, *Hubbert's Peak*, p. 7.

24 H. W. Menard and George Sharman, "Scientific Uses of Random Drilling Models," *Science* (October 24, 1975), pp. 337–343.

25 Yergin, *The Prize*, p. 219.

26 Robert Stoneley, *An Introduction to Petroleum Exploration for Non-Geologists* (Oxford, UK: Oxford University Press, 1995), pp. 73–74.

27 Deffeyes, *Hubbert's Peak*, p. 81.

28 Yergin, *The Prize*, p. 576.

29 National Research Council, *Cumulative Environmental Effects of Oil and Gas Activities on Alaska's North Slope* (Washington, DC: National Academies Press, 2003), pp. 3–4.

30 Yergin, *The Prize*, pp. 571–573.

31 William J. Pike, "Reflections on Rough Seas," *Ocean Industry* 26, no. 1 (February 1991), p. 15.

32 Stoneley, *An Introduction to Petroleum Exploration for Non-Geologists*, p. 103.

33 Kenneth S. Deffeyes, letter to the author, March 12, 2003.

34 Proven oil reserves as of January 1, 2003. Energy Information Administration, "Country Analysis Briefs: North Sea," http://www.eia.doe.gov/emeu/cabs/northsea.html.

35 Deffeyes, *Hubbert's Peak*, p. 4.

36 Kenneth S. Deffeyes, interview by the author, December 28, 2002.

37 Ibid.

Chapter Three

1 Energy Information Administration, *Annual Energy Review 2001* (Washington, DC: U.S. Department of Energy, November 2002), Table 11.5, p. 287.

2 *Microsoft Encarta Encyclopedia 2002*.

3 Bob Vavra, "1973: The Arab Oil Embargo Transforms the World," *National Petroleum News* (November 2000), p. 18.

4 David Hackett Fischer, *The Great Wave: Price Revolutions and the Rhythm of History* (New York: Oxford University Press, 1996), pp. 203–208.

5 David Brian Robertson, ed., *Loss of Confidence: Politics and Policy in the 1970s* (University Park, PA: Pennsylvania State University Press, 1998), pp. 1–10.

6 Fischer, *The Great Wave*, pp. 203–208; Lizette Alvarez, "Britain Says U.S. Planned to Seize Oil in '73 Crisis," *New York Times*, January 2, 2004, p. 4.

7 Alan S. Miller, "Energy Policy from Nixon to Clinton: From Grant Provider to Market Facilitator," *Environmental Law* 25, no. 3 (1995), pp. 715–731.

8 Michael Klare, *Resource Wars: The New Landscape of Global Conflict* (New York: Henry Holt, 2002), p. 59.

9 Miller, "Energy Policy from Nixon to Clinton."

10 Fischer, *The Great Wave*, pp. 203–208.

11 Department of Energy, "D O E History," http://www.oakridge.doe.gov/pmab/
    restore/History/DOEHistory.htm.

12 Brian Trumbore, "The Arab Oil Embargo of 1973–1974," http://Stocksand-
    Newscom/.

13 Robertson, ed., *Loss of Confidence*, pp. 1–10.

14 Klare, *Resource Wars*, p. 33.

15 See, for example, Vandana Shiva, *Stolen Harvest: The Hijacking of the Global Food
    Supply* (Boston, MA: South End, 1999), and http://www.oxfam.org/.

16 Jeremy Rifkin, *The Hydrogen Economy: The Creation of the World-Wide Energy Web
    and the Redistribution of Power on Earth* (New York: Tarcher, 2002), pp. 7–8.

17 Seamus O'Cleireacain, *Third World Debt and International Public Policy* (New York:
    Praeger, 1990), p. 3.

18 Trumbore, "The Arab Oil Embargo of 1973–1974."

19 Michael Economides and Ronald Oligney, *The Color of Oil: The History, the Money,
    and the Politics of the World's Biggest Business* (Katy, TX: Round Oak, 2000), p. 3.

20 National Research Council, *Cumulative Environmental Effects of Oil and Gas Activities
    on Alaska's North Slope* (Washington, DC: National Academies Press, 2003), pp.
    27–29, 66, 151.

21 Will Harvie, "On Guard: Ice Patrol Out to Make Sure the Oil Platform Is No
    Second Titanic," *Oilweek* (December 1, 1997), pp. 20–22.

22 *Microsoft Encarta Encyclopedia* 2002.

23 Douglas Martin, "Oil Drillers off Canada Battle Nature and Politics," *New York
    Times,* March 15, 1981, p. 1.

24 Economides and Oligney, *The Color of Oil*, p. 29.

25 Rhonda Duey, "Stuck at the Starting Gate?" *Hart's E&P*, December 2001.

26 Economides and Oligney, *The Color of Oil*, p. 31; Kenneth S. Deffeyes, *Hubbert's
    Peak: The Impending World Oil Shortage* (Princeton, NJ: Princeton University
    Press, 2001), pp. 73–75.

27 Dan Mueller, quoted in Rick von Flatern and Marshall DeLuca, "Advisory Notes,"
    Offshore Engineer (April 2003), p. 19.

28 Martin, "Oil Drillers off Canada Battle Nature and Politics," p. 1.

29 Christian Williams, "Drilling Farther, Deeper; Offshore Oil Rigs Breed New
    Hazards," *Washington Post*, October 28, 1994, p. A1.

30 Christian Williams, "Command Splintered on Sea Rigs," *Washington Post*, October
    29, 1984, p. A1.

31 Williams, "Drilling Farther, Deeper," p. A1.

32 Don Sutton, "Widow of Oil Rig Victim Tries to Cope with Her Loss," *Toronto
    Star*, September 22, 1994, p. 6.

33 A. Kevan Parry, "Reflecting on End of Ocean Ranger," *Ottawa Citizen*, August
    24, 1993, p. A8.

34 Daniel Yergin, *The Prize: The Epic Quest for Oil, Money, and Power* (New York:
    Simon & Schuster, 1991), p. 733.

35 Matthew R. Simmons, "The World's Giant Oilfields: How Many Exist? How

Much Do They Produce? How Fast Are They Declining?" (Simmons & Company International, December 18, 2001), p. 1.

36 Walter Youngquist, *GeoDestinies: The Inevitable Control of Earth Resources over Nations and Individuals* (Portland, OR: National, 1997), p. 183.

37 Simmons, "The World's Giant Oilfields," p. 9.

38 Vavra, "1973."

Chapter Four

 1 Energy Information Administration, *Annual Energy Review 2001* (Washington, DC: U.S. Department of Energy, November 2002), Table 5.4, p. 133.

 2 Richard Heinberg, *The Party's Over: Oil, War, and the Fate of Industrial Societies* (Gabriola Island, British Columbia: New Society, 2003), p. 75.

 3 Alan S. Miller, "Energy Policy from Nixon to Clinton: From Grant Provider to Market Facilitator," *Environmental Law* 25, no. 3 (1995).

 4 Ibid.

 5 Michael Klare, *Resource Wars: The New Landscape of Global Conflict* (New York: Henry Holt, 2002), pp. 64–65.

 6 ExxonMobil, "ExxonMobil Today," http://www.exxonmobil.com/Corporate/About/History/Corp_A_H_XOMToday.asp; Chevron, "A long affiliation," http://www.chevron.com/learning_center/history/time/1980-now/pg5.asp.

 7 Matthew R. Simmons, "The World's Giant Oilfields: How Many Exist? How Much Do They Produce? How Fast Are They Declining?" (Simmons & Company International, December 18, 2001), p. 12.

 8 Michael Economides and Ronald Oligney, *The Color of Oil: The History, the Money, and the Politics of the World's Biggest Business* (Katy, TX: Round Oak, 2000), p. 100. Total world GDP = US $31,283,839 million. From World Bank, "Total GDP 2001," http://www.worldbank.org/data/databytopic/GDP.pdf.

 9 ExxonMobil 2001 Summary Annual Report, "Letter to Shareholders," and "Long-Term Returns," http://www.exxonmobil.com/.

10 See Table 4.

11 U.S. Department of Transportation Bureau of Transportation Statistics, *National Transportation Statistics 2004* (Washington, DC: U.S. Government Printing Office, February 2005), Tables 4-11 and 4-14, 336, 340.

12 Patricia S. Hu et al., "Summary of Travel Trends: 1995 Nationwide Personal Transportation Survey," U.S. Department of Transportation and Federal Highway Administration; INFORM, "The need for sustainable transportation," fact sheet, http://www.informinc.org/fact_needsus.php ; U.S. Census Bureau, "U.S. POPClock Projection," http://www.census.gov/cgi-bin/popclock/.

13 Average time Americans spend with children is 1.3 hours/day. See Table 9, "Average hours per day spent by persons 18 years and over caring for household children under 18 years, by sex of respondent and age of youngest household child, 2004 annual averages," from Bureau of Labor Statistics 2004 American

Time Use Survey Summary. Also Douglas E. Morris, "Transit missteps leave us trapped," *Baltimore Sun*, September 29, 2005, 17A.

14 Idling in traffic burned 506 million gallons in 2000, on average. National Transportation Statistics 2002, Table 4-27.

15 Molly O'Meara Sheehan, "City Limits: Putting the Brakes on Sprawl," Worldwatch paper 156, June 2001, pp. 18, 22, 24; Patricia S. Hu, "Americans and Their Vehicles," Center for Transportation Analysis, Oak Ridge National Laboratory, Department of Energy, May 1, 2003.

16 Thirty thousand Americans die annually from respiratory illnesses directly attributed to toxic emissions from vehicles. See INFORM, "The need for sustainable transportation"; 40,000 Americans die in car crashes. See Partnership for Safe Driving, http://www.crashprevention.org/. More than 5,000 die in truck-related crashes. Ron Bradley et al., "Technology Roadmap for the Twenty-first-Century Truck Program," p. xv.

17 Keith Bradsher, *High and Mighty: SUVs—The World's Most Dangerous Vehicles and How They Got That Way* (New York: PublicAffairs, 2002), pp. 20–27, 267.

18 Hu, "Americans and Their Vehicles"; Jack Doyle, "The Autocrats: Detroit and the Politics of Pollution," *Earth Island Journal* (autumn 2000), p. 36; Energy Information Administration, *Annual Energy Review 2001* (Washington, DC: U.S. Department of Energy, November 2002), Table 2.9, p. 61; Environmental Protection Agency, "Light-Duty Automotive Technology and Fuel Economy Trends: 1975 Through 2003," http://www.epa.gov/otaq/fetrends.htm.

19 Micheline Maynard, "S.U.V.'s stumbled and sedans gained as 2005 focused on fuel," *New York Times*, January 5, 2006.

20 Kozo Mayumi, Mario Giampietro, and John M. Gowdy, "Georgescu-Roegen/Daly versus Solow/Stiglitz revisited," *Ecological Economics* (November 1998); Lee Schipper, "On the Rebound: The Interaction of Energy Efficiency, Energy Use, and Economic Activity," *Energy Policy* (June 2000), pp. 351–353.

21 Annabelle Garay et al., "Phoenix Gasoline Problems Persist As Pipeline Remains Shut Down," Associated Press, August 18, 2003.

22 Nick Madigan, "Gasoline Crisis Changes Car Culture of Phoenix," *New York Times*, August 24, 2003, p. 16.

23 International Fertilizer Industry Association, "Nitrogen fertilizer nutrient consumption - Million tonnes N," October 2004, available at http://www.fertilizer.org/ifa/statistics/indicators/tablen.asp. A single ton of nitrogen fertilizer requires six barrels of oil equivalent. Charles A. S. Hall, Cutler J. Cleveland, and Robert Kaufmann, *Energy and Resource Quality: The Ecology of the Economic Process* (New York: Wiley, 1986), p. 125.

24 V. Smil, p. 226.

25 Brian Halweil, "Home Grown: The Case for Local Food in a Global Market," Worldwatch paper 163, November 2002, pp. 6, 9.

26 Total land area: 9,158,960 sq km. Arable land: 19.32 percent, or 1,769,511 sq. km. 1,769,511 square kilometers = 437,255,691 acres. *CIA World Factbook* 2002,

http://www.cia.gov/cia/publications/factbook/geos/us.html#Geo; Michael Pollan, "When a Crop Becomes King," *New York Times,* July 19, 2002, p. 17.

27   Pollan, "When a Crop Becomes King," p. 17.

28   Emily Matthews et al., *The Weight of Nations: Material Outflows from Industrial Economies* (Washington, DC: World Resources Institute, 2000), pp. 22–23.

29   Total petroleum consumption for the industrial sector, 2001 = 4,667,000 barrels/day or 1.7 billion barrels/year out of total consumption of 6.5 billion barrels. Energy Information Administration, *Annual Energy Review 2001* (Washington, DC: U.S. Department of Energy, November 2002), Table 5.12b, p. 151; Energy Information Administration, "Manufacturing Consumption of Energy 1994," p. 6.

30   The following is from an interview of Frank Hewetson by the author, February 2003.

31   Hall et al., *Energy and Resource Quality,* pp. 51–53. By 1989, the relation between GNP growth and energy consumption weakened. See Energy Information Administration, *Annual Energy Review 1989* (Washington, DC: U.S. Department of Energy).

32   INFORM, "The need for sustainable transportation," fact sheet, http://www.informinc.org/fact_needsus.php; Hall et al., *Energy and Resource Quality,* p. 49.

33   Rex Tillerson, "Current Sources—A Global View" (London: Institute of Petroleum, February 17, 2003).

34   Daphne Wysham, "Sustainable Development South and North: Climate Change Policy Coherence in Global Trade and Financial Flows," Institute for Policy Studies, March 25, 2003; "Project Underground, Drilling to the Ends of the Earth," http://www.moles.org/ProjectUnderground/motherlode/drilling/frontier.html.

35   "Striking a better balance: The World Bank Group and extractive industries," Final Report of the Extractive Industries Review, Volume 1, October 2003, p. xiii.

36   Energy Information Administration, *International Energy Outlook 2003* (Washington, DC: Department of Energy, May 2003), p. 30.

37   Sheehan, "City Limits," pp. 16, 61.

38   BP Annual Report 2002, p. 9.

39   Sheehan, "City Limits," p. 17.

40   Charles W. Petit, "A Smoky Shroud over Asia Blocks Both Sun and Rain," *U.S. News & World Report,* March 17, 2003, p. 46.

41   "EIA Sees Developing Nations As Key to Energy Demand Jump," *Oil & Gas Journal,* April 15, 2002, p. 26.

42   John H. Wood et al., "World Conventional Oil Supply Expected to Peak in Twenty-first Century," *Offshore* (April 2003).

Chapter Five

1   David Knott, "Britain's Approach to Petroleum Taxes," *Oil & Gas Journal,* January 15, 1996, p. 31.

2   Energy Information Administration, "Country Analysis Briefs: United Kingdom," February 2003, http://www.eia.doe.gov/emeu/cabs/uk.html.

3 Deborah Hargreaves, "Sweep of a Dustbin and Brush—North Sea Oil Prospects," *Financial Times*, December 18, 1991, p. 28.

4 "Apache, TotalFinaElf Expand into Uncommon Areas," *Oil & Gas Journal*, January 20, 2003, p. 32.

5 Bill Mongelluzzo, "Alaskan Boom Cools; Tankers Redeployed," *Journal of Commerce*, July 12, 1990, p. 1A; Matthew R. Simmons, "The World's Giant Oilfields: How Many Exist? How Much Do They Produce? How Fast Are They Declining?" (Simmons & Company International, December 18, 2001), p. 25.

6 Mohammad Al-Gailani, "Iraq's Significant Hydrocarbon Potential Remains Relatively Undeveloped," *Oil & Gas Journal*, July 29, 1996, p. 108.

7 Rules about foreign investment are being relaxed in many countries, often against public opinion. See, for example, Energy Information Administration, "Country Analysis Briefs."

8 "PIW Ranks the World's Top Oil Companies," *PIW-Special Supplement Issue*, December 23, 2002, p. 1.

9 "The 112 Billion Barrel Question," *International Petroleum Finance* (April 2003), p. 1.

10 Ian Vann, "New Oil Provinces—The Opportunities and Constraints," (Speech given at the Institute of Petroleum in London, February 17, 2003).

11 "Global E&P outlays to rise 'materially' in '06," *Oil & Gas Journal*, December 19, 2005, 5; "Global Exploration and Development Spending Expected to increase," *Alexander's Gas & Oil Connections*, February 6, 2003; International Bank for Reconstruction and Development, "World Development Indicators," 2001, p. 14.

12 Andrew McBarnet, "Customers Shun Shiny New Toys: Just When 3D Data Acquisition Seemed Commercially Viable, the Bottom Fell Out of the Market," *Financial Times,* June 10, 1999, p. 2.

13 Ibid.

14 Vann, "New Oil Provinces."

15 Kathy Shirley, "Forecast: Fair to Partly Cloudy? Future Exploration Investing Uncertain," *AAPG Explorer*, April 2004.

16 IHS Energy, interview by the author, March 3, 2003.

17 Lee C. Lawyer, letter to the author, 2003.

18 Lee C. Lawyer and Kenneth S. Deffeyes, letters to the author, 2003.

19 David Kaplan, "BP project Now Thunder Horse; Capitulation on Name Eases Lakota Objection," *Houston Chronicle,* February 21, 2002, p. 1.

20 Kathy Shirley, "GOM Deep Water + Subsalt Plays: The Promise of the Best of Both Worlds," *Explorer* (October 2000).

21 Lee C. Lawyer, letter to the author, 2003.

22 Linda R. Sternbach, "West Africa—A Special Issue on an Emerging World Petroleum Province," *Leading Edge* (November 2002), pp. 1101–1102.

23 "West Africa: Potential for Oil Brings New Problems to São Tomé," *Offshore* (February 2003), p. 38.

24 Jon Lee Anderson, "Our New Best Friend: Who Needs Saudi Arabia When You've Got São Tomé?" *New Yorker*, October 7, 2002, p. 74.

25 Martin Quinlan, "West African Discoveries Edging Towards Development," *Petroleum Economist* (June 1997), p. 44.

26 Interstate Oil and Gas Compact Commission, "Who Will Fund America's Energy Future? Petroleum Research and Development in the Twenty-first Century" (summer 2002), Table 2, p. 12.

27 Kenneth S. Deffeyes, interview by the author, December 28, 2002.

28 Alain Delaytermoz, "Ultra-Deepwater E&P Challenges Ahead," *Offshore* (December 2001), p. 32.

29 *U.S. News & World Report*, "America's Best Graduate Schools 2004," http://www.usnews.com/usnews/edu/grad/rankings/eng/brief/engsp12_brief.php#year.

30 Kenneth S. Deffeyes, *Hubbert's Peak: The Impending World Oil Shortage* (Princeton, NJ: Princeton University Press, 2001), pp. 161, 202.

31 Offshore Technology Research Center, "Mission Statement," http://otrc.tamu.edu/Pages/mission.htm.

32 "TU, ChevronTexaco to Start Model Partnership," press release, University of Tulsa, July 26, 2002.

33 Malcolm Brown, "London Links," *Frontiers* (December 2002), p. 11.

34 Corporate Watch et al., "Degrees of Capture: Universities, the Oil Industry, and Climate Change," 2003, pp. 2, 5.

35 Michelle Markley, interview by the author, December 2002.

36 Albert Bally, letter to the author, March 14, 2003.

37 American Petroleum Institute, "Focus on Innovation," http://www.classroom-energy.org/students/technology/index.html.

38 U.S. Department of Energy, Office of Fossil Energy, "Environmental Benefits of Advanced Oil and Gas Technology," March 5, 1999.

39 Rick Donoghue, "4-D: Back to the Future," *Hart's E&P Net* (March 2003).

40 John R. Fanchi, "State of the Art 4D Seismic Monitoring: The Technique, the Record, and the Future," *Oil & Gas Journal*, May 31, 1999, p. 38.

41 Will Harvie, "On Guard: Ice Patrol Out to Make Sure the Oil Platform Is No Second Titanic," *Oilweek*, December 1, 1997, p. 20.

42 Alan Boras, "Hibernia: The Question Asked: 'Does It Make Economic Sense, Here and Now, Today and For the Future?'" *Calgary Herald*, January 10, 1993, p. A9.

43 Douglas Martin, "Oil Drillers off Canada Battle Nature and Politics," *New York Times*, March 15, 1981.

44 Brian Bergman, "One of a Kind: The Hibernia Rig Is an Engineering Wonder," *Maclean's*, March 3, 1997, p. 30.

45 George Peer, "Engineering Marvel," *Oilweek*, December 1, 1997, p. 26.

46 Bergman, "One of a Kind," p. 30.

47 Harvie, "On Guard," p. 20.

48 Lawrence Lack, "Hibernia Oil Project Started at Last," *Christian Science Monitor*, December 12, 1990, p. 7.

49 Hibernia, "The Hibernia Reservoir," http://www.hibernia.ca/html/about_ hibernia/reservoir.html.

50 "Analysis: Angola: Deeply Ambitious," *Petroleum Economist,* March 31, 2002, p. 12.

51 Jeremy Beckman, "TotalFinaElf Prepares to Launch Two Further Developments in Angola Block 17," *Offshore* (February 2003), p. 26.

52 See, for example, SPG Media Limited, "Industry Projects: Abana, Gulf of Guinea, Nigeria," Offshore Technology, http://www.offshore-technology. com/projects/abana/index.html.

53 Robert E. Snyder, "FPSO Allows Fast-Track Development," *World Oil* (July 1996), p. 33.

54 "TotalFinaElf's Girassol Project and Geologist Bally Selected to Receive 2003 OTC Distinguished Achievement Awards," press release, Offshore Technology Conference.

55 "Deep-Water Technology; Gulf of Guinea: New Ideas," *Petroleum Economist,* October 17, 2002, p. 28.

56 American Petroleum Institute, "Focus on Innovation," http://www.classroom- energy.org/students/technology/index.html; Joe W. Key, "FPSO Market Projected at $8.5 Billion for 1990s," *Ocean Industry* (June 1991), p. 56.

Chapter Six

1 National Research Council, *Cumulative Environmental Effects of Oil and Gas Activities on Alaska's North Slope* (Washington, DC: National Academies Press, 2003), p. 152.

    Some innovations meant to soften the industry's environmental footprint in Alaska had actually created new, potentially more troubling problems. The oil industry injected wastes into holes in the ground—"disposal wells"—rather than shoving it into ugly open pits, but this could end up contaminating the groundwater. They built roads out of ice rather than the more intrusive gravel, but this required siphoning billions of gallons of water from lakes. The depleted lakes have been left so shallow they are liable to freeze solid. Fish can't live in them anymore. National Research Council, *Cumulative Environmental Effects of Oil and Gas Activities on Alaska's North Slope,* pp. 77, 115–116.

2 Project Underground, "Drilling to the Ends of the Earth," September 13, 1998, http://www.moles.org/ProjectUnderground/motherlode/drilling/intro.html.

3 Greenpeace UK, "Seismic Exploration: Greenpeace Media Briefing Notes."

4 Deborah Hargreaves, "Sweep of a Dustbin and Brush—North Sea Oil Prospects," *Financial Times,* December 18, 1991, p. 28.

5 "Injuries to International Petroleum Drilling Workers, 1988–1990," *Morbidity and Mortality Weekly Report,* February 26, 1993, p. 128.

6 Charles Woolfson, John Foster, and Matthias Beck, *Paying for the Piper: Capital and Labour in Britain's Offshore Oil Industry* (London: Mansell, 1996), pp. 106–108.

7 Stuart Millar, "Blood and Black Gold: A Decade After the Piper Alpha Disaster,

for the Survivors and Bereaved There Are Still Burning Questions of Recognition and Responsibility," *The Guardian*, July 6, 1998, p. 2.

8   This and following are from an interview of Jake Molloy by the author, February 2003.

9   Bureau of Transportation Statistics, National Transportation Statistics 2000, "Crude Oil and Petroleum Products Transported in the United States by Mode," Table 1-51M.

10   Allan J. Mayer et al., "How to Make Tankers Safer," *Newsweek*, January 17, 1977, p. 60.

11   René De La Pedraja, *A Historical Dictionary of the U.S. Merchant Marine and Shipping Industry: Since the Introduction of Steam* (Westport, CT: Greenwood, 1994), p. 456.

12   Jeremy Leggett, *The Carbon War: Global Warming and the End of the Oil Era* (New York: Routledge, 2001), pp. 114–115.

13   Sonia Shah, "The Quest for Oil Under the Great Barrier Reef," *Progressive* (July 2003), p. 33.

14   "SeaRiver Commissions Double-Hull Alaska Tanker Design," *Oil & Gas Journal*, February 3, 2003, p. 40.

15   Greg Muttitt and James Marriott, "Some Common Concerns: Imagining B P 's Azerbaijan-Georgia-Turkey Pipelines System," PLATFORM (November 2002), p. 129.

16   ExxonValdez Oil Spill Trustee Council, "Oil Spill Facts," available at http://www. oilspill.state.ak.us/facts/qanda.html.

17   De La Pedraja, *A Historical Dictionary of the U.S. Merchant Marine and Shipping Industry*, p. 194.

18   "SeaRiver Commissions Double-Hull Alaska Tanker Design," p. 40.

19   Leggett, *The Carbon War*, p. 114.

20   Molloy interview.

21   ExxonValdez Oil Spill Trustee Council, "Oil Spill Facts," http://www.oilspill. state.ak.us/facts/qanda.html.

22   De La Pedraja, *A Historical Dictionary of the U.S. Merchant Marine and Shipping Industry*, p. 194.

23   David Brinkerhoff, "U.S. Petroleum Engineers Become Rare Commodity," Reuters News Service, February 18, 2004.

24   CBS News Transcripts, "Readin', Writin', and Commercials: Marketing Strategies of Many Large Corporations Now Target Public Classrooms," *60 Minutes*, October 10, 1993.

25   Peter Morris (International Commission on Shipping), interview by the author, May 30, 2003.

26   "SeaRiver Commissions Double-Hull Alaska Tanker Design," p. 40.

27   Leggett, *The Carbon War*, p. 115.

28   International Transport Workers' Federation, "Flags of Convenience Campaign Report 2001/02."

29 United Nations Conference on Trade and Development, *Review of Maritime Transport 2002* (New York and Geneva: United Nations, 2002), Table 8, p. 21.

30 International Association of Independent Tanker Owners, "INTERTANKO Tanker Facts 2002," http://www.intertanko.com/about/annualreports/2001/2_8.html.

31 Siamack Shojai, ed., *New Global Oil Market: Understanding Energy Issues in the World Economy* (Westport, CT: Praeger, 1995), pp. 178–179.

32 "Shipping: Follow the Flag of Convenience," *Economist*, February 22, 1997, p. 75.

33 U.S. Maritime Administration, Waterborne Databank, "United States Waterborne Commerce," April 3, 2003, http://www.marad.dot.gov/Marad_Statistics/.

34 International Transport Workers' Federation, "Sweatships: Fact Sheet About the Cruise Industry," http://www.itf.org.uk/itfweb/publications/sweatships/factsheet.htm.

35 International Confederation of Free Trade Unions et al., "More Troubled Waters: Fishing, Pollution, and FOCs," August 2002, p. 19.

36 Morris interview.

37 Peter Morris, "Ships, Slaves and Competition," International Commission on Shipping, 2000.

38 Peter Ford, "Why Aging Oil Tankers Still Ply the Seas," *Christian Science Monitor*, November 21, 2002.

39 Owen Bowcott and Linus Gregoriadis, "Chirac Leads Calls to Outlaw Single-Hull Tankers After Spate of Accidents," *The Guardian*, November 20, 2002.

40 Emma Daly, "The Sinking of the *Prestige*," *Observer*, November 24, 2002, p. 18.

41 Emma Daly, "Oil from Crippled Ship Fouling Beaches in Spain," *New York Times*, November 19, 2002, p. 19.

42 Bowcott and Gregoriadis, "Chirac Leads Calls to Outlaw Single-Hull Tankers After Spate of Accidents."

43 Op-ed, "Cracking Open an Oil Tanker," *New York Times,* November 20, 2002.

44 Emma Daly, "Oil Tanker Splits Apart off Spain, Threatening Coast," *New York Times,* November 20, 2002, p. 6.

45 Emma Daly, "Oil Spilled off Spanish Coast Threatens Shellfishing Grounds," *New York Times*, December 5, 2002, p. 19.

46 Matthew R. Simmons, "Are Oil and Murphy's Law About to Meet?" *World Oil*, February 2003.

47 Giles Tremlett, "Sunken *Prestige* Tanker Will Leak Oil for Another Three Years," *The Guardian*, December 12, 2002, p. 18.

48 "Four-fifths of remaining fuel in sunken tanker Prestige pumped out," *Platts Oilgram Price Report*, September 7, 2004.

49 Bowcott and Gregoriadis, "Chirac Leads Calls to Outlaw Single-Hull Tankers After Spate of Accidents."

50 Ford, "Why Aging Oil Tankers Still Ply the Seas."

51 Morris interview.

52 "The Pending Formalization," *Oil & Gas Journal,* April 14, 2003, p. 7.

53 "SeaRiver Commissions Double-Hull Alaska Tanker Design," p. 40.

54 "The Price of Oil," *New Statesman*, November 25, 2002, p. 6.

55 Jon P. Davidson et al., *Exploring Earth: An Introduction to Physical Geology*, 2nd ed.
    (Upper Saddle River, NJ: Prentice-Hall, 2002), p. 465. Although dumping oil-
    contaminated ballast water, a common practice within the oil industry, has yet
    to attract regulators' ire, between 1993 and 2002, the U.S. Justice Department
    fined several of the hundreds of cruise ships touring the world's more pleasant
    ports over $48 million for regularly dumping the plastic trash, toxic waste, and
    oil-contaminated water produced by their thousands of vacationing passengers
    onboard directly into the sea. Marilyn Adams, "Cruise-Ship Dumping Poisons
    Seas, Frustrates U.S. Enforcers," *USA Today*, November 8, 2002, p. 1.

56 Leggett, *The Carbon War*, p. 113.

57 International Transport Workers' Federation, "Flags of Convenience Campaign
    Report 2001/02."

58 Veronica Murillo, "Floating Technology: Tanker Lightering, Transport Leaks
    Carry Highest Risk in FPSO Operations," *Offshore* (November 2000), p. 68.

59 World Wildlife Fund, "The Status of Natural Resources on the High Seas," 2001,
    p. 33.

60 M. H. Kim, interview by the author, April 4, 2003. Rene Coenen (Office for
    the London Convention 1972), letter to the author, April 16, 2003.

61 Minerals Management Service, "MMS Reaches Decision About FPSO's in Gulf
    of Mexico," press release, January 2, 2002.

62 "Lots of FPSO, FSO, FSU Contracts, Except U.S. Gulf," *Offshore* (November
    2000), p. 32.

63 John Morrison (telecoms technician for Bluewater on the Glas Dowr FPSO off
    South Africa), letter to the author, April 6, 2003.

64 R. S. Carney, ed., "Workshop on Environmental Issues Surrounding Deepwater
    Oil and Gas Development: Final Report," OCS Study MMS 98-0022 (New Orleans,
    LA: U.S. Department of the Interior, Minerals Management Service, Gulf of
    Mexico OCS Region, 1997), p. 9.

65 Robert S. Carney, letter to the author, March 29, 2003.

66 Jonathan Wills, "Muddied Waters: A Survey of Offshore Oilfield Drilling Wastes
    and Disposal Techniques to Reduce the Ecological Impact of Sea Dumping,"
    Ekologicheskaya Vahkta Sakhalina (Sakhalin Environment Watch), May 25, 2000,
    http://www.offshore-environment.com/drillcuttings.html.

67 F. Olsgard et al., "A Comprehensive Analysis of the Effects of Offshore Oil and
    Gas Exploration and Production on the Benthic Communities of the Norwegian
    Continental Shelf," *Marine Ecology Progress Series* 122 (1995). See http://www.
    oilandgas.org.uk/.

68 Ian MacDonald, "The Edge of the Gulf: Deep Sea Expedition to the Gulf of
    Mexico," 2000, http://www.nurp.noaa.gov/.

69 Erwin Suess et al., "Flammable Ice," *Scientific American* 281, no. 5 (1999), p. 76.

70 Leggett, *The Carbon War*, pp. 45–46.

71 Comments by Bill Dillon, Geologist, u s g s, ˙http://woodshole.er.usgs.gov/
    project-pages/hydrates/bermuda.html.

72 National Oceanic and Atmospheric Administration, "Fire in Ice," *Ocean Explorer/
    Explorations*, http://oceanexplorer.noaa.gov/explorations/deepeast01/back-
    ground/fire/fire.html.

73 Gregory J. Hatton et al., "Cold Reality: Ice-Like Hydrates Can Spell Trouble for
    Deepwater Hydrocarbon Flow Lines," *SwRI Technology Today* (spring 1998).

74 Hatton et al., "Cold Reality."

75 Jeremy Beckman, "Subsea Installations Running Smoothly at Girassol," *Offshore*
    (February 2003), p. 30.

76 "A Survey of the Relationship of the Australian Spotted Jellyfish, Phyllo-
    rhiza Punctata, and o c s Platforms," http://www.gulfbase.org/project/view.
    php?pid=asotrotasjppaop.

77 Robert S. Carney, interview by the author, March 28, 2003.

78 William J. Broad, "Legendary Monster of the Deep, 26-foot-squid, Captured
    on Film," *New York Times*, September 28, 2005, p. 6.

79 Carney, ed., "Workshop on Environmental Issues," p. 37.

80 Carney interview.

81 National Science Foundation, Summary of f y 2003 Budget Request to Congress,
    "Ocean Sciences," http://www.nsf.gov/bfa/bud/fy2003/atmos_os.htm.

82 Interstate Oil and Gas Compact Commission, "Who Will Fund America's Energy
    Future? Petroleum Research and Development in the Twenty-first Century"
    (summer 2002), p. 3.

83 Pennsylvania State University, "Scientists Discover Methane Ice Worms on Gulf
    of Mexico Sea Floor," press release, July 29, 1997.

84 Carney interview.

85 Molloy interview.

Chapter Seven

1 Terry Lynn Karl and Ian Gary, "Bottom of the Barrel: Africa's Oil Boom and the
   Poor," Catholic Relief Services report, June 2003, pp. 1–18.

2 Jerry Useem, "The Devil's Excrement: Perez Alfonzo's Different Name for Oil,"
   Fortune, January 21, 2003.

3 United Nations Development Program, "Human Development Report 2002."

4 World Bank, "GNI per capita 2004, Atlas method and PPP," available at http://
   siteresources.worldbank.org/DATASTATISTICS/Resources/GNIPC.pdf.

5 Karl and Gary, "Bottom of the Barrel," p. 30.

6 Andy Denwood, "Gabon's oil boom hangover," b b c News, October 11, 2004,
   available at http://news.bbc.co.uk/2/hi/africa/3733578.stm.

7 Ibid., pp. 19–32.

8 Duncan Austin and Amanda Sauer, *Changing Oil: Emerging Environmental Risks and
   Shareholder Value in the Oil and Gas Industry* (Washington, DC: World Resources
   Institute, 2002), p. 27.

9   Lydia Polgreen, "Blood flows with oil in poor Nigerian villages," *New York Times*, January 1, 2006.

10 Ike Okonta and Oronto Douglas, *Where Vultures Feast: Shell, Human Rights, and Oil in the Niger Delta* (San Francisco: Sierra Club, 2001), pp. 5, 61–63.

11 Thomas Hodgkin, *Nigerian Perspectives: An Historical Anthology*, ed. Gerald S. Graham (London: Oxford University Press, 1960), pp. 92–94.

12 Okonta and Douglas, *Where Vultures Feast*, pp. 6–11, 15, 21–22.

13 Energy Information Administration, "Country Analysis Briefs: Nigeria," http://www.eia.doe.gov/emeu/cabs/nigeria.html.

14 Okonta and Douglas, *Where Vultures Feast*, pp. 81–83.

15 Ibid., pp. 67, 78–79.

16 Ibid., pp. 81, 93, 104, 202.

17 Ken Wiwa, *In the Shadow of a Saint: A Son's Journey to Understand His Father's Legacy* (London: Black Swan, 2001), p. 85.

18 Okonta and Douglas, *Where Vultures Feast*, p. 39.

19 Kwesi Owusu, "Drops of Oil in a Sea of Poverty," New Economics Foundation and Jubilee Plus, September 2001, p. 8.

20 Wiwa, *In the Shadow of a Saint*, p. 80.

21 United Nations Development Program, "Human Development Report 2002."

22 Okonta and Douglas, *Where Vultures Feast*, pp. 19, 110.

23 "World Summit Highlights Range of Clean Energy Plans," *Oil & Gas Journal*, September 19, 2002, p. 32.

24 Okonta and Douglas, *Where Vultures Feast*, p. 202.

25 Wiwa, *In the Shadow of a Saint*, pp. 81–86.

26 Okonta and Douglas, *Where Vultures Feast*, p. 117.

27 Wiwa, *In the Shadow of a Saint*, p. 87.

28 Okonta and Douglas, *Where Vultures Feast*, pp. 119–127.

29 Wiwa, *In the Shadow of a Saint*, pp. 153–157.

30 Okonta and Douglas, *Where Vultures Feast*, p. 129.

31 Melissa Crow, "Nigeria: The Ogoni Crisis: A Case-Study of Military Repression in Southeastern Nigeria," Human Rights Watch, July 1995.

32 Okonta and Douglas, *Where Vultures Feast*, pp. 133–135, 171.

33 Wiwa, *In the Shadow of a Saint*, pp. 200–201.

34 Nadine Gordimer, "In Nigeria, the Price for Oil Is Blood," *New York Times*, May 25, 1997, p. 11.

35 Okonta and Douglas, *Where Vultures Feast*, pp. 146–154.

36 This and the following quotes are from Isioma Daniel, "Protests in the Nigerian Delta: Women's Tactics Stymie Oil Giant, *Ms.* (December 2002).

37 Norimitsu Onishi, "Left Behind: As Oil Riches Flow, Poor Village Cries Out," *New York Times,* December 22, 2002, p. 1.

38 Okonta and Douglas, *Where Vultures Feast*, p. 186.

39 Christian Aid, "Behind the Mask: The Real Face of Corporate Social Responsibility," January 21, 2004.

40 "Shell Advertises Nigerian Woes," BBC News, April 28, 2003, http://news.bbc.co.uk/1/hi/business/2981477.stm.

41 Michael Peel, "Oil Groups to Restart Work in Nigeria," *Financial Times,* April 5, 2003, p. 13.

42 Daniel Balint-Kurti, "Oil, Poverty Ignite Nigerian Delta," Reuters News Service, April 4, 2003.

43 Somini Sengupta, "Ethnic Dispute Stills Nigeria's Mighty Oil Wells," *New York Times,* April 1, 2003, p. 3.

44 "Shell Advertises Nigerian Woes."

45 Peel, "Oil Groups to Restart Work in Nigeria," p. 13.

46 Association for the Study of Peak Oil, "Country Assessment Series: Colombia," July 2002.

47 Frank Safford and Marco Palacios, *Colombia: Fragmented Land, Divided Society* (Oxford: Oxford University Press, 2002), p. 282.

48 Ibid., pp. 272–274, 281, 283.

49 James D. Henderson, *When Colombia Bled: A History of the Violencia in Tolima* (Tuscaloosa, AL: University of Alabama, 1985).

50 Safford and Palacios, *Colombia,* pp. 348–354.

51 Association for the Study of Peak Oil, "Country Assessment Series: Colombia."

52 Safford and Palacios, *Colombia,* p. 356.

53 Harvey F. Kline, *State Building and Conflict Resolution in Colombia, 1986–1994* (Tuscaloosa, AL: University of Alabama Press, 1999).

54 Al Gedicks, "Resource Wars Against Native Peoples in Colombia," *Capitalism, Nature, Socialism* (June 2003), pp. 85–111.

55 Occidental Petroleum, "History–Colombia," http://www.oogc.com/world_oper/latin_america/hist_colo.htm.

56 Gedicks, "Resource Wars Against Native Peoples in Colombia."

57 Bob Williams, "Giant Caño Limón Discovery Thrusts Colombia to Forefront," *Oil & Gas Journal,* April 15, 1985, p. 23.

58 Energy Information Administration, *Annual Energy Review 2001* (Washington, DC: U.S. Department of Energy, November 2002), p. 133.

59 Kline, *State Building and Conflict Resolution in Colombia.*

60 Washington Office on Latin America, "Colombia Monitor," May 2003, p. 10.

61 Cited in Gedicks, "Resource Wars Against Native Peoples in Colombia."

62 "The Real Costs of Pipeline Protection in Colombia: Corporate Welfare with Dangerous Consequences," Witness for Peace report from Aruaca, Colombia, July 2002, p. 8.

63 Washington Office on Latin America, "Colombia Monitor," p. 8.

64 Gedicks, "Resource Wars Against Native Peoples in Colombia."

65 Karl Penhaul, "Along the Pipeline: Tracking Colombia's Revolt," *Boston Globe,* April 21, 2002, p. A12.

66 Washington Office on Latin America, "Colombia Monitor," p. 5.

67 Keri Geiger, "Running Out of Time," *LatinFinance* (October 2003), p. 32.

68 Daphne Eviatar, "Striking It Poor: Oil As a Curse," *New York Times*, June 7, 2003, p. 9.

69 Karl and Gary, "Bottom of the Barrel," pp. 1, 18, 38–40.

70 Dan Gardner, "Ethics and Oil: A Canadian Company with a Sterling Image Navigates a Brutal Regime in Equatorial Guinea," *Ottawa Citizen*, November 5, 2005, p. B1.

71 Nicholas Shaxson, "African Islands, Awaiting Oil Cash, Also Prepare for Trouble to Flow," *Washington Post,* January 18, 2004, p. 18.

72 Celia W. Dugger, "World Bank suspends loans to Chad over use of oil money," *New York Times*, January 7, 2006, p. 5.

73 Neela Banerjee, "U.S. Oil Still Pours from a Mideast Barrel," *New York Times*, October 22, 2002, p. C1.

74 Daniel Fisher, "Dangerous Liaisons: Selling Oil Means Cutting Deals with Dictators. Nobody Does It Better Than ExxonMobil," *Forbes*, April 28, 2003.

75 Ibid.

Chapter Eight

1   Energy Information Administration, *Emissions of Greenhouse Gases in the United States 2001* (Washington, DC: U.S. Department of Energy, December 2002), p. 10.

2   Gale E. Christianson, *Greenhouse: The Two-Hundred-Year Story of Global Warming* (New York: Penguin, 1999), pp. 111–115.

3   Woods Hole Research Center, "The Warming of the Earth: A Beginner's Guide to Understanding the Issue of Global Warming," http://whrc.org/resources/online_publications/warming_earth/index.htm.

4   Keith Bradsher, *High and Mighty: SUVs—The World's Most Dangerous Vehicles and How They Got That Way* (New York: PublicAffairs, 2002), p. 27.

5   Energy Information Administration, *Emissions of Greenhouse Gases in the United States 2001*, pp. 5–6.

6   J. T. Houghton et al., eds., *Climate Change 2001: The Scientific Basis* (Cambridge, UK: Cambridge University Press and the Intergovernmental Panel on Climate Change, 2001), p. 39.

7   Christianson, *Greenhouse*, p. 222.

8   Houghton et al., eds. *Climate Change 2001*, p. 52.

9   Christianson, *Greenhouse*, p. 222.

10 O. Hoegh-Guldberg et al., *Pacific in Peril: Biological, Economic, and Social Impacts of Climate Change on Pacific Coral Reefs* (Sydney: Greenpeace Australia Pacific, October 2000), pp. 10–12. Also, William Steif, "Experts Are Puzzled by Widespread Coral 'Bleaching' in Caribbean," *New York Times*, December 15, 1987, p. 4.

11 Hoegh-Guldberg et al., *Pacific in Peril*, p. 4.

12 Houghton et al., eds. *Climate Change 2001*, p. 4.

13 Greenpeace London, "Nature's Bottom Line: Climate Protection and the Carbon

Logic," July 1998, http://www.greenpeace.org.uk/MultimediaFiles/Live/Full-Report/2159.pdf.

14 Jeremy Leggett, *The Carbon War: Global Warming and the End of the Oil Era* (New York: Routledge, 2001), p. 46.

15 David Keys, "Global Warming: Methane Threatens to Repeat Ice Age Meltdown," *Independent*, June 16, 2001, p. 11.

16 Christianson, *Greenhouse*, p. 239.

17 Houghton et al., eds. *Climate Change 2001*, pp. 13–14.

18 Leggett, *The Carbon War*, p. 141.

19 Ibid., pp. vii–viii.

20 Ibid., pp. ix–x.

21 Darcy Frey, "How Green Is BP?" *New York Times*, December 8, 2002, p. 99.

22 Energy Information Administration, *Emissions of Greenhouse Gases in the United States 2001*, p. 23.

23 Christianson, *Greenhouse*, pp. 201–209, 236.

24 Leggett, *The Carbon War*, p. 85.

25 Ibid., pp. 89–90.

26 Jon P. Davidson et al., *Exploring Earth: An Introduction to Physical Geology,* 2nd ed. (Upper Saddle River, NJ: Prentice-Hall, 2002), p. 425.

27 Jared Diamond, *Guns, Germs, and Steel: The Fates of Human Societies* (New York: W. W. Norton, 1997), pp. 336–341.

28 Patrick Barkham, "Going Down," *The Guardian*, February 16, 2002, p. 24; Genevieve Sheehan, "Tuvalu Little, Tuvalu Late," *Harvard International Review* 24, no. 1 (2002), p. 11; Richard C. Paddock, "Tuvalu's Sinking Feeling," *Los Angeles Times*, October 4, 2002, p. 1; Piers Moore Ede, "Come Hell or High Water: Rising Sea Levels and Extreme Flooding Threaten to Make the South Pacific's Tuvalu the First Victim of Global Warming," *Alternatives Journal* (winter 2003), p. 8; *Microsoft Encarta Encyclopedia* 2002; and Tuvalu Online, http://www.tuvaluislands.com/.

29 Leggett, *The Carbon War*, p. 136.

30 Ibid., p. 141.

31 Sallie Baliunas et al., "Evidence on the Climate Impact of Solar Variations," *Energy* (December 1993), pp. 1285–1295.

32 Greenpeace International, "Exxon's weapons of mass deception." October 2002, http://www.greenpeace.org.uk/MultimediaFiles/Live/FullReport/5292.pdf.

33 William J. Cromie, "Brightening Sun Is Warming Earth, May Account for Major Part of Global Warming," *Harvard University Gazette,* November 6, 1997.

34 Sallie L. Baliunas, "The Writing on the Wall: Finding New Sources of Funding for Research," *Mercury* (January–February 1996), p. 18.

35 Greenpeace International, "Exxon's weapons of mass deception."

36 Houghton et al., eds. *Climate Change 2001*, p. 25.

37 "Harvard Expert Debunks Global Warming 'Models,'" *Consumers' Research* (May 2001), p. 20.

38 Christianson, *Greenhouse*, pp. 160–164, 253.

39 S. Fred Singer, "Global Warming Lucency," *Washington Times*, October 15, 1998; also, Leggett, *The Carbon War*, pp. 84–85.

40 Houghton et al., eds. *Climate Change 2001*, pp. 43, 45.

41 Leggett, *The Carbon War*, pp. 173–175.

42 Ibid., pp. 198, 229–230, 268, 299, 301.

43 Mark Pinsky, "Battle of the Origins: Americans Remain Divided over Creationism and Evolution," *San Diego Union-Tribune*, January 21, 2000, p. E1; Chris Mooney, "Survival of the Slickest: How Anti-Evolutionists Are Mutating Their Message," *American Prospect*, December 16, 2002, p. 18.

44 Global Vision video transcript, "Colin Campbell: The decline of the Petroleum Age," November 2002, http://www.global-vision.org/wssd/campbell.html.

45 "Technical Summary of the Working Group I Report," in Houghton et al., *Climate Change 2001*, p. 53.

46 Fred Pearce, "Is Broken Ocean Pump a Global Warning?" *New Scientist*, March 19, 1994.

47 Greenpeace International, "Exxon's weapons of mass deception."

48 Houghton et al., eds. *Climate Change 2001*, p. 39.

49 Ibid., pp. 306, 309.

50 Worldwatch Institute, "Report Calls for Rapid Scaling Up of Efforts to Preserve Health of Forests and Provide Economic Benefits," press release, April 2, 1998.

51 Rainforest Action Network, "Cattle Ranching," http://www.rainforestweb. org/Rainforest_Destruction/Cattle_Ranching/.

52 Two million hectares = 7,722.0431708 square miles. Project Underground, "Shrinking Frontier Ecosystems," http://www.moles.org/.

53 Christianson, *Greenhouse*, pp. 258–268.

54 Greenpeace International, "Exxon's weapons of mass deception."

55 Leggett, *The Carbon War*, p. 16.

56 Ross Gelbspan, "Beyond Kyoto Lite," *American Prospect*, February 25, 2002, p. 26.

57 Christianson, *Greenhouse*, p. 274.

58 Frey, "How Green Is B P ?," p. 99.

59 Jeremy Leggett, "Solar P V: Talisman for Hope in the Greenhouse," *Ecologist* (March–April 1999), pp. 133–135.

60 Hoegh-Guldberg et al., *Pacific in Peril*, pp. 10–12.

61 Sonia Shah, "The Quest for Oil Under the Great Barrier Reef," *Progressive* (July 2003), pp. 32–35.

62 O. Hoegh-Guldberg, interview by the author, November 2002.

63 Energy Information Administration, *Emissions of Greenhouse Gases in the United States 2001*, pp. 5–6.

64 Barkham, "Going Down"; Sheehan, "Tuvalu Little, Tuvalu Late," p. 11; Paddock,

"Tuvalu's Sinking Feeling"; Ede, "Come Hell or High Water"; *Microsoft Encarta Encyclopedia* 2002; and Tuvalu Online, http://www.tuvaluislands.com/.

65   Mark Townsend and Paul Harris, "Now the Pentagon Tells Bush: Climate Change Will Destroy Us," *Observer,* February 22, 2004.

66   BP, 2001 Annual report on form 20-F (London: BP, 2002), p. 58, cited in Duncan Austin and Amanda Sauer, *Changing Oil: Emerging Environmental Risks and Shareholder Value in the Oil and Gas Industry* (Washington, DC: World Resources Institute, 2002), p. 35.

67   David Ritson, "Fuel for Thought: Stanford Has Signed Up for a Ride on a Tiger. Will It Survive the Journey Intact?" *Nature,* February 6, 2003, p. 575. See Stanford University Global Climate & Energy Project, "Faculty," s.v. Lynn Orr, http://gcep. stanford.edu/about_faculty.html.

68   Jeremy Leggett, interview by the author, February 2003.

69   Energy Information Administration, *Emissions of Greenhouse Gases in the United States 2001,* p. 14.

70   World Resources Institute, "Analysis of Bush Administration Greenhouse Gas Target," February 14, 2002.

71   See William G. Moseley, "Voodoo Environmentalism," *Christian Science Monitor,* February 27, 2002, p. 9.

72   Elizabeth Shogren, "Thirteen Industries Set Emissions Targets As Part of Bush Initiative," *Los Angeles Times,* February 13, 2003, p. 30.

73   Ross Gelbspan, "Beyond Kyoto Lite," *American Prospect,* February 25, 2002, p. 26.

74   "Some triumph . . . In the cold light of day what did Montreal really deliver?" *New Scientist,* December 17, 2006.

Chapter Nine

1   Energy Information Administration, *International Energy Outlook 2003,* p. 31; also, Pierre Jungels and Energy Information Administration, *Annual Energy Review 2001,* p. 297.

2   Pierre Jungels, "Future Outlook of Oil and Gas Supply and Demand," (presentation, Institute of Petroleum, London, UK February 17, 2003).

3   Bill Powers, "House of Saud = House of Cards," *Canadian Energy Viewpoint,* June 29, 2003.

4   E-mail post by Gregson Vaux, DOE staffer, to Energy Resources group, February 4, 2004.

5   Matthew R. Simmons, "Are Oil and Murphy's Law About to Meet?" *World Oil* (February 2003).

6   Jungels, "Future Outlook of Oil and Gas Supply."

7   Kenneth S. Deffeyes, *Hubbert's Peak: The Impending World Oil Shortage* (Princeton, NJ: Princeton University Press, 2001), p. 10.

8   Neela Banerjee, "Oil Companies Are Said to Balk on Production," *New York Times,* February 11, 2003, p. C1.

9   Kenneth S. Deffeyes, interview by the author, December 28, 2002.

10 Goldman Sachs, *Energy Weekly,* August 11, 1999, cited in Colin J. Campbell, "Peak Oil: A Turning Point for Mankind" (presentation, Technical University of Clausthal, Clausthal, Germany, December 2000).

11 "Profit Leader Exxon Opts to 'Stay the Course,'" *International Petroleum Finance* (April 2003), p. 1.

12 Rick von Flatern and Marshall DeLuca, "Advisory Notes," *Offshore Engineer* (April 2003), p. 15.

13 Global Vision video transcript, "Colin Campbell: The Decline of the Petroleum Age," November 2002, http://www.global-vision.org/wssd/campbell.html.

14 von Flatern and DeLuca, "Advisory Notes."

15 Energy Information Administration, *Annual Energy Outlook 2005 with Projections to 2025* (Washington, DC: Department of Energy, February 2005), p. 45.

16 Robert Stoneley, *An Introduction to Petroleum Exploration for Non-Geologists* (Oxford, UK: Oxford University Press, 1995), p. 90.

17 Kenneth S. Deffeyes, letter to the author, March 2003.

18 Colin J. Campbell, "Depletion and Denial: The Final Years of Oil Supplies," *USA Today* (magazine; November 2000),

19 Cutler J. Cleveland and Robert K. Kaufmann, "Modeling Discovery," Oil Analytics, http://www.oilanalytics.com/discotop.html.

20 Colin J. Campbell and Jean H. Laherrere, "The End of Cheap Oil," *Scientific American* (March 1998), pp. 78–83.

21 Reuters, "Kuwait Oil Reserves Only Half Official Estimate-PIW," *Reuters.com*, January 20, 2006; "Shell's Chairman Philip Watts Reassures Employees," *Oil & Gas Journal*, January 21, 2004.

22 Deffeyes, *Hubbert's Peak*, p. 6.

23 "BP Statistical Review of World Energy," June 2002, p. 4, http://www.bp.com/downloads/1087/statistical_review.pdf. See also Energy Information Administration, "Country Analysis Briefs," http://www.eia.doe.gov/emeu/cabs/contents.html.

24 Eric Niiler, "Awash in Oil: There's Plenty of Cheap Oil, Says the U.S. Geological Survey," *Scientific American* (September 2000).

25 Stoneley, *An Introduction to Petroleum Exploration for Non-Geologists*, pp. 90–95.

26 See U.S. Geological Survey, "World Energy Resources," http://energy.cr.usgs.gov/oilgas/wep/.

27 Campbell, "Peak Oil: A Turning Point for Mankind."

28 Comments by Colin Campbell, posted on EcoSystems Web site The Coming Global Oil Crisis, http://www.oilcrisis.com/.

29 Niiler, "Awash in Oil."

30 Colin Campbell, letter to the author, April 22, 2003.

31 Niiler, "Awash in Oil."

32 Energy Information Administration, *International Energy Outlook 2003* (Washington, DC: U.S. Department of Energy, May 2003), p. 37.

33 Colin Campbell, letter to the author, May 1, 2003.

34 Kenneth S. Deffeyes, letter to the author, May 1, 2003.

35 Colin J. Campbell, "The Fuel That Fires Political Hotspots," *Times Higher Education Supplement*, May 17, 2002.

36 Jean Laherrere, "Forecasting Future Production from Past Discovery" (presentation, OPEC seminar, "OPEC and the Global Energy Balance: Toward a Sustainable Energy Future," Vienna, Austria, September 28–29, 2001).

37 Deffeyes, *Hubbert's Peak*, p. 191, note 8.

38 Jean Laherrere, "Hydrocarbons Resources: Forecast of Oil and Gas Supply to 2050" (presentation, Petrotech, New Delhi, India, January 10, 2003).

39 Deffeyes, *Hubbert's Peak*, p. 7.

40 Total transportation sector petroleum consumption is about 13 million barrels/day or 4.7 billion barrels/year. Defense department fuel use is approximately 1.8 percent of the country's total transportation fuel. Energy Information Administration, *Annual Energy Review 2001* (Washington, DC: U.S. Department of Energy, November 2002), Table 5.12c, p. 152; Elizabeth G. Book, "Pentagon Needs Accurate Accounting of Fuel," *National Defense* (March 2002), p. 36.

41 Defense Science Board Task Force on Improving Fuel Efficiency of Weapons Platforms, *More Capable Warfighting Through Reduced Fuel Burden* (Washington, DC: Office of the Undersecretary of Defense for Acquisition, Technology, and Logistics, January 2001), pp. 39–45.

42 Book, "Pentagon Needs Accurate Accounting of Fuel," p. 36; Defense Science Board Task Force on Improving Fuel Efficiency of Weapons Platforms, *More Capable Warfighting Through Reduced Fuel Burden*, p. ES-1.

43 Ibid., pp. 31–35.

44 On FORTRAN, see User Notes on Fortran Programming, "A Brief History of FORTRAN/Fortran," http://www.ibiblio.org/pub/languages/fortran/ch1-1.html. Book, "Pentagon Needs Accurate Accounting of Fuel," p. 36.

45 Victor Mallet, "China Is Biggest Oil Consumer After U.S.," *Financial Times*, January 21, 2004, p. 10. Also, Energy Information Administration, "Country Analysis Briefs: United States," April 2004, http://www.eia.doe.gov/emeu/cabs/usa.html#oil.

46 "Tonnes of Problems," *Economist*, April 19, 2003.

47 Barbara Freese, *Coal: A Human History* (Cambridge, MA: Perseus Publishing, 2003), pp. 207–208.

48 "Tonnes of Problems."

49 "Asia's Biggest Strip Coal Mine to Take a Green Look," Xinhua News Agency [wire service], July 12, 2002.

50 James Brooke, "Russia's Latest Oil and Gas Oasis," *New York Times*, May 13, 2003. p. W1.

51 "World Gas: Shell in Asia; Cracking China," *Petroleum Economist*, May 19, 2003, p. 17.

52 "BP Bites the Russian Bullet," *Petroleum Economist*, March 18, 2003, p. 38.

53 Michael T. Klare, "Oiling the Wheels of War," *Nation*, September 19, 2002.

54 National Energy Policy Development Group, "Reliable, Affordable, and Environmentally Sound Energy for America's Future," May 2001, p. xiii.

55 "Night Fell on a Different World—A Year On," *Economist*, September 7, 2002.

56 "Supplement on Canadian Energy," *Petroleum Economist*, January 14, 1998, pp. 18–24.

57 "Non-Conventional Hydrocarbons: Scratching the Surface," *Petroleum Economist*, March 31, 2002, p. 31.

58 "Supplement on Canadian Energy, pp. 18–24."

59 Lesley Curwen, "Shell Moves Mountains to Take Oil from the Land of the Cree," *Independent on Sunday*, January 26, 2003, p. 5.

60 Greenpeace International, "Greenpeace Calls on Prime Minister to Cut Carbon Subsidies," November 4, 1997, http://archive.greenpeace.org/~climate/archive/kdates/november04.html.

61 "Supplement on Canadian Energy," pp. 18–24

62 See "News in Brief," *Petroleum Economist*, November 30, 1999, pp. 42–43, and December 21, 1999, p. 65.

63 "News in Brief," *Petroleum Economist*, September 30, 1999, p. 74.

64 "Pooling Expertise in Oil Sands," *Petroleum Economist*, October 29, 1999, p. 39.

65 L. F. Ivanhoe, "Canada's Future Oil Production: Projected 2000–2020," *Hubbert Center Newsletter* #2002/2 (Golden, CO: Colorado School of Mines, 2002).

66 Richard Heinberg, *The Party's Over: Oil, War, and the Fate of Industrial Societies* (Gabriola Island, British Columbia: New Society Publishers, 2003), p. 112.

67 "Oil Sands Threatened by Environmental Concerns," *Petroleum Economist*, November 19, 2002, p. 33.

68 Ibid.

69 "Canada: Oil Sands Under Pressure," *Petroleum Economist*, August 19, 2002, p. 32.

70 "Undeterred by the low oil price," *Petroleum Economist,* February 10, 1999, p. 101.

71 Heinberg, *The Party's Over*, p. 112.

72 Hanneke Brooymans, "Oil and Water: A Volatile Mix," *Edmonton Journal*, March 2, 2003, p. D5.

73 Ivanhoe, "Canada's Future Oil Production," p. 2.

74 "Supplement on Canadian Energy," p. 21.

75 "Cost Over-Runs Hit Oil-Sands Investors," *Petroleum Economist*, September 20, 2001, p. 43.

76 "Book on Wiebo Ludwig Saga Pegs RCMP As Incompetent," *Ottawa Citizen*, October 23, 2001, p. D10.

77 "Cost Over-Runs Hit Oil-Sands Investors," p. 43.

78 "Could Canada's Vast Tar Sands Prove the Ultimate Anti-OPEC Resource?" *Economist*, June 26, 2003.

79 Clifford Krauss, "In Canada's wilderness, measuring the cost of oil profits," *New York Times*, October 9, 2005.

80 Global Vision video transcript, "Colin Campbell: The Decline of the Petroleum Age," November 2002, http://www.global-vision.org/wssd/campbell.html.

81 Dev George, "Caspian Equal to Mideast Gulf," *Offshore* (March 1996), p. 34.

82 Michael Klare, *Resource Wars: The New Landscape of Global Conflict* (New York: Henry Holt, 2002), pp. 84–85.

83 Elaine Sciolino, "It's a Sea! It's a Lake! No. It's a Pool of Oil," *New York Times*, June 21, 1998, p. 16; Theodore C. Jonas, "'Parting the Sea': Caspian Littoral States Seek Boundary Disputes' Resolution," *Oil & Gas Journal*, May 28, 2001, p. 66.

84 Greg Muttitt and James Marriott, *Some Common Concerns: Imagining BP's Azerbaijan-Georgia-Turkey Pipelines System* (London: PLATFORM, 2002), pp. 26, 107.

85 Greg Muttitt, interview by the author, February 2003.

86 After the invasion of Iraq in 2003, word started to leak out that the United States might be willing to bless a pipeline project through Iran, in return for Iran's help "fashioning a post–Saddam Hussein Iraqi government." See Darius Snieckus, "Caspian Commitment Plays the Waiting Game," *Offshore Engineer* (May 2003), p. 18.

87 Jeremy Leggett, *The Carbon War: Global Warming and the End of the Oil Era* (New York: Routledge, 2001), p. 67.

88 Klare, *Resource Wars*, p. 95.

89 Muttitt and Marriott, *Some Common Concerns*, pp. 31, 57.

90 Global Vision video transcript, "Colin Campbell."

91 Paul Brown, "Oil Money Threatens to Make Killing Fields of Kazakhstan: Wild East Could End the West's Dependence on OPEC but at a Heavy Cost," *The Guardian*, December 4, 2002, p. 28.

92 Energy Information Administration, "Country Analysis Briefs."

93 Arik Hesseldahl, "Saddam's Oil Fit," *Forbes*, April 8, 2002, http://www.forbes.com/2002/04/08/0408oil.html.

94 Marego Athans, "Does Oil Fuel U.S. Plan?" *Vancouver Sun*, February 14, 2003, p. A9.

95 "Despite Crisis, Iraq Outlines Plan to Boost Crude Production," *Oil Daily*, February 20, 2003; *International Petroleum Encyclopedia 2002* (Tulsa, OK: Pennwell, 2002), p. 99.

96 *International Petroleum Encyclopedia 2002*, p. 99.

97 John Diamond, "U.S. in Combat Under Constraints," *USA Today*, March 26, 2003, 4A.

98 John M. Broder, "Fuel Supplies Are a Top Concern of Military Planners," *New York Times*, March 19, 2003; Neela Banerjee, "Army Depots in Iraqi Desert Have Names of Oil Giants," *New York Times*, March 27, 2003.

99 Peter Pae, "Military Wants to Lease 100 Boeing 767 jets," *Los Angeles Times*, May 24, 2003, p. C1; also, Air Force Media Center, "DoD Announces Details of Tanker Lease Program," April–June 2003; and Airforce Technology, "KC-767 Tanker Transport Aircraft, USA," http://www.airforce-technology.com/projects/kc767/.

100   Broder, "Fuel Supplies Are a Top Concern of Military Planners."

101   Sabrina Tavernise, "Harried G.I.'s Keep Order in Mosul's Gas Lines," *New York Times*, May 7, 2003.

102   Jeff Gerth, "Oil Experts See Long-Term Risks to Iraqi Underground Reserves," *New York Times*, November 30, 2003, p. 1.

103   Eric Watkins, "Disputes Flare Anew over Iraqi E&D Contracts," *Oil & Gas Journal*, May 28, 2003.

104   Sabrina Tavernise, "U.S. Tells Iraq Oil Ministers Not to Act Without Its O.K.," *New York Times*, April 30, 2003.

105   Neela Banerjee, "U.S. Official Treads Carefully in Overseeing Iraqi Oil Industry," *New York Times*, May 12, 2003.

106   Oliver Morgan and Nick Mathiason, "Amec Loses Out to U.S. in Iraq Deal," *Observer*, January 18, 2004, p. 1.

107   Daniel Fisher, "Dangerous Liaisons: Selling Oil Means Cutting Deals with Dictators. Nobody Does It Better Than ExxonMobil," *Forbes*, April 28, 2003.

108   "Shell to participate in integrated reservoir study in Iraq," *Shell in the Middle East* magazine, April 2005, available at http://www.shell-me.com/english/apr05/news-me2.htm.

109   Maureen Lorenzetti et al., "Rebuilding Iraqi Oil Sector Must Navigate Feuds Old and New," *Oil & Gas Journal*, April 21, 2003, p. 18.

110   Ed Vuillamy, "U.S. Discussed Plan to Pump Fuel to Its Regional Ally and Solve Energy Headache at a Stroke," *Observer*, April 20, 2003; "Tel Aviv Seeks to Tap War Dividend," *Petroleum Economist*, May 19, 2003, p. 38.

111   White House Office of the Press Secretary, "Dr. Condoleezza Rice Discusses the President's Trip to Africa," press release, July 3, 2003, http://www.whitehouse.gov/news/releases/2003/07/print/20030703-14.html.

112   Energy Information Administration, "Country Analysis Briefs."

113   "Iraqi Production," *Oil & Gas Journal*, January 5, 2004, p. 6.

114   Jeff Gerth, "Doubts Raised on Saudi Vow for More Oil," *New York Times*, October 27, 2005.

115   James Sterngold, "Cheney's Grim Vision: Decades of War," *San Francisco Chronicle*, January 15, 2004, p. 3.

116   Heather Timmons and Vikas Bajaj, "BP Details Its Damages from Hurricanes," *New York Times*, October 5, 2005.

117   David Teather, "Republicans Turn on the Oil Industry as Petrol Prices Soar," *The Guardian*, November 10, 2005.

118   Jad Mouawad, "With Oil Prices off Their Peak, Are Supplies Assured?" *New York Times*, December 5, 2005.

119   Jad Mouawad, "Oil Producers Are Urged to Invest in More Capacity," *New York Times*, November 7, 2005.

120   Jeff Gerth, "Doubts Raised on Saudi Vow for More Oil," *New York Times*, October 27, 2005.

Chapter Ten

1   "The average solar energy influx in North America is about 22 watts per square foot." Richard Heinberg, *The Party's Over: Oil, War, and the Fate of Industrial Societies* (Gabriola Island, British Columbia: New Society Publishers, 2003), p. 142. 22 watts (joules/sec) = 75.117345 BTU/hour. 4 BTU ~ 1 kilocalorie.

2   Jeremy Leggett, letter to Lord John Browne (CEO of BP), September 27, 2001.

3   Jeremy Leggett, *The Carbon War: Global Warming and the End of the Oil Era* (New York: Routledge, 2001), p. 205.

4   Kenneth S. Deffeyes, *Hubbert's Peak: The Impending World Oil Shortage*, (Princeton, NJ: Princeton University Press, 2001), p. 183.

5   Leggett, *The Carbon War*, p. 205.

6   Rex Tillerson, "Current Sources—A Global View" (presentation, Institute of Petroleum, London, UK, February 17, 2003).

7   U.S. Photovoltaic Industry Roadmap Steering Committee, "Solar-Electric Power: The U.S. Photovoltaic Industry Roadmap," April 2001, p. 26.

8   Interstate Oil and Gas Compact Commission, "Who Will Fund America's Energy Future? Petroleum Research and Development in the Twenty-first Century," summer 2002, p. 3.

9   Shell, "Shell Renewables - Shell WindEnergy - Facts and Figures," http://www.shell.com/home/Framework?siteId=rw-br&FC2=&FC3=/rw-br/html/iwgen/about_shell/wind/facts_0603.html.

10 "The Unrepentant Oilman," *Economist,* March 15, 2003.

11 Leggett, letter to Browne.

12 Leggett, *The Carbon War*, pp. 244, 272.

13 Leggett, letter to the author.

14 Heinberg, *The Party's Over*, pp. 141, 152–153.

15 Nolan Fell, "Sun Block: A Rush on Microprocessors Is Good News for Silicon Chip Makers, but It Could Spell Disaster for the Solar Energy Revolution," *New Scientist*, May 10, 2003, p. 38.

16 Deffeyes, *Hubbert's Peak*, p. 183.

17 "Twenty-second World Gas Conference: Fulfilling the Potential for Gas," *Petroleum Economist,* July 16, 2003, p. 13.

18 Tillerson, "Current Sources—A Global View."

19 "The Unrepentant Oilman."

20 Seth Dunn, *Hydrogen Futures: Toward a Sustainable Energy System* (Washington, DC: Worldwatch Institute, August 2001), p. 6.

21 "These Fuellish Things," *Economist*, February 15, 2003.

22 Dunn, *Hydrogen Futures*, p. 6.

23 "These Fuellish Things."

24 Dunn, *Hydrogen Futures*, p. 7.

25 Amory B. Lovins, "Twenty Hydrogen Myths," Rocky Mountain Institute, June 23, 2003, http://www.rmi.org/sitepages/pid171.php#20H2Myths.

26 Donald L. Barlett and James B. Steele, "The U.S. Is Running Out of Energy," *Time*, July 21, 2003, p. 36.

27 "Making Gas from Gas," *Economist*, January 18, 1997, p. 78.

28 "The Third Age of Fuel," *Economist*, October 25, 1997, p. 16.

29 Pembina Institute, "Fuel Cells: A Green Solution?" press release, March 2000.

30 "The Third Age of Fuel," p. 16.

31 Dunn, *Hydrogen Futures*, p. 53.

32 John Vidal, "Tomorrow's Petrol Is a Gas," *The Guardian*, November 11, 2004, 6.

33 "The Billion-Dollar Bet," transcript, 60 *Minutes II*, April 2, 2003.

34 Department of Energy, "FY 2002 Progress Report for Hydrogen, Fuel Cells, and Infrastructure Technologies Program," Energy Efficiency and Renewable Energy Office of Hydrogen, Fuel Cells, and Infrastructure Technologies, November 2002, p. 6.

35 "The Fuel Cell's Bumpy Ride," *Economist*, March 24, 2001.

36 Rob Coppinger and Julia Pierce, "Fuelling a Myth," *Engineer*, February 20, 2003, http://www.e4engineering.com/story.aspx?uid=c435d6af-ef2b-466a-b020-ea3d068ac8ef.

37 Jack Doyle, "Fool Cells: How Detroit Plays Americans for a Bunch of Suckers," February 6, 2003, http://tompaine.com/scontent/7210.html.

38 John Vidal, "Tomorrow's Petrol Is a Gas," *The Guardian*, November 11, 2004, 6.

39 White House Office of the Press Secretary, "Statement by the President," February 27, 2003.

40 Thomas F. Armistead, "Prototype Will Generate 275 MW, Produce Salable By-Products," *Engineering News-Record*, March 10, 2003, p. 16.

41 See Stanford University Global Climate & Energy Project, http://gcep.stanford.edu/.

42 Barbara Freese, *Coal: A Human History* (Cambridge, MA: Perseus Publishers, 2003), p. 194.

43 E-mail post by Gregson Vaux to Energy Resources group, 2003.

44 Freese, *Coal*, p. 194.

45 Heinberg, *The Party's Over*, p. 130.

46 "Senate Adds Rule to Energy Bill to Double Ethanol in Gasoline," *New York Times*, June 6, 2003, p. 20.

47 Dan Morgan, "Under the Influence of Ethanol: Pressure to Help Corn Farmers Is Key Part of Energy Deal," *Washington Post*, August 26, 2002, p. 13.

48 Keith Bradsher, *High and Mighty: SUVs—The World's Most Dangerous Vehicles and How They Got That Way* (New York: PublicAffairs, 2002), pp. 257–259.

49 T. W. Patzek et al., "Ethanol from Corn: Clean Renewable Fuel for the Future or Drain on our Resources and Pockets?" June 4, 2003, University of California, Berkeley, http://www.ce.berkeley.edu/Courses/E11/PatzekEthanolPaper.pdf.

50 "Fuel for Thought," *Los Angeles Times*, January 13, 2006, 10.

51 Jamie Miyazaki, "Natural Gas's New Global Role," *Asia Times*, November 11, 2003.

52 "BP plans to double renewables spend," *Petroleum Economist*, January 4, 2006.

53 Simon Romero, "A New Old Way to Make Diesel," *New York Times*, January 18, 2006 [online].

54 Charles F. Conaway, *The Petroleum Industry: A Nontechnical Guide* (Tulsa, OK: PennWell, 1999), pp. 222–227.

55 Ike Okonta and Oronto Douglas, *Where Vultures Feast: Shell, Human Rights, and Oil in the Niger Delta* (San Francisco: Sierra Club, 2001), pp. 88–89.

56 Heinberg, *The Party's Over*, p. 127.

57 Miyazaki, "Natural Gas's New Global Role."

58 Claudia H. Deutsch, "Natural Gas: The Stealth Energy Crisis," *New York Times*, December 17, 2005, B3.

59 Heinberg, *The Party's Over*, p. 126.

60 Frank Clemente, "Canada Cannot Solve Our Natural Gas Problem," *Energy Pulse*, June 17, 2003.

61 "Residents, Energy Interests Clash in Rockies: Many Moved to the West for the Environment, but Drilling Has Marred Land," Associated Press, February 1, 2004.

62 Tom Doggett, "Energy Firms Get $1 Billion Break in Fees," Reuters, January 23, 2004.

63 Simon Romero, "Short Supply of Natural Gas Raises Economic Worries," *New York Times*, June 17, 2003, p. 1.

64 Nelson Antosh, "Using an Innovative Platform, Project in Alaska Aims to Tap Vast Source of 'Ice That Burns,'" *Houston Chronicle*, February 23, 2003, p. 1.

65 Antosh, "Using an Innovative Platform, Project in Alaska Aims to Tap Vast Source of 'Ice That Burns,'" p. 1.

66 "Vehicles: Navy Reveals Research Efforts," *Fuel Cell Technology News* (September 2002).

67 Robert S. Carney, interview by the author, March 28, 2003.

68 ChevronTexaco, "2001 Annual Report," p. 24.

69 "Twenty-second World Gas Conference: Fulfilling the Potential for Gas," *Petroleum Economist*, July 16, 2003, p. 13.

70 Leggett, *The Carbon War*, p. 126.

71 Sonia Shah, "The New Oil," *Salon.com*, March 16, 2004, http://archive.salon.com/tech/feature/2004/03/16/methane_hydrates/.

72 According to IPCC's Third Assessment Report, the global warming potential of methane, over 100 years, is 23 times that of an equivalent amount of carbon dioxide. Over 100 years, the GWP of 60 Mt of methane the IEA predicts the oil and gas industry will emit is equal to 1,380 Mt of carbon dioxide, or 3,042,375,600,000 pounds of carbon dioxide. Since burning a gallon of oil produces about 19 pounds of carbon dioxide and 42 gallons of oil equal a barrel, it would require the burning of over 3.8 billion barrels of oil to produce this

quantity of carbon dioxide. See International Energy Agency, "Unit Converter," http://www.iea.org/Textbase/stats/unit.asp.

73 Elisabeth Bumiller, "If You Can't Take the Heat Get Out of the West Wing," *New York Times*, October 3, 2005.

74 Jim VandeHei and Justin Blum, "Bush Signs Energy Bill, Cheers Steps Toward Self-sufficiency," *Washington Post*, August 9, 2005.

75 U.S. PIRG et al, "Summary of the harmful provisions in the energy bill," July 28, 2005.

Conclusion

1 Owen Bowcott, "Private Sector Will Defeat Climate Change, US Tells Anti-Kyoto Summit," *The Guardian*, January 12, 2006, 17.

2 Chris D. Thomas et al., "Extinction Risk from Climate Change," *Nature,* January 8, 2004, pp. 145–148.

3 John Vidal and Paul Brown, "Eco Soundings: Act of Faith," *Guardian,* March 12, 2003, p. 8.

4 "GM Aims to Cut Costs by Dollars 14b a Year," *Financial Times*, January 14, 2006, 1; BP Annual Report 2004; "Oil Sands to Play Even Greater Role in Securing North American Energy Supply," CNW, January 30, 2004.

5 Michael Richardson, "Plugging into Wind, Sun, and Water," *South China Morning Post*, January 6, 2006, 13.

6 Amy Waldman, "Mile by Mile, India Paves a Smoother Road to Its Future," *New York Times*, December 4, 2005, 1.

7 "Congestion Charging: Capital Lessons," *Guardian,* February 18, 2004, p. 23.

8 Keith Bradsher, "China's Car Culture Hits Some Potholes," *New York Times,* January 11, 2004, p. 4; Oliver August, "Cars Drive Bikes from City Streets," *Australian*, reprint of *Sunday Times* story, December 29, 2003, p. 8.

Index

Acknowledgments

First, thanks to my friend and agent, Anthony Arnove, without whom this book would not have been written. For cheerful research assistance, I thank Josephine Worsfold; for generously sharing their expertise, Colin Campbell, Bob Carney, Kenneth S. Deffeyes, Al Gedicks, Frank Hewetson, Jeremy Leggett, Andrew MacKillop, Michelle Markley, Roy Morrison, Jake Molloy, and Greg Muttitt, among others. For their support and thoughtful suggestions, I thank Seven Stories Press, especially Dan Simon and Anna Lui.

Background for this book draws heavily on the so-called grey literature—unpublished reports, reviews, and commentary. I am indebted to the careful, committed work of organizations such as World Resources Institute, Worldwatch, Greenpeace, and the Catholic Relief Services; as well as the insightful and always thought-provoking commentary and analysis from the group of Hubbertian engineers, environmentalists, and others on the energy resources list and their associated websites.

Finally, I acknowledge a deep debt to the various familial editors, reviewers, and supporters lurking amidst the Shah-Bulmer family. You know who you are. Molecular ecologist Mark Bulmer, in particular, painstakingly reviewed each draft of this book, which is dedicated, in hopes for a safe, fair, happy world full of whizzing bicycles, to our boys, Zakir and Kush.

About the Author

SONIA SHAH IS an independent journalist and author of *The Body Hunters: Testing New Drugs on the World's Poorest Patients*. Her writing on science and politics appears regularly on www.soniashah.com as well as in *The Nation*, *Orion*, *Salon*, and elsewhere.